Based on Peter Holland's wide experience as a reviewer of stage productions, *English Shakespeares* explores the full extent of Shakespeare performances in England over the last decade.

As a regular reviewer for *Shakespeare Survey* and the BBC, Holland has examined the variety, the strengths and the problems of English productions. His introductory chapter points to themes which are taken up in the detailed accounts that follow: the size and scale of different theatres, the difficulties of over-familiarity, the power of director's theatre, the possibilities of design, the excitement of new actors, the discoveries of regionalism and the variety of playing spaces in which Shakespeare is performed. The main part of the book is a chronological account of productions which charts the work of several English companies, including the Royal Shakespeare Company, the Royal National Theatre, Cheek by Jowl, Northern Broadsides and the English Shakespeare Company. A final chapter compares the English experience with productions elsewhere, including America, France, Germany and Russia.

Peter Holland's reviews are individually thoughtful, provocative and illuminating; cumulatively they show that there is no one English Shakespeare style but a rich and often bewildering variety.

ENGLISH SHAKESPEARES

ENGLISH SHAKESPEARES

Shakespeare on the English stage in the 1990s

PETER HOLLAND

Director, The Shakespeare Institute, The University of Birmingham

CAMBRIDGE
UNIVERSITY PRESS

PUBLISHED BY THE PRESS SYNDICATE OF THE UNIVERSITY OF CAMBRIDGE
The Pitt Building, Trumpington Street, Cambridge CB2 1RP, United Kingdom

CAMBRIDGE UNIVERSITY PRESS
The Edinburgh Building, Cambridge CB2 2RU, United Kingdom
40 West 20th Street, New York, NY 10011–4211, USA
10 Stamford Road, Oakleigh, Melbourne 3166, Australia

© Cambridge University Press 1997

First published 1997

Printed in the United Kingdom at the University Press, Cambridge

Typeset in 11/12.5pt Monophoto New Baskerville   [SE]

A catalogue record for this book is available from the British Library

Library of Congress cataloguing in publication data
Holland, Peter, 1951–
English Shakespeares: Shakespeare on the English stage in the
1990s / Peter Holland.
    p.   cm.
Includes bibliographical references and index.
ISBN 0 521 56405 0 (hardback) – ISBN 0 521 56476 x (paperback)
1. Shakespeare, William, 1564–1616 – Stage history – England.
2. Shakespeare, William, 1564–1616 – Stage history – 1950–
3. Theater – England – History – 20th century.   I. Title.
PR3106.H65   1997
792.9'5–dc21   97-5758 CIP

ISBN 0 521 56405 0 hardback
ISBN 0 521 56476 x paperback

Contents

Illustrations

Preface

Theatre reviewing is an ephemeral and parasitic art. It is parasitic because without the performance there can be no review, and it is ephemeral because the review's meaning is bound up with the performance. But, unlike the transience of performance itself, the review can be returned to and re-evaluated long after the performance is over. Yet reviews are written for a precise context: the daily paper, the weekly magazine, the radio broadcast or the academic journal. Divorced from their circumstances, their meanings change and they seem like documents witnessing an invisible experience.

This book is primarily the product of my moments of pretending to be working as a professional reviewer. Yet I have always been aware as a reviewer of being more an academic than a professional critic. As the academic study of performance has developed by leaps and bounds in recent years so the activity of watching productions, particularly Shakespeare productions, has itself been explored and theorised. The change is exemplified by the difference, within American academic analysis, between the writing in the fine special issue of *Shakespeare Quarterly* in 1985 devoted to 'Reviewing Shakespeare'[1] and that in an equally exhilarating collection put together ten years later, *Shakespeare, Theory, and Performance* (ed. James C. Bulman, 1996). The new sophistication witnesses an increased academic anxiety about the possibility of analysing performance at all, and is distinctly self-conscious about its theoretical position. Where the contributors to the earlier collection were comfortable about admitting that they reviewed productions, the later collection is full of disclaimers: Barbara Hodgdon's provocative analysis of reviews of Robert Lepage's production of *A Midsummer Night's Dream* at the Royal National Theatre opens with a careful definition of her article as one that:

moves beyond text-centred analyses and takes a contextual and material-ist approach which situates historical spectators and their reading strate-gies as the primary objects of investigation. Consequently, I offer neither a self-referential thick description nor a performance-driven account of the theatrical aesthetics or semiotics of either 'Shakespeare's' or 'Lepage's' *Dream*, except in so far as to note what textual and/or theatri-cal signs might prompt a particular reading.[2]

Professional reviewers rarely theorise their activity. Irving Wardle's account in his study *Theatre Criticism* (1992) is a rare example of a practising critic analysing that practice. More often critics simply bring together what they perceive as their best columns into a single view of the English stage. I have aimed to do more than that.

My aim in this volume is both to describe in detail (giving what Hodgdon, following Clifford Geertz, calls a 'thick description') and to offer a materialist reading of the circumstances within which Shakespeare production takes place. My ideal of writing about theatre performance is still the work of theatre critics like Beerbohm and Shaw, writers who can describe in such a way as to make the reader see what they saw. It is a style I admire in the work of Richard David and, when a friend wondered whether this book was intended in some way to be a successor to Richard David's *Shakespeare in the Theatre* (Cambridge, 1978), I could only say that I would be proud if it were to prove so.

As Hodgdon understands, 'thick description' is necessarily 'self-referential' and my accounts of productions are, I hope, properly aware of my own position in relation to them. Part of chapter 1 is concerned with the necessary fragmentation of that mythical col-lective: the audience. My writing about productions is unembar-rassedly subjective. If it sometimes seems in current academic practice that other people can read a book for a student, it is cer-tainly the case that no one has been able to see a production for me, even if my response has inevitably been transformed by the other viewers with whom I discussed it or whose reviews I encoun-tered.

Theatre-going is a complex cultural practice and my first chapter explores intervals, audience sizes and textual cuts as examples of constructions of performance that surround and transform any production and which are themselves defined by materialist circumstances far beyond the control of the individual actor, director or even theatre company. The succeeding chapters document, year by year, the Shakespeare productions I saw between late 1989 and late 1995. The first year's stint is divided into two: chapter 2 looks at some of the work in the Royal Shakespeare Theatre and the Royal National Theatre; chapter 3 examines the more populist work in the Royal Shakespeare Theatre and work in the Swan Theatre. Chapters 4 to 8 complete the narrative and the last chapter explores productions of Shakespeare by non-British companies from numerous countries, especially within the context of their appearance in English theatres. Each year's productions are a richly various group. While each chapter provides a particular focus (e.g. on history in chapter 7), the concerns reappear in every chapter. There can be no single definition of English Shakespeare production; this book both witnesses and celebrates its diversity.

Well over half of the productions I consider in this book were by the Royal Shakespeare Company. From one perspective the RSC's position is dominant and imperialist, a cultural institution whose significance in the perception of Shakespeare in performance is out of proportion to values that might be ascribed to its productions. Although, throughout this study, I am sharply critical of many RSC productions, I am unashamedly an RSC fan. But I have tried to analyse the nature of its practice, the constrictions forced on it as well as its freedoms, as a means of demonstrating that the performances constitute only one strand of the culture of English Shakespeare production.

This book began in 1989 when Stanley Wells invited me to contribute the annual review of Shakespeare productions in England to *Shakespeare Survey*. For six years he put up with the late arrival of overlength pieces and hardly complained or cut a line. Without his invitation and support I would not have found myself trying to see as many major Shakespeare productions as possible year by year, let alone trying to turn my views of them into coherent arguments about the state of English Shakespeare production. I am also grateful for his detailed comments on the first draft of this book. My thanks, too, to Catherine Alexander for help with the annual struggle over photographs, and to Sarah Stanton for advice both throughout my reviewing stint and with the preparation of this book. I was saved from many errors of style and fact by the meticulous and exemplary copy-editing of Helen Southall.

I am also grateful to a whole host of BBC radio producers for *Kaleidoscope, Nightwaves* and *Third Opinion* for inviting me to review productions for them, and to Giles Foden and the *TLS* for frequent invitations, including the long piece on the 'Everybody's Shakespeare' Festival which lies behind my concluding chapter. Jennifer Bowen and Anne Theroux took a shot in the dark in asking me to present a series of six programmes for BBC World Service Radio on 'Shakespeare's Globe'. I hope they were happy with the result since the experience was for me thrilling, taking me to Moscow and Hamburg, Paris and Alabama, and, most excitingly, to Delhi, Bangalore, Lucknow and Bombay, in search of Shakespeare productions.

I am grateful too for the kind friendship of many of the professional theatre reviewers, particularly Michael Billington, Michael Coveney and, especially, John Peter, whom I came to know on the circuit of first nights. Their reviews can be found in that invaluable and indispensable source, *Theatre Record*. If I occasionally quote from them to take issue with their views, I am still lost in admiration for the intelligence and perceptiveness that they bring to bear on their work, day in, day out.

First versions of the *Survey* pieces were given to the RSC Summer School in Stratford – again thanks to the kindness of Stanley Wells and Robert Smallwood and to those most tolerant but expert audiences. Robert, who wrote rival annual accounts of Stratford productions for *Shakespeare Quarterly*, will recognise how often my views as expressed at the Summer School have been tempered in the light of his genial doubt. Early versions of other sections were heard at the meeting of the Deutsche Shakespeare Gesellschaft in Bochum in 1994 (my thanks to Dieter Mehl) and at the meeting of the Société Française Shakespeare in Paris in 1996 (my thanks to Ruth Morse and Richard Marienstras).

Above all, my thanks go to the many friends who have accompanied me to the theatre, talked to me about their views on the productions and tolerantly listened to mine. If I name some, I have not forgotten others, but I must mention Paul Hartle (and all the students who took courses with me on the University of New Hampshire summer programme in Cambridge), Jean Chothia, Wilbur Sanders, Adrian Poole and Claire Preston (and all the Cambridge students who came to Stratford as part of the 'Shakespeare in Performance' paper), Albert Braunmuller (and his UCLA students), Michael Cordner, Anne Barton and, above all, my constant theatre-companion and sternest critic, Angela Ritter. Without her judgement, memory and acuity I would have made many more errors than are left in this book; many of the best ideas ought to be acknowledged as hers, not mine.

Last, but not least, my gratitude to the many actors and directors, especially the members of the RSC whose views I heard in seminars at the Shakespeare Centre each January, for talking with me about their work. I hope they forgive my use of their thoughts so freely offered.

References to Shakespeare throughout are keyed to *The Complete Works*, eds. Stanley Wells and Gary Taylor (Oxford, 1986). Reviews cited can be found in *Theatre Record* unless otherwise stated. For other works cited in the text and notes, place of publication is London unless otherwise indicated.

CHAPTER 1

Measuring performance

Mention statistics and measurement in an analysis of Shakespearean performance and most people will wonder what the connection is. My concern in this chapter is not simply to set out some of the apparently marginal aspects of the experience of Shakespeare plays in production but to try to use them to demonstrate some different determinants on audience experience and thereby indicate the theoretical position from which my analysis of individual productions is written.

Theatre performance, a system of such immense complexity that most theory has collapsed in the face of it, is a burgeoning field of academic study, for Shakespeare and beyond, yet it is rarely perceived as an area of precise measurement. However, within the practice of theatre, for theatre practitioners and playgoers alike, precise measurement figures far more substantially and visibly. By considering those calculations, some of the systems of theatre practice can be uncovered.

In the programme for the production of *Julius Caesar* by Peter Hall at the Royal Shakespeare Theatre in 1995, the reader was informed that 'The performance is approximately 2¼ hours in length.' Such gestures towards precision have both external and internal implications. The length of a performance has significant consequences for an audience. Perhaps in Stratford the announcement of the brevity and rapidity of this *Julius Caesar* served primarily only to reassure audiences that they would be out of the theatre long before the pubs closed. But in London, the length of a performance has distinctly different resonances. Anyone attending a long performance at the Barbican – Adrian Noble's *Hamlet* with Kenneth Branagh, for instance, in 1992 – is used to seeing various members of the audience leave towards 11 p.m., not because they dislike the production but in order not to miss the last train home.

1

The example may seem trivial but the experience of performance and the playgoer's ability to comprehend the implications of production are affected so that the measurement of a performance's length has significance for the receptivity and pleasure of an audience. Assumptions about the audience's ability to assimilate meaning may be contradicted by such external factors. In an important passage in *The Tragic Muse*, Henry James has Gabriel Nash express something of the effects of the temporal constrictions of performance in his analysis of 'the essentially brutal nature of the modern audience':

[The dramatist] has to make the basest concessions. One of his principal canons is that he must enable his spectators to catch the suburban trains, which stop at 11.30. What would you think of any other artist – the painter or the novelist – whose governing forces should be . . . the suburban trains? [1]

The effect of length on audience perception is something of which theatre companies are acutely aware. British theatre companies know well that there are economic implications in performance length: a long performance may mean that the stage crew needs to be paid overtime, with a consequentially severe effect on a company's finances, the profitability of a production or even on the company's willingness to mount the production at all. The measurement of length can, then, be a powerful index both of response and of economic function.

In other cultural circumstances the effect of performance length on ticket-sales may be acute. In Moscow in 1994, I was made aware of the radically different position theatre now occupied in the post-Soviet state. Audience attendances were down, partly, I was told, because the real theatre was now to be found on television, in the daily experience of the political theatre of social upheaval. But long performances were especially at risk. The first question people asked at the box-office was no longer 'What is the performance about?' but 'What time does it finish?', a concern driven by the fact that, in a largely non-car-owning society, audiences were reliant on public transport, and that, in the aftermath of the new rule by gangsterism, travelling home late at night was dangerous. Personal safety in London is also seen as a major contributory factor in the reluctance of women to attend theatres on their own, making the gender composition of audiences a direct consequence of performance length. For a play like *The Taming of the Shrew* such changes in audience make-up may be crucial to the interaction of production and spectators.

But the programme for Hall's *Caesar* also informed audiences that the play 'will be played without interval', and signs in the foyer each night reinforced the information. In this it followed Terry Hands' 1987 production, also for the RSC. The information matters, not only for the theatre's bar-sales, an important source of company income, but also for the audience's comfort: such a long single span would never be allowed on Broadway where the difficulties of middle-aged men with prostate problems sitting so long are taken seriously. As Tom Stoppard found shortly before the Broadway opening of *Travesties*, his play had to be cut to accommodate the demands of '"Broadway Bladder" (a term . . . which refers to the alleged need of a Broadway audience to urinate every 75 minutes)'.[2]

Intervals are a feature of performance that await proper investigation. They constitute one of theatre's sharpest means of defining interpretation, controlling articulation. For some plays the choice is ready-made: I have never seen a production of *The Winter's Tale* that has not placed the interval immediately before the speech of Time as Chorus, as natural a break as one could wish for. But in *Troilus and Cressida*, for instance, the modern convention of placing the interval as the lovers head off to bed both defines the shaping of the play, framing its two movements with Pandarus's two moments of direct audience-address, and mutes the dramatic sharpness of Calchas's entry to demand the exchange of Cressida viciously hard on the heels of the lovers' one night of love. Other productions take intervals in mid-scene: Trevor Nunn's 1991 *Measure for Measure*, for instance, stopped halfway through 3.1, transposing some lines from later in the scene to provide a conveniently emphatic close; John Caird's *Antony and Cleopatra* in 1992 halted after 3.6.19, at the end of Octavius's description of Antony, Cleopatra and their children in the market-place, an event that was seen as well as described. Sometimes intervals are taken disproportionately late: productions of *King Lear* often go through to the blinding of Gloucester before the interval.

The theatrical articulation accomplished by this choice of the placing of the interval can be acute but it can also be determined by factors other than directorial interpretation of the performance structure. The RSC's previous production of *Julius Caesar* in the Royal Shakespeare Theatre, directed by Stephen Pimlott in 1991, held back the interval until after 4.1, the scene in which the triumvirs mark names for execution. Only when the action of the play left Rome did Pimlott allow a break, so that the interval was as much geographic as structural. But the massive set of columns and a doorway, designed by Tobias Hoheisel, needed to be struck by the stage crew for the remainder of the performance; on some nights the interval lasted forty minutes, longer than the second half of the performance which usually ran for only thirty-five minutes. Such intervals, common enough in the opera house, are unknown in British theatres and audiences were confused and unsettled both by the interval length and by the performance's manifest imbalance of its parts.

For *Julius Caesar*, Hall – and Hands before him – identified the sweep of the play as one that denies or at least resists a performance's articulation by the interposition of an interval, choosing instead to follow Elizabethan practice and allow the play its single arch. Our academic understanding of Shakespearean dramatic structures, helped by Emrys Jones's innovative *Scenic Form in Shakespeare* (Oxford, 1971), now recognises the predisposition of Shakespearean tragedy towards a central plateau, a long sequence of unbreakable action across the centre of the play. Theatre directors, attempting to accommodate performances to companies' and audiences' expectations of intervals, had long understood the problem. But *Julius Caesar* and *Macbeth* are the only plays permitted to articulate their construction without the artificial structuring device on audience perception that an interval constitutes.

The length of Hall's *Caesar* was a direct consequence of Hall's attitude to pace. Actors were driven by the director towards an unusually rapid delivery. The impetus was partly derived from Hall's entirely reasonable perception of the play's rapidity, the delivery matching and illuminating the pace of the dramatic action. But it was also a consequence of Hall's belief in the necessity of Elizabethan verse being spoken at speed. Hall has become especially concerned with a metronomic approach to Shakespearean verse, counting out five stresses for each verse-line in rehearsal and demanding a pause at the end of the line, whatever the syntax may be doing. Hugh Quarshie, who played Mark Antony in Hall's *Caesar*, has dubbed the approach 'iambic fundamentalism' and complained that it was deeply inhibiting for actors, less the discovery of meaning in the rhythm of the verse than a constriction on that discovery, a denial of the provocative tensions between verse rhythm and syntactical meaning in Shakespearean language.[3] Its inhibition on the actors' freedom was also an inhibition on audience comprehension. I was painfully aware, on the first occasion on which I saw the production in 1995, that actors seemed to be speaking with one eye on the clock, determined to bring the performance in on time.

Chekhov complained to his wife Olga Knipper about Stanislavsky's production of *The Cherry Orchard*: some relatives had reported that in the last act Stanislavsky 'drags things out most painfully. This is really dreadful! An act which ought to last for a maximum of twelve minutes – you're dragging it out for forty. The only thing I can say is that Stanislavsky has ruined my play.'[4] Chekhov saw that speed is meaning, that the act played as fast as he intended denied the fatalist tragedy that Stanislavsky's approach was designed to reveal. But in the equally extreme case of Hall's *Caesar*, speed denied meaning, preventing the audience following the drama's and the production's argument. It was striking that, when I saw the production again in January 1996, it took ten minutes longer, the actors now taking control and finding some of the detailing in the language that they had previously had to refuse themselves.

The timing of the performance offered by the programme was deliberately phrased as '*approximately* 2¼ hours in length'. Such measurements are necessarily imprecise but the differences can be highly significant. In a production heavily laden with stage mechanics the running time can change significantly: David Troughton, who played Richard III in Stephen Pimlott's production in Stratford in 1995, proudly announced to a Shakespeare Centre seminar in January 1996 that the previous night's performance had shaved seven minutes off the running time, partly because the machinery had all worked smoothly but also because the actors felt confident to let the performance move more quickly. In any case, the programme's measurement of performance length derives from an estimate made in the later stages of rehearsals, at the point when the copy for the programme needs to reach the printers. Subsequent to that, the production may decide to cut speeches or whole scenes, to eliminate slow-moving effects or to speed up over-portentous delivery. The programme for Pimlott's *Richard III* announced a length of 'approximately 4 hours' but an inserted slip corrected that to 'approximately 3½ hours'.

Performance analysis is inhibited both by the imprecision and the inadequacy of its data. It is not only the exact measurement of a performance that may be lacking but also the range of variation within which a particular performance may be placed. Internal timings may also be highly significant. Jonathan Miller's 1987 production of *The Taming of the Shrew* for the RSC defined the major switch in Katherine's relationship to Petruccio through a long pause in the sun/moon scene (4.6). As Katherine (Fiona Shaw) observed the sun, looking at it through her wedding-ring, she silently meditated on her marriage and analysed the relationship before resolving to accept it and value it. The prompt-book for the production indicates that the stage-managers became intrigued by this pause, timing it each night as they waited for the next lighting cue, as the pause lengthened and lengthened in the course of the run. Like the famous pause in Peter Brook's 1950 *Measure for Measure* before Isabella would kneel to intercede for Angelo's life in the last scene, or the one before the first entry of King Lear in Robert Sturua's 1987 production in Tbilisi, each performance allowed the moment the maximum space the performers believed the audience could or would tolerate. The pause's length becomes an indication of the actor's silent investigation of the action and of the audience's understanding of the import of an event that the production found outside language.

The measurement of the maximum capacity of the Royal Shakespeare Theatre in Stratford in 1996 is 1,508. I want to use this fact both in relation to the measurement of theatre space and to the measurement of audience size. The three theatres that the Royal Shakespeare Company runs in Stratford – the Royal Shakespeare Theatre, the Swan and The Other Place – attract the most particular and peculiar audiences. It may possibly constitute the largest audience for Shakespeare in the world but it certainly constitutes the most heterogeneous. International Shakespeare scholars, the world's theatre experts, regular theatre-goers, local residents and tourists – both English-speaking and those without a word of English in their vocabularies – are to be found there Brian

Cox, playing King Lear in Deborah Warner's production for the Royal National Theatre, recognised that such diversity extended to London:

Clearly, if you are doing a play by Shakespeare the audience must comprise people who are interested in the plays of Shakespeare . . . but how interested? At the NT there are schoolchildren dragged there unwillingly for the sake of their GCSEs, husbands who would rather be asleep in front of the television, socialites who go because it is the place to be seen, sponsors whose product is patronising the event, tourists there in error. Ian McKellen says that only nice people go to the theatre; they do, but sometimes on automatic pilot.[5]

The rhetoric of the disgruntled actor is not trustworthy as audience research, but there is little hard evidence for the social composition, the age range, nationality or cultural and commercial interests of audiences in Stratford or London. Like all theatre companies, the RSC knows the size of its nightly audiences. It can identify and measure both its percentage capacities and also its percentage of the maximum potential figure for box-office takings, performance by performance. The two measures are significant in their differences: a production may be nearly full but the box-office significantly lower as a percentage of its maximum, a consequence of, for instance, the number of customers paying full price for their seats compared with the number coming on a group booking at a discounted rate, or the number paying a high price for a seat in the stalls compared with the number paying much less for the balcony. A play that appeals more to those unable or unwilling to pay a high price per ticket may be nearly full but the distribution of the audience within the house will be a measure of the nature of the production's or the play's appeal. The two ranges of appeal – play or production – are eloquent distinctions of measurement. Some plays in the repertoire will attract near-capacity audiences irrespective of the quality of the production: Adrian Noble's disappointing 1995 production of *Romeo and Juliet*, trashed by the reviewers, still did 'good business', as the jargon has it, while Trevor Nunn's 1981 production of *All's Well That Ends Well*, starring Peggy Ashcroft, one of the finest Shakespeare productions of the century, often played in Stratford to tiny audiences.

The RSC has come to believe that a particular Shakespeare play will produce a particular size of audience, completely irrespective of the production. As Trevor Nunn, the RSC's sole artistic director from 1968 to 1978, expressed it in 1973, 'We are dedicated to the works of Shakespeare. To put it in a slightly livelier way, Shakespeare is our house dramatist.'[6] Yet the financial constrictions, consequent on that crucial measurement of 1,508, mean that the repertory for that theatre is far less than the full range even of the Shakespeare canon. We cannot now, given the current state of theatre economics, expect to see large-scale main-house productions of plays like *Timon of Athens*, *Two Gentlemen of Verona* or even *All's Well That Ends Well*. Financial measurement precludes them. Shakespeareans might find that disappointing but some further statistics might be a helpful corrective: in the six years covered by the reviews in this book, the RSC produced forty-two productions of twenty-nine different Shakespeare plays, twenty-five of which were seen in at least one production in the Royal Shakespeare Theatre (six in the Swan and four in The Other Place – some, of course, in more than one theatre).

None the less particular plays come round for production with surprising frequency. The RSC is on a cycle or perhaps a treadmill which is becoming increasingly arduous, a strain on the demand for invention and originality. While Nunn recognised over twenty years ago that the company must preserve Peter Hall's founding principle, 'that whenever the Company did a play by Shakespeare, they should do it because the play was relevant, because the play made some demand upon our current attention',[7] he also recognised that 'To present the plays of Shakespeare relevantly, but also to present them (roughly) once every five or six years, is contradictory . . . The difficulty is to avoid novelty but remain fresh.'[8] What was true in 1973 is all the more emphatically true now: the pressures of the contradiction have only intensified.

The choices of repertory for the RSC are particular. The decisions made for a season derive from the question 'Which Shakespeare plays shall we do this season?', not from the question 'Shall we do a Shakespeare play?'. Any description of the reasons for the choice of a particular play is inevitably tentative but when, in 1993, the RSC mounted a production of *King Lear*, the conditioning factors might reasonably be set out as follows: Adrian Noble had begun an extremely successful collaboration with Robert Stephens two years earlier when Stephens, after a long absence from the English stage, played Falstaff in Noble's production of both parts of *Henry IV*, winning awards for Stephens and garnering for him the highest praise as one of the great classical actors of his generation. Noble's first production of *King Lear* in 1982 had been his debut on the main stage and, in spite of the brilliance of Antony Sher as Fool, had not been a success. Recognising that he had found the actor he wanted to play Lear, Noble felt it was time to try the play again. The company's previous production of the play in 1990, directed by Nicholas Hytner and starring John Wood, highly praised by many, was now just far enough in the past to justify another (three years, the minimum gap in the current frequency of return).

The decision to produce *King Lear* in 1993 was then conditioned entirely by theatrical concerns: the nature of the company's repertory, the availability of the right combination of leading actor and director, as well as the marketability of a major tragedy in that season's repertory. There is no socio-political reason here as a primary cause for the production's inception, even if one could certainly disentangle socio-political implications in the production's interpretative decisions, and even if such interpretative decisions might be important to the commitment of director or actor. The Royal Shakespeare Company sees itself as a cultural institution, its decisions primarily aesthetic, its politics submerged. It would not, of course, be wrong to read the production politically but the reasons would not be primary, self-evidently present in the decision to create the performance. Even in those cases where an RSC Shakespeare production does seem to be driven by its interpretative purpose, the production's existence within the RSC's repertory for a given season is unlikely to be a result of the interpretation; its place in the frequency cycle is always likely to be far more important.

This sense of the under-interpreted nature of mainstream British Shakespeare is particularly visible when observed from the outside. Laxmi Chandrashekhar, a lecturer in English in Bangalore, India, commented to me that Indian audiences look forward to British touring productions because

there is always this illusion that a British director understands Shakespeare better than an outsider can . . . Sometimes of course one is slightly disappointed because there is no attempt at any particular interpretation or to make it relevant . . . When a local group does Shakespeare in the local language we always find a justification for doing Shakespeare.[9]

This drive for justification in Indian productions is, as Chandrashekhar recognises, an anxiety about the legacy of colonialism, a need to justify the choice on other than British terms. Relevance to the Indian social and political situation is a primary means of denying the colonial imprimatur. For the RSC, obviously, no such anxieties pertain. Noble's *King Lear* has no need of a justification, least of all one of relevance: it is justified by the very existence of the Royal Shakespeare Company. Hall's criterion of immediacy, the sense that a play should be considered 'as if that morning it had dropped through the letterbox on to the front doormat',[10] seems less efficacious by now. The institution has its own momentum and its own necessities that justify its work in general without ever needing to justify a particular Shakespeare production. In 1974 Trevor Nunn had defined his aims: 'I want an avowed and committed popular theatre. I want a socially concerned theatre. A politically aware theatre.'[11] Nunn's choice for the 1972 Stratford season of a cycle of Shakespeare's Roman plays was driven by his belief that the plays seemed to him 'to have the most meaning and the most point and the most relevance'.[12] But such a search for the right response to the demands of relevance has disappeared from the company's practice.

The cyclicality of the process, the inevitability of needing to return to a play and hence of needing to find a new way of doing it, has its consequences. Some of the company's work seems to have forgotten the limited knowledge of the bulk of its audience; it often speaks more directly to those whose theatre-going is within a frame of repeated Shakespeare productions, those for whom the narrative is familiar, the production does not need justification and whose perception of the production is always in relation to other productions and to a knowledge of the text itself. There is a closed circuit of theatrical communication here, something that is not, of course, in itself undesirable but which may function to exclude other parts of the audience.

Even so, marketing, that mysterious part of the theatre industry, can produce surprising effects. David Thacker's *Coriolanus* in 1994, starring Toby Stephens, did reasonably but not remarkably well in the Swan Theatre (capacity 458). Since the opening of the Swan in 1986, the RSC has always had the problem of finding the right London theatre to which to transfer the Swan productions. Apart from experiments in using the Mermaid Theatre and the

Young Vic, they have either moved to the Pit or to the main stage at the Barbican, neither of which in any way reproduces the stage size or audience configurations of the Swan. With *Coriolanus*, the company took the bold decision, in the light of its Stratford takings, to move the production up into the much larger expanse of the Barbican main stage. An aggressive marketing poster campaign used a photograph of Toby Stephens, face and shirt terrifyingly drenched in blood, charging violently at the camera. It built on the cult success of the film *Natural Born Killers* and carried the slogan 'A natural born killer too'. There were protests in the newspapers but the effect on the box-office was extraordinary: sales, particularly of cheaper seats and stand-by tickets, were exceptionally high. The campaign may have put off middle-aged theatregoers but had plainly helped to attract an enormous audience of young people, many of whom had never been to a Shakespeare production and may have had no idea what the play was going to be about.

Marketing Shakespeare and measuring the response to marketing is a precise indication of the cultural placing of Shakespeare in late twentieth-century Britain. Academic analysis of contemporary Shakespeare production hardly ever takes any notice of the profound implications of audience measurement. If the analysis may not be vitiated by the evidence of measurement, it can certainly frequently be transformed, placed into a precisely evidenced context to define production reception on the one hand and, on the other, the company's understanding of the implications of its own history for its decisions.

Yet the details of audience measurement for box-office and capacity are acknowledged to be inaccurate about the exact composition of the audience. The very heterogeneity of Stratford audiences, the most extreme example of the problem, means that the reception of production is never unified. This is not simply a matter of taste. I regularly find myself in strong disagreement with other Shakespeare performance scholars about the value and meaning of an event within a production. But scholars fall within one category of consumption, that bizarre subset of Shakespeare audiences constituted by academic Shakespeareans, a group that may imagine itself to be the sole arbiters of taste yet one to which theatre companies pay little attention since their economic value is small. Even at those times, for example during the biennial

International Shakespeare Conference in Stratford, when the theatre seems to be full of Shakespeare scholars, they do not amount to more than 15 per cent of the theatre's capacity. But that substantial segment of a Stratford audience that does not understand a word spoken on stage perceives the production in a markedly different way. Analyses of audience response are premised on an assumption that the audience can be treated as a coherent, single-minded mass, but that is clearly not the case. The proper understanding of cultural consumption, of Shakespeare as consumerist product, would necessitate a much more exacting measurement of the varieties of audience and their discrepant perceptions than anything currently available.

But even if it were possible to identify the statistical breakdown of the audiences it would not signify, for the myth of the audience is far more potent and pervasive than mere statistical evidence. Actors tend to assume that audiences are of a particular type, that their ingredients can be analysed and responded to. Mid-week matinee performances in Stratford or in London contain parties from schools, and actors often report that they have played up to (or down to) that part of the audience, as if the rest of the theatre were empty. Participants in a production, consciously or not, gear and re-gear performances according to their assumptions about the audience. From the moment of their inception, whole productions will set out to define a form of relationship to the composition of their future audiences, be it an intractable refusal to compromise, like Deborah Warner's, or the firm belief, not necessarily intellectually cheap, that the production has a primary responsibility to please those whom it assumes will come to see it.

I have been suggesting that assumptions about the audience affect choice of play and the nature of actors' work but the argument applies equally strongly to production style. The most common complaint heard from actors in main-house Shakespeare productions at the RSC concerns the set designs, an objection often echoed by theatre critics and academic Shakespeareans. In 1985, Ralph Berry identified the RSC's addiction to visible production extravagance as a policy response to falling box-office income in 1981:

At that point the Governors of the RSC, the makers of manners, determined that there was an urgent need to increase investment in productions . . . This change of policy coincided with much better business in 1982. It can be argued that the RSC's success in 1982 was attributable to the muscular US dollar (which is reflected directly in visits to Stratford-upon-Avon) and the presence of Derek Jacobi in several major roles throughout that season. Such an argument does not modify the main thesis. The policy of higher investment in productions is now officially regarded as a success; it is the key fact of the Shakespeare we now see at the most influential contemporary stages.[13]

Berry's argument attributes more power to the RSC's Governors than they possess but it was and continues to be assumed that those members of the Stratford audience who are willing to pay the high prices of seats in the Royal Shakespeare Theatre are also to be found in the London theatres (be they tourists or wealthy Londoners). Hence, the argument goes, they are used to expecting to find in the theatre the sort of visual extravagance and dominance that characterises the late twentieth-century musical from *Cats* to *Les Misérables*. The connection between the RSC and the successful London musical is, of course, direct and identifiable in directors: Trevor Nunn was artistic director of the RSC and directed musicals, including both *Cats* and *Les Misérables*, before succeeding Richard Eyre as artistic director of the Royal National Theatre. The commercial managements responsible for musicals turn to the country's most talented directors to help ensure a musical's success and that talent is most often apparent in a director's success with Shakespeare. By an illogical extension of the argument, it is assumed by the RSC that the theatrical values and especially visual values and elaborations of the musical must be transferred back to their Shakespeare work.

The 'good night out' principle – that theatre-going in Stratford should be an experience closely modelled on theatre-going in London – resulted in the creation of a general visual style for Shakespeare production in the RSC in the 1980s that was unlike the more specific styles of the RSC in the 1960s and 1970s and more like the styles for London musicals. The empty stages, massive walls of metal and leather costumes that seemed so distinctively RSC in its earlier phases have their own theatrical roots but they were never to be found in the West End theatre. Minimalism gave way to splendour and the philosophy of the 1980s lasted throughout the period I shall be considering.

Increasingly, design-concept seemed dominant over directorial concept or at least it seemed that the latter was made most explicitly visible through the former, as the collaboration between directors and designers began to make it appear that the designers might be controlling directors, the designer as director, rather than the traditional pattern. Design-dominance has its own consequences, as Berry notes:

The installation of the designer as a major, perhaps a stellar member of the cast is not unmixed good news, certainly not for actors. Derek Jacobi has said that he could scarcely stand comfortably, let alone move about safely, on the irregular terrain of the 1982 *Tempest* set. In the past, critics reviewed actors; more recently directors. Today one reviews the designer.[14]

Designs can be so massive as to dwarf and fundamentally redefine the actor on the stage. But the time it takes to construct a set for a major production at a theatre like the Royal Shakespeare Theatre is never less than the whole of the available rehearsal period. That, together with the nature of the director–designer relationship, means that actors arrive on the first day of rehearsal expecting to be shown a model of a set over which they can have no influence. The elaborate sets define interpretation before the actors can have any influence on the development of the production and, unsurprisingly, they feel as a result excluded from the processes of creating interpretation. The set-model can loom in the rehearsal room as an object suggesting an unequal struggle. It was one thing to see a model of David Fielding's set for Nick Hytner's production of *King Lear* in 1990 and even to rehearse with an enormous rotating cube implicitly present in the room, but quite another thing to transfer the rehearsal room work on to the cube itself. What appeared in the rehearsal room to be actor-centred comes, for actors and audience alike, to be set-dominated, the actors inevitably losing the battle.

Actors are also often presented with a stage-set that is complex and, as Jacobi found, even dangerous for them to work on. Its mechanical devices can be restrictive and prone to break-down. Stephen Pimlott's 1995 *Richard III*, designed, like his *Julius Caesar*, by Tobias Hoheisel, made extensive use of an inner-stage platform which rolled out from a huge sliding door in the back wall of the set. Dubbed by the actors 'the CD player', the platform's movement was entirely dependent on electrical stage machinery without any manual override. It often stuck, either in or out. At one preview, when it had been particularly liable to eccentric and unexpected movement, David Troughton, playing

Richard, looked straight at the audience, knelt down beside the platform and crossed himself, praying that this time it would move on cue. In discussion, Troughton has made it clear that he would have preferred to play on a bare stage with a curtain in the back wall.

But the elaboration of the sets for the main house at Stratford, even when they work efficiently and are approved of by actors, can be seen as a direct consequence of an assumption about audience measurement. The RSC's extravagant sets for the Royal Shakespeare Theatre, and its house style of strong and elaborate design, are not solely the result of an aesthetic decision consequent on directors' and designers' theories about the most effective or important way of interpreting a Shakespeare text. The house style is also driven by the assumption that the audience the company needs to attract into those 1,508 seats is the audience for *Cats,* and that the audience wants the RSC's visual style to rival the theatrical experience of such musicals. To some extent, economics mean that the RSC must give its audience what it understands the audience to demand. The sets are measured not against the play but within the system of sets for big theatres that seek a tourist audience. Other considerations, for example about the appropriateness of the sets to late twentieth-century readings of the plays, may be subordinated to theatre economics.

The programme for Adrian Noble's 1995 *Romeo and Juliet* stated 'The text used in this production is the New Cambridge Shakespeare from which approximately 564 lines have been cut.' Measurement suggests the comparison of something to a standard, a definition of relationship. In the case of cutting the text, the performance is measured against a preceding text, the playscript, the assumed authority for the words spoken.

Of course, the cutting of a Shakespeare play has a long history. It may well be that *Hamlet,* in its second Quarto guise, was never played complete in the Jacobean theatre. When Davenant's mildly adapted version of the play was published in 1676 it carried the following information, directed 'To the Reader':

This Play being too long to be conveniently Acted, such places as might be least prejudicial to the Plot or Sense, are left out upon the Stage: but that we may no way wrong the incomparable Author, are here inserted according to the Original Copy with this Mark "[15]

The statement is a complex and resonant one. It marks one step in the opening of an explicit gap between text and performance in the representation of the text, a gap that needs identifying as a space between the conceptualisation of Shakespeare as a location of value, 'the incomparable Author', and the theatre as a place with its own constrictions, where that which is 'too long to be conveniently Acted' must be abbreviated. The consequences are substantial. Many speeches which no modern full-scale performance would dream of eliminating are marked as having been cut in performances of this version: for example, Hamlet's instructions to the players, 'Speak the speech, I pray you' (the first forty-five lines of 3.2) are marked as having been omitted, lines which we recognise as able to be cut without being 'prejudicial to the Plot' but whose significance to modern understandings of the play defines the cut as certainly prejudicial to 'Sense'.

But the treatment here of the text for a scene like 1.1 suggests a very different process at work. A modern edited text of the scene based on Q2 usually runs to 176 lines (the scene is nearly twenty lines shorter in F1). Of those, the 1676 Quarto marks fifty-four for cutting, reducing the scene by nearly a third. The longest single cut is fourteen lines, the description of the portents in Rome 'A little ere the mightiest Julius fell', but many of them are single lines.

Scholars investigating a play's stage-history minutely identify such cuts, examining their significance for interpretative choices made in production. Irene Dash has eloquently argued that the perception of Shakespeare's female characters in the history of performance has been deeply affected by the often savage cuts in their lines, eliminating for example material that was perceived as too explicitly sexual.[16] Occasionally there is a recognition that cutting is also a matter of theatrical expedience, of an acting company's awareness of different priorities in performance.[17] As Boris Pasternak, whose translation of *Hamlet* Grigori Kozintsev used both for stage and film productions, commented in a letter to the director,   .

Cut, abbreviate, and slice again, as much as you want. The more you discard from the text, the better. I always regard half of the text of any play, of even the most immortal and classic work of genius, as a diffused remark that the author wrote in order to acquaint actors as thoroughly as possible with the heart of the action to be played. As soon as a theatre

has penetrated his artistic intention, and mastered it, one can and
should sacrifice the most vivid and profound lines (not to mention the
pale and indifferent ones), provided that the actors have achieved an
equally talented performance of an acted, mimed, silent, or laconic
equivalent to these lines of the drama and in this part of its development.[18]

The cuts marked in 1.1 in the 1676 text generate a scene that is
more dynamic, less prone to digressive accounts of material that
disrupt the forward momentum of the scene. It ensures, for
instance, that the theatre audience has less time to wait for the
moment they are eagerly anticipating, the first entrance of Hamlet
himself, the star's first appearance. Significantly, no line is
'pricked' down while the Ghost is on stage, only in the lengthy
conversations before and after his appearances. This cut version
can be precisely measured against the conflated text, noting that
much of the material omitted in the Folio is cut here.

But my interest in the activity of cutting and the measurement
of performance that it enables is not mathematical and scholarly
but perceptual. Almost the whole of an audience is totally unaware
of cuts, even when they may, at Stratford, have read their programmes carefully and watch armed with the information that a
certain number of lines have been cut. I saw Adrian Noble's 1995
Romeo and Juliet twice but I must admit that I cannot confidently
identify more than a few of the 'approximately 564' lines which
were not spoken. I also have to state that I feel unembarrassed
about admitting that I cannot. I do not find myself seated in the
theatre checking off the lines in my mind against my knowledge of
the play. My consciousness of the text against which I measure the
performance is not a matter of putting mental ticks and crosses
against the lines. Even in Noble's *Romeo*, which I found myself
watching with considerable disengagement as it dutifully
unfolded, the text of a play with which I claim a fair familiarity was
not strongly present within my activity of watching. When Jay Halio
suggests that 'the critic must depend upon having a complete
knowledge of the play',[19] he is asking for a kind of perception that
cannot allow any comfortable commitment to the pleasures of the
performance, for all the scholarly rigour that he reasonably
requires.

Of course there are moments at which the text and its absences
can be immanent for a particular member of the audience. One of

my students noted – I had not – that, in Pimlott's *Richard III* (from which some 700 lines had been cut), Hastings' speech as he was led off for execution in 3.4 did not begin with the lines 'Woe, woe for England! Not a whit for me, / For I, too fond, might have prevented this'. The playing of the scene denied the self-conscious revaluation in the lines: Hastings' awareness that his own stupidity did not warrant grief and his redirection of the significance of the event towards its consequences for the country rather than the personal tragedy he might have seen it as constituting. The production played Hastings' last exit as personal, denied the political resonances – of that I was perfectly aware – but the precise textual mechanism by which such a reading was enabled, the cuts, went, for me, unremarked. Here the cut performed the inverse of Pasternak's recommendation, denying any performance 'equivalent to these lines of the drama', changing 'this part of its development'.

I was shocked that, at the end of Gale Edwards' production of *The Taming of the Shrew* for the RSC in 1995, after the dark, bleak reading Josie Lawrence gave Katherine's final speech, Petruccio did not say 'Why, there's a wench! Come on, and kiss me, Kate' as he knelt, appalled by what had happened. There was, in the tormented account of the play's ending that the production argued for, simply no way in which the line could have been spoken, its cutting a necessary consequence of the production's reading of the play against its grain. But a colleague of mine, seated next to me, did not note the cut of such a famous and familiar line, even though he was fully aware of what the production was arguing about the text. I do not find this anecdote critical of my colleague, even though I leave him anonymous; it is, rather, a definition of the ways in which the text is being made differently manifest, divergently present for spectators in the course of the experience of production.

Measuring the treatment of the text in this manner is not necessarily part of the way a particular audience member accepts or rejects a production's interpretation, even though spectators often measure productions for their willingness to align with the interpretation the playgoer wishes all productions of the play to offer. But the measuring of the presence of text – in the examples I have been using, through the awareness of its local absences – is a measure of playgoers' varying awarenesses of the text's immaıence, of the ways that their particular perception of performance ınd knowledge of the text conjoin and interrelate.

In 1983, Patrice Pavis used a questionnaire for his students ıtudying theatre semiotics. One of the questions asked 'what role ıs given to dramatic text in production' and Pavis comments that the text in performance does not always have the same status'.[20] ı would go further. In a rich variety of ways, both the processes of ıroduction and the experiences of the spectators are measured ıgainst a concept of the text. The production of a Shakespeare ıext constructs an intention for the communication of meaning ıased on its own location of the text within a wide range of deter-minants: for example, its assumptions about the play, the work's ːultural and theatrical history, the theatre company's cultural ɔlacing and the assumed nature of its audiences. Within a ɔoreign-language Shakespeare production, a non-Anglophone ɔroduction, the spoken text is itself processed and consumed in ɹelation both to a range of degrees of knowledge of the ঌhakespeare text and in relation to the history of translations of ːhat text, its variances from culturally normative presentations of ːhat play.

We can, as theatre researchers or as students of Shakespeare, ınvestigate with comparative ease the construction of the presenta-ːion of meaning. We can explore the structures of intentionality ₋vithin a production, for example by interviewing a number of the ːheatre workers associated with the generation of the production. But we have no mechanism to understand the degrees of imma-ɹence of the text in the consciousness of the consumers of the per-ɸormance. This is not simply a matter of awareness of cuts, of the ₋visible absences of segments of the generating text, even though I have used that as the basis for my examples. It can, just as easily, be ıssumptions about character and action, about the historical or ɕontemporary placing of meaning, about the relationship of a pro-duction to the history of the play in performance.

Shakespeare is not and cannot be measured precisely in per-ɸormance. The audience fragments into its constituent ındividualities, dissolving the myth of a unity of reception and ɕreating instead an unassimilable and unmeasurable diversity. I ঌhall frequently mention the audience in the following chapters; ɣet it is only a rhetorical fiction, a device of suggestion, not ın accurate measurement of response. Theatre critics and

Shakespeare scholars, our most frequent sources of information about audience response to a production, are a statistical aberration, a deviation from anything approaching a median reception, let alone the illusion of a normative one. My accounts of particular productions in the subsequent chapters are probably similarly aberrant, skewed, abnormal. For, in the end, our reactions only measure ourselves.

CHAPTER 2

1989–1990: the Royal Shakespeare Company and the Royal National Theatre

All's Well That Ends Well, Coriolanus, Much Ado About Nothing, King Lear (RSC, Royal Shakespeare Theatre); *King Lear, Richard III* (Royal National Theatre)

At the end of the 1980s the pattern of Shakespeare production in England had not changed greatly from the beginning of the decade with the Royal Shakespeare Company's dominance almost unchallenged. The Royal National Theatre offered at most two Shakespeare productions a year. There were occasional productions by the major touring companies like the Cambridge Theatre Company and Cheek by Jowl but the sheer cost of touring with a large enough company to play Shakespeare allowed most groups to explore the possibility only rarely. The only major challenge had come from the English Shakespeare Company, founded by Michael Bogdanov and Michael Pennington. Their name offering a national pride to set against the RSC's monarchical overtones, the English Shakespeare Company had built up a cycle of Shakespeare's history plays over three years of touring in the UK and beyond between 1986 and 1989.[1] I shall be exploring their later work in chapter 4 but by the end of 1989 the ESC was unsure of its next step. Hence, at this point, Shakespeare in England still substantially meant the RSC and I must begin by considering its nature.

In 1989 the Royal Shakespeare Company decided to split its Stratford season in two, opening a new repertory in Stratford at the end of August, including three new Shakespeare productions in the Royal Shakespeare Theatre and one in the Swan. The experiment of the split season was not a success; administratively, indeed, it proved a complete nightmare. But it reflects a sustained

anxiety within the RSC about the form of its work. At both the
beginning and end of the period this book covers, the usually sub-
terranean rumblings about the strait-jacketing that the pattern of
the RSC's work causes surfaced and resulted in substantial change.
If Adrian Noble's plans for change after 1996 derive from both the
difficulties of playing at the Barbican Theatre and Noble's passionate and powerful belief in the company's obligation to be genuinely national, the impetus for change derives from some of the
same causes that led to the split-season experiment of 1989–90: a
justifiable anxiety that the company would continue to work in a
particular circular way, moving between Stratford and London,
only because it had always done so, not because this was necessarily the way to produce the best work for the acting company or for
the audiences. The split-season experiment of 1989–90 survived
only a single year and in 1990 the company reverted to its then
traditional March to January schedule, but the causes of the
experimental change lie deep in the RSC's sense of itself as a
company.

     As early as 1964, Peter Hall announced 'I could contribute little
unless I could develop a company with a strong permanent
nucleus.'[2] But the company Hall created – flexible, inclusive,
gently left-liberal in its politics – defined its permanence without a
policy, its continuity residing in its personnel. Yet it is clear that the
RSC is not a company of actors. Actors come and go, came and
went year by year. Some start at the bottom and work their way up
through the ranks to prestigious roles. Some come in at the top or
the bottom and then leave, never to return. The coherence that
might define a company of actors, a shared knowledge and experience, does not exist. Directors new to the RSC are often surprised
to find that the actors hardly know each other, let alone represent
a coherent group whose ability to work together on stage and in
the rehearsal room can short-cut the rehearsal process. Actors and
audiences alike are aware of the sheer number of actors who have
worked with the RSC. For a number of reasons, some of which I
shall explore later in this chapter, Deborah Warner's cast for her
King Lear for the Royal National Theatre was ironically known as
'the RSC at the National Theatre'.

     Sally Beauman has argued that the failure to create an ensem-
ble company at the RSC was intrinsic to its dependence on
Shakespeare whose plays 'do not naturally lend themselves to

ensemble work' since the plays 'are hierarchic in cast terms; they contain one or two roles that remain mountain peaks of theatre, then a range of strong supporting parts, then a large number of brilliantly observed but tiny parts'.[3] The company has had recurrent problems over finding major actors to take on the 'mountain peaks' or, rather, who are sufficiently stellar to encourage an audience to want to see their mountaineering. The contractual demands of a two-year schedule (Stratford followed by London) were, from the start, likely to be seen as undesirable by actors working in the hope of film and television roles.

But the assumptions of an ensemble also embody implications about the RSC as a repository of knowledge about performance practice for Shakespeare. The continuities of the company's voice-work in the career of Cicely Berry[4] suggest a coherent company policy about the relationship between voice and body, between actor and role. Berry has been adored and revered by generations of RSC actors as a benign guru who taught them how to use their voices in Shakespeare. Her approach, based on freeing the actor's body to allow it to be open and responsive to the demands of the text, assumes that the text is a natural series of sounds susceptible to interpretation only if allowed to function in its own right. Hence her work is based on the sound and metre of the text, though that text is a modernised edited text, with its punctuation and lineation often strikingly at variance with any early printed text. The Shakespeare text becomes, in her work and in her books, a sacred text communicated through the actor whose body must be subservient to the demands of the voice. This primacy of language is a modern version of the talismanic approval accorded to verse-speaking in the golden traditions of Shakespeare acting. In the work of directors like Peter Hall – traditional RSC directors – Berry's emphasis on verse and language continued. But even in productions by directors barely interested in the details of Shakespearean language, Berry's status within the company as a cross between coach and first-aider ensured that her principles of work continued to exemplify the RSC style.

Of course the RSC is the inheritor of a long tradition of English Shakespeare production, a tradition that it has rarely sought fundamentally to radicalise. It also has become the embodiment of that tradition, the cultural epitome of the centrality of Shakespeare in British theatre. At the end of Sally Beauman's book on Shakespeare in Stratford, she quotes Trevor Nunn, then the RSC's artistic director, describing the achievements and responsibilities of the company: 'For all our good work, for all our discoveries, our insistence on continuity, for all our present audience response, and for all our earnestness, I do not think we have – yet – ensured a future for Shakespeare.'[5] Nunn envisaged the RSC as the last shield against the eradication of Shakespeare, a company whose duty was to preserve the performance tradition into the future. Yet the actors who make up the company are often unaccustomed both to the company's way of working and to the experience of acting Shakespeare at all, particularly in large performance spaces like the Royal Shakespeare Theatre. The RSC style is something into which actors have to be trained and the training is both through the voice-work with Berry or her younger colleague Andrew Wade and through the experience of working alongside actors more accustomed to the RSC's responses to the demands of Shakespeare. But the company does comparatively little to train its actors into an ensemble, to create a company style as a matter of policy. The hectic scheduling of new productions (incomprehensible to theatre workers elsewhere in Europe) is the osmotic carrier of a style.

At times the RSC has appeared like a company of directors. The four productions of the autumn season in 1989 involved five directors: Terry Hands directed *Coriolanus* with John Barton, the company's artistic director working alongside one of the company's most senior resident directors; the two other directors of productions in the Royal Shakespeare Theatre, John Caird (*As You Like It*) and Barry Kyle (*All's Well That Ends Well*) had both worked for the company frequently over the previous few years. The final autumn production, *Pericles*, in the Swan Theatre, was directed by David Thacker, then artistic director of the Young Vic. Given the company's strong awareness of the difficulties of the main-house stage, it had become increasingly common for directors new to the company to work first in one of their other venues. While in subsequent years both Caird and Kyle ended their official position with the company as associates and returned rarely to work with the RSC, Thacker would leave the Young Vic and become for a while the RSC's resident director, a new post created for him. By the end of the 1980s, the list of directors who constituted the RSC as a company was substantial. While Peter Hall,

Trevor Nunn, John Barton and others now appeared like elder statesmen, the new group of Caird and Kyle, Adrian Noble, Ron Daniels and Bill Alexander usually each directed one production a year, leaving little room for others to be brought in. Since the directors tended to work with the same group of designers the RSC's style was defined directorially and visually, rather than through a performance ensemble.

If the experimental organisation of the season in 1989–90 was designed to help change the company's work on stage it was not a success. The new work of the autumn was largely disappointing, as if the company had run out of ideas and energy: directorial clichés and excesses replaced substantive re-investigation of the texts; glib concepts dominated without offering illuminating rediscoveries. A company style can also become a set of company clichés. The often considerable worth of aspects of the main-house productions was lost within the tired and predictable nature of the conceptual framework. Only in David Thacker's *Pericles* in the Swan, his first production for the company, was there the fresh inventiveness that the RSC ought usually to be capable of generating.

No one could accuse Barry Kyle's production of *All's Well That Ends Well* of being short of ideas. Three separate concepts vied for dominance in the production; the problem was their local inadequacy and mutual incompatibility. Any one of them might, conceivably, have permitted a view of the play to develop, though each had its own particular limitations, but the cumulative effect was of directorial inventiveness unable to reach a decision about the play or even to demonstrate a legitimate inconclusiveness. Instead the play was simplified to a point of banal unrecognisability, leaving a few actors to fight back on the play's behalf through their awareness of what could have been achieved.

Hanging over the stage as the audience entered the theatre were two banners representing James I and Elizabeth I. Whisked away before the action began, they were brought back for the final scene. By this time, the King of France had acquired a plaid doublet, making him some kind of representation of King James, while the Countess was placed on stage and costumed to echo the banner showing Elizabeth. There is no reason why directors should feel obliged to play up the Frenchness of the play's France, for this France is an aspect of England, but that is not the same as translating it to an exactly defined moment of English history.

Kyle's unusual reading of the play as a precise historical analogue is one that might produce an imaginative production.

But any equivalence that might have been achieved was blurred by the gentle Scots accent of Helen (Patricia Kerrigan) and the much stronger and at times impenetrable Scots of Lavatch (Geoffrey Freshwater), thereby moving Roussillon to Scotland and conjuring up, in the relationship of the Countess and Lavatch, bizarre echoes of Queen Victoria and John Brown. If the King of France was to be seen as James I, then Roussillon should have been purged of its Scottishness. A gesture towards historical meaning was being offered in such a way that the historical sense was denied. It is conceivable that it would still be worth reading or seeing the King of France as a complement to or attack on James, a choice depending on one's view of the character's intelligence and perceptiveness, but that does not help to place the Countess as some historicised figure, least of all as Elizabeth. Elementary historical knowledge, so often a problem for such typological reading, produced an effect of meaninglessness.

Once the banners had gone, the audience was presented with a full-scale rustic festival complete with upstage violinist leading a rustic dance, a table adequately laden with bread and fruit and an actor carrying a corn-sheaf. As productions of *The Winter's Tale* regularly prove, actors are not adept at seasonal exuberances – they were no better here. Rusticity and the cycle of the seasons became key points of departure for numerous scenes, often providing a literalist source for a character's comments. In 4.5, for instance, the stage was set for autumn, with estate workers sweeping up leaves and a bonfire burning in a tidy incinerator. The Countess's despair over Bertram's actions was neatly fixed by her casting his toy soldiers and a bundle of his letters into the fire, while Lavatch's chilling image of hell (4.5.47–55) was simplistically justified by having him stoking 'a good fire' (4.5.48–9).

But, while the seasonal cycle has obvious connections with the play's rhythm, such ideas need to be followed through, not left as dangling possibilities. In 1.3 Lavatch was accompanied by an onstage Isbel, clearly hoping he would do the decent thing by her, but Lavatch's comments on sowing and ploughing ('He that ears my land spares my team, and gives me leave to in the crop', 1.3.44–5) have a curiously ironic effect if the Countess is sowing corn in the same scene.

Sometimes the agricultural hints seemed purely tangential to the scene. In 3.2, for instance, a rectangular patch of ground with beanpoles was dragged on to the stage but its only purpose appeared to be its convenient provision of a bunch of sticks for actors to hurl at each other at the end: as Helen's soliloquy left her exhausted and prone, a bunch of French lords rushed whooping on to the stage dressed as *Boys' Own* images of Red Indians, complete with face-paint, turning the set into an adventure playground of ropes and slides, and treating the beanpoles as spears to stick into the large rocking-horse left upstage.

Throughout the production the strongest and most effective idea was this treatment of the world of the war as a bunch of school-boys playing out fantasy playground games. The night-time manoeuvres became nothing more than a Boy Scouts' wide game. Much given to hurrahing, practising their sword-drill with preening self-regard or posing in front of a line of mirrors, the lords of the French court seemed apt companions for a very boyish Bertram, a nice lad who has barely stopped playing with toy soldiers when he discovers that this is apparently a perfectly acceptable gentlemanly and chivalric way of living in the wider world beyond Roussillon. The war may be, as the Second Lord Dumaine suggests, 'A nursery to our gentry' (1.2.16) and that provided the clue for the production's exploration of the play as if it were taking place in some Edwardian nursery.

Roussillon's garden contained a splendid tree-house which metamorphosed into a lookout post for the scenes of war. Paris too was a nursery with its dominant rocking-horse and a king costumed like a children's book illustration of an ermine-cloaked monarch. It was appropriate here that the King should wait for Helen curled up on the floor like a small child clutching a pillow in 2.1, that the triumphant Bertram of 3.3 (the first scene after the interval) should be mounted on the toy horse and that the discomfited Paroles should end up in 4.3 with a toy drum round his neck.

Set against the naivety and outright childishness of this male world the production offered Helen, Diana and the Widow a sisterhood support group: the four people playing Florentine citizens in 3.5 were all women, with Mariana clutching a baby, as a literal explanation for her stringent warnings about the consequences of 'the wreck of maidenhood' (3.5.22). These women accompanied

1. *All's Well That Ends Well* 2.3, RSC, 1989: The King of France (Hugh Ross) gives Helen (Patricia Kerrigan) to Bertram (Paul Venables)

Helen to the Widow's house, reappeared again in 4.4, having apparently agreed to act as travelling companions to the Widow (who seemed to be journeying in a cart borrowed from Brecht's Mother Courage), but vanished thereafter. The male world, characterised by its self-perpetuation of boyhood, finding in all its actions a means of reasserting childhood, was, then, set against an image of suffering women. But the image had become a stereotypical gesture towards an alternative feminist reading of the play. There was nothing in the representation of Helen or the Countess to support this demand. The historical basis of the King of France analogy was thus set beside a different moment of history in the Victorian values of a view of a boy-male world and beside a gestured modernity in the production's attitude towards women.

The single outstanding performance came from Suzan Sylvester as Diana whose arrival was like an immense burst of energy and joy. Her infectious delight in the games of sexual desire and her happiness in virtue suggested that Montaigne's description of virtue as 'a pleasant and buxom quality' could have been coined for such a Diana. There was no doubt about her chastity – she fully lived up to her name – but there was nothing cold about it either. Teasing the court with the riddle of Helen showed her radiant with the plea-sures of paradox, so that her control over the mystery made her a young anticipation of Paulina's role in the statue scene at the end of *The Winter's Tale*. But Diana was also enjoying being at court, making her preferable to the rather dour pregnant Helen, dressed in bridal white under her pilgrim's cloak: Bertram might reasonably have complained that his second thoughts were far more sensible.

But much else was simply flattened. I had never thought to see again an *All's Well That Ends Well* in which Bertram and Helen (and, in this case, the Countess) embrace at the end of the play in a full reconciliation, as if nothing very much has happened and all will live happily ever after. In this production nothing very much had happened and in the tradition of good children's stories every-thing could be satisfactorily resolved. But that is only a small frag-ment of the play. The three structures Kyle used – the historical analogy, the seasonal rhythm and the perception of male behav-iour as rooted and trapped in its boyish games – were each serious and reasonably valid responses to the forms of the play's struc-tures. However, the three strands did not support each other, unconnectedly lying athwart the production, glimpsed and dis-carded, only to be glimpsed again. The complexity of the play was not made apparent through the multiplicity of strands of directo-rial conceptual overlay. Concept is not in itself a revelation of complexity. As Kyle's *All's Well* switched between its concepts, the lucidity with which this difficult play sets out its complexities, however unresolvable, was never intensified, only added to. The RSC's previous production of the play, Trevor Nunn's version in 1981, had been of tremendous import for the play and the company, an unarguably superb achievement. Inevitably it had taken time for the RSC to feel ready to tackle the play again. Kyle's work, brave and imaginative in some respects, also gave in to the pressures that were inevitably created by the company's and some of the audience's memories of Nunn. Determinedly different, it did not achieve an internally coherent validity.

Kyle's three negotiations with history (Renaissance, Victorian, contemporary) were controlled intentions of directorial inter-pretation. But sometimes history catches a production unawares and watching *Coriolanus* in December 1989 was a strange experience. Though Terry Hands' production (with help from John Barton) did nothing whatsoever to conjure up the analogy, the tumultuous events in Eastern Europe inevitably became a point of comparison. As the citizens of Rome flexed their political muscles in search of food and freedom from oppression, images from the countries of the dissolving Warsaw Pact whirled through my mind. The patrician world is, of course, nothing like a Soviet-supported regime but the exhilaration of the discovery of the strength of mass protest was powerfully present. Hands' refusal to explore the analogies could have been seen as an admirable exercise in restraint in a disciplined rejection of the immediately topical for a production that would have a lifespan of many months. But it could equally be seen as a theatrically reactionary avoidance of the licit demands of immediacy, providing a safe piece of theatre for generalised cultural consumption rather than a production that saw in *Coriolanus* a necessary means of coping with the complete transformation of European politics (as Grass depicted Brecht doing in his play *The Plebeians Rehearse the Uprising* (1966)), keeping the headline news and the arts pages a safe distance apart. The English Shakespeare Company's 1991 production (which I shall discuss in chapter 4) was to take the analogy far more seriously.

The analogy was, though, operating beyond the production's control and it was present only in my mind as a reaction to the text; little on stage offered support for such a weighty comparison, since the production never managed to explore the social context for the plebeian revolt, even though, when Sicinius asked 'What is the city but the people?' (3.1.199) there was a sudden moment of arrest in the impetus of the scene, a shocked realisation of the potential revolutionary power of the crowd, that could have been fed effectively into the rest of the production.

By 1989 the RSC was unrecognisable as the company once firmly identified, by itself and others, with a broad left-liberalism in politics: as Ralph Berry commented, 'While there was no question of the theatre promulgating an ideology, it was generally understood that the beliefs and ideals of the RSC were left of centre.'[6] It is possible, of course, to play *Coriolanus* from almost any political perspective but the RSC, by the end of the 1980s, seemed to be eschewing any acknowledgement of having a political position at all, either generally or particularly, so that Hands, whose

2. *Coriolanus* 2.3, RSC, 1989: Coriolanus (Charles Dance) meets the people

work on productions of Shakespeare's English histories earlier in his career was clear and forthright in the political self-definition of an attitude towards the plays' political meaning, seemed to have tried to occlude any suggestion that a politics was necessary or desirable in tackling an exact depiction of the workings of the state and its people in *Coriolanus*. In itself that could be seen as a post-Thatcherite position, a pulling-away from a visible politics to leave an assertion of the play as cultural object, an object within a commerce of theatre. But the production seemed to lack what it would not be overcruel to term the courage of its lack of convictions.

As it was, the crowd suffered from the tension between realism and stylisation, a stylistic insecurity that bedevilled the production. Occasionally individualised, the plebeians were more often treated as an undifferentiated mass, arranged formally into groups to fill the stage but never appearing comfortable with each other, as if the actors, not the plebeians, had hardly ever met before. Their black costumes connoted a uniformity, parallel to their choric responses. As usual, the director(s) had found no way of making sense of speeches by 'All', the most ungainly of all Shakespearean speech prefixes.

Rome, a consistently brightly lit city, was obviously a place where a great deal of civic work was being done: in 2.1, for instance, after the victory over the Volscians, plebeians were hard at work cleaning the frieze on the bronze monument that dominated the stage, and in 4.6, once Coriolanus had been banished, Roman citizens could be seen taking up basket-weaving (a sure sign of peace) while the tribunes, now dressed in gleaming white, wandered around patting babies, conveniently presented by passing mothers for them to pat. In the latter scene, admittedly, the babies were a part of the production's determination to ridicule the tribunes at every opportunity (exemplified by casting two comic actors in the roles) but the basket- weaving looked like a serious gesture at fleshing out the reality of Rome. It was, however, not the presentation of a theatrical context but a continuous distraction, trivialising the play's vision of the city. It was directly comparable to the representations of the Volscian society in 4.3, set, it would appear, in some Volscian nightclub with two appalling dancers swaying in a fake Tartar routine upstage, a couple canoodling on a bench and four other Volscians seated at a table, indicating, I presume, the depths of Volscian depravity and decadence by playing dice and drinking. Throughout the production, the bright daylight of Rome was contrasted with the Volscian gloom broken by fiery torches. But the play's finely detailed contrasts between the two communities were coarsened and trivialised by such business, providing only a distraction and not a context for the play's politics.

What was much more intriguing was the careful and thoughtful use of the women in the two crowds, Roman and Volscian. In 2.3 it was the women plebeians who provided the switch of mood against Coriolanus with the Third Citizen's speech (2.3.166–73) divided between a group of women. In 5.1 there was a strong emphasis on the men arming for the threat of war and, by the end of the scene, a powerful image of the women left behind, the city unmanned. The tiny scene of the women's triumphant return to Rome (5.5) was handed over to the women as well. The speech by the Senator was spoken by Valeria but the scene was dominated by Volumnia who paraded Young Martius, now in full military costume, as the new Coriolanus, receiving his father's sword from Valeria. As the people knelt to this image of patrician authority in triumph, Coriolanus's fall became Volumnia's victory, her power transferred from son to grandson, the matriarchal control still unquestioned. Even more emphatically, the voices of the Volscian people in 5.6 shouting against Coriolanus were all women, a female recognition of the costs of Coriolanus's actions by the people who are 'widowed and unchilded' (as Aufidius calls them at 5.6.152). The Volscian women urged their men to attack Coriolanus who was knifed by Aufidius and then mobbed and beaten to death by the crowd. Such moments created exactly the notion of a society, a community of people, against which Coriolanus himself was set. This was far more coherent as a revision of the position of women within the play's culture than Kyle had achieved in *All's Well*. It built on the play's strong presence of women in Rome's politics, dominated by Volumnia, and allowed for the action to be seen in relation to both genders within the city. The Volscian women who bayed for Coriolanus's death, shouting their losses ('He killed my son! My daughter! . . . He killed my father', 5.6.122–3) and finding revenge the only consequence, were offered as relatives of a Volumnia whose diet of anger ('Anger's my meat, I sup upon myself', 4.2.53) had transferred to them.

The production's publicity was dominated by a photograph of Charles Dance as Coriolanus. What the production revealed consistently was a glaring gap between characters' reactions to Coriolanus and Coriolanus himself. On his first entrance the citizens scurried away terrified as he stalked magisterially on to the stage, cradling an unsheathed sword in his arms, as so often throughout the play; in 3.3 his glowering at Sicinius across a small table was enough to reduce Sicinius (Geoffrey Freshwater) to a gibbering, quaking jelly whose papers rustled uncontrollably in his hands, so that the tribune became a disconcerting depiction of what a Thatcherite leader might wish to do to a trade unionist. Again and again Hands used stagey devices to increase the menace and authority of Dance's performance. At 1.7.21, the entry of 'Martius, bloody' became an entry of a ghostly figure of power coming down an avenue of light, with another spot glancing flashes of light from the blade of the sword he cradled and with his speech backed up by an exaggerated atmospheric echo, used again for 'There is a world elsewhere' (3.3.139).

But such devices only served to emphasise all the more strongly that Dance needed such support to cover his own deficiencies of technique and imagination. At his best as the child of Barbara Jefford's tigerish and authoritarian mother, Dance found it easy to underline the potential comedy of the struggle between them in 3.2; 'Look, I am going' (134) sounded like nothing so much as 'Look, I really am off to tidy my bedroom', instantly made serious by the force of Volumnia's implied threat of giving up on him in 'Do your will' (137). But at too many other moments the lightness and comedy that Dance finds so much closer to his natural acting style surfaced inappropriately: the battlefield request 'Have we no wine here?' (1.10.91) is not a dinner-party enquiry about the contents of the cocktail cabinet. The attempts at demonstrating a vitality and frustrated power were unconvincing: Dance spent too much time pacing the stage as a poor theatrical indication of restless energy.

Dance had played Aufidius to Alan Howard's Coriolanus in 1977. His own Aufidius was Malcolm Storry who demonstrated that he should have been cast as Coriolanus. Shaven-headed, Storry effortlessly produced an aura of brutality and viciousness, a social contempt and an arrogant physicality, all of which Dance lacked. Storry switched between the cold excitement of dominance and the horrified shame and disbelief at defeat. The meeting with Coriolanus in 4.5 transformed magically from the cold, hard threat of the repeated question 'What's thy name?' to an exhilaration of recognition, the realisation that Coriolanus had come to him. By the end of the play, standing astride Coriolanus's corpse, Storry's Aufidius was both triumphant and yet emptied by the triumph; as the crowd shuffled off and sneaked away, Aufidius and the nobles, left alone on stage with the corpse, picked it up and bore it off, the last one extinguishing the last torch to leave the stage in darkness, a downbeat ending that showed a confidence rarely visible elsewhere.

In 1990 Stratford reverted to a March to January programme, opening with Bill Alexander's production of *Much Ado About Nothing*, inaugurating a season plagued by the extravagances of designers. There are times when I wonder whether designers have ever read the play they are working on. *Much Ado About Nothing* is hardly the most demanding of Shakespeare's plays for a designer, but there are certain things one cannot do without if the production is to have anything approximating to a realist set at all: there must be somewhere that at least suggests a church for Hero and Claudio not to get married in; there must be something approximating to a convincing monument for Hero not to have been buried in; and it is not unreasonable to expect something for both Benedick and Beatrice to hide behind for their respective gulling scenes. Kit Surrey's set failed to meet the first two demands. The RSC's previous and disastrous production of the play in 1988 (with a Benedick trying to hide behind a deckchair on an empty stage) ought to have taught them much but the 1990 production exercised a sexually discriminatory policy that gave Benedick a cypress tree to climb up and fall out of in 2.3 but left Beatrice in 3.1 propped up against the proscenium arch looking unsure whether she was effectively invisible or not – indeed, the lighting, which left her in semi-sepulchral gloom, seemed equally unsure whether she was on stage or not. By this point the audience felt sorry for the actress, not Beatrice, with no place to hide.

Beatrice's or, rather, Susan Fleetwood's plight in 3.1 was of a piece with the production's difficulties with Beatrice all through. Things started well with the discovery of her at the play's opening, fencing with Leonato and comfortably beating him, even if it could be seen as a rather literal analogy to the wit combats to follow. This opening dumb-show – and the RSC's house style seemed to require a production to open with an ever more substantial piece of action before the first word is spoken[7] – here served to underline Beatrice's independence, at least in relation to her uncle, and her transgressive skill in a defiantly masculine art. The fencing gloves anticipated the glove that Beatrice and Benedick used to throw down their challenge to each other, its transfer marking the oscillations of power: hurled down by Beatrice on her exit at 1.1.153, for instance, it was returned by Benedick, equally emphatically, on his exit at 2.1.257.

Susan Fleetwood's confident and intelligent handling of the language, mature and effective, was rather helped by being set against a Hero and company who were all too like characters in *The Mikado* 'full to the brim with girlish glee'. But Beatrice's defencelessness in the face of Hero and Ursula was more than a consequence of the set. Instead the character had lost her comic defences, the vivacity and control of the opening scenes becoming brittle in retrospect, the pain and loneliness beneath now more openly apparent to the audience. But, sentimentally spotlit on a darkening stage for her stanzaic soliloquy (3.1.107–16), Beatrice was left to reach for a genuine weight and seriousness that the production seemed unwilling to allow her.

This was consistent with the production's argument about the play's attitude towards women, for clearly they were of far less importance than male bonding and an awareness of social hierarchies. Beatrice's mocking of Don Pedro's offer of marriage ('Will you have me, lady?', 2.1.305) was especially disruptive not only because his status was ridiculed but even more so because Don Pedro's offer was plainly serious. His admiration of her seemed to matter because such feelings so rarely surfaced. This male focus was visible in the church scene (4.1), where the focus of attention was most often on Leonato, not Hero. His distress and fury led him to assume the truth of the accusations and to come close to putting into practice the violence against her that he promises ('These hands shall tear her', 4.1.193). In this context Beatrice's near-hysteria at Benedick's refusal to kill Claudio was a logical response to her powerlessness and her cry 'O that I were a man!' (4.1.304) sounded like a rational ambition, for the production opened a decisive gap between her success at the pretence of duelling and her exclusion from the transfer of the skill into direct action: beating Leonato was within her domain, killing Claudio could never be.

Within the context of a markedly traditionalist production, the problems of Beatrice's butting up against the parameters of female action reflected the RSC's sustained problem of negotiating an alternative, post-feminist approach to female performance both by the actor and in the Shakespearean text. *Much Ado* was of a piece with the awkward exploration of sisterhood in Kyle's *All's Well* and Hands' investigation of the Volscian women in his *Coriolanus*. Susan Fleetwood's Beatrice was never going to be a member of the group of 'clamorous voices'[8] for the production denied her a space even while gesturing towards one. The exploration of Beatrice's difference, so firmly structured into the play, was endlessly compromised by the production's self-congratulatory and comforting return to a fascination with the difficulties of masculinity. Such treatment of gender looks ostensibly modern, in being prepared to critique the male world at all, but it is a regression and evasion of the challenge to masculinity that could be achieved by a sustained re-examination of the spaces left by patriarchy.

When later Benedick advised Beatrice, with great seriousness, to 'Serve God, love me, and mend' (5.2.84), he seemed to be offering her the protection of a male world and the production did not begin to suggest why she might have good grounds for feeling a little dubious about the offer. By the end of this production the relationship of Beatrice and Benedick mattered much less than that between Claudio and Benedick, a relationship still as venomous after the rebirth of Hero as it had been after her death. Benedick's barely controlled fury at 'my lord Lackbeard' (5.1.188) had not at all abated. Only Beatrice's intervention stopped Benedick continuing the quarrel after this Claudio's sneering delivery of his final speech in the play (5.4.111–15) and her intervention was a kiss of such passion and length that the watchers, on stage and off, began to become embarrassed. Female sexual desire, Beatrice's for Benedick, was marked as an efficient social device to divert male attention from the anger and awkwardness of male friendship. But since the play's and production's climax was effectively the reconciliation of the two men with a handshake, it relegated women to fashionable and attractive accessories for men. As Kyle found in *All's Well* a depiction of men as boys, so Alexander found in *Much Ado* a depiction of a male need for camaraderie far beyond the significance of marriage. The RSC seemed far more adroit and perceptive in its investigation of male bonding than of female friendship or heterosexual desire. It was disappointing that too many performances were perfunctory when the production's argument was perfectly clear and interesting, for all its limitations.

The two productions of *King Lear* which opened a few weeks apart, Nicholas Hytner's for the RSC and Deborah Warner's for the Royal National Theatre, could not have been more unlike. Newspaper critics found themselves unable to praise both: those who had admired Hytner's expressed deep disappointment with Warner's; those who damned the RSC seemed to do so in anticipation of their pleasures at the National. That it seemed difficult to like both was a direct consequence of the nature of the two productions.

It is not uncommon for the same Shakespeare play to be on at the country's two most prestigious theatres at the same time. It had happened before in 1988 with *The Tempest* when Hytner's RSC production with John Wood played at the same time as Peter Hall's at

the National with Michael Bryant. But the co-existence of the two
King Lears was a product of a queue. After Deborah Warner's production of *Titus Andronicus* for the RSC with Brian Cox as Titus in
1987, it was widely seen as inevitable that the two would move on
to *King Lear.* Brian Cox opens his account of the rehearsals and
tour with a telephone conversation:

'So we're in a queue, are we?' I asked.
'Yes. Barry Kyle and Bob Peck, then it looks like Nick Hytner and John
Wood.'
'All that hype about me following *Titus* with *Lear* – somebody ought to
tell Michael Billington there's a queue for Lear.'[9]

When Bob Peck decided not to play Lear, Warner and Cox moved
up the queue, then Richard Eyre, the artistic director of the
National Theatre, decided to send a company led by Ian McKellen
on an international tour of two plays, and Warner was invited to
direct *King Lear* for it. International theatre culture and the commercial implications for the National Theatre of such a prestigious
tour produced a clash which neither company saw reason to avoid,
though Cox's diaries are full of anxiety about the closeness of the
two opening nights. The theatrical economy means that the
competition is seen as healthy: the increasing hype it causes gener-
ates audience interest and, it is assumed, a desire to see both productions in order to compare and contrast. But it is precisely that
that becomes most disturbing: the productions are only seen as an
opportunity for choice. The distinctiveness is submerged in difference: Cox is 'not-Wood', Hytner 'not-Warner'.

What the comparison never defines is any way in which the RSC
is 'not-the-National-Theatre'. The companies have only a geographical distinctiveness. If the visual and directorial style of
Warner's production was unlike Hytner's, Eyre's 1990 National
Theatre production of *Richard III* could have sat comfortably
alongside Hytner's *Lear* at the RSC, a company for which Eyre has
never directed Shakespeare. After her productions with Kick
Theatre, a small-scale touring company she created, Warner had
moved to the RSC, even if her method there emphatically defined
a difference from the conventional forms of British Shakespeare
production. What was unusual about Warner's *King Lear* was a consequence of the intense nature of her work, not the theatre
company for which she was working. A distinctive company style

becomes invisible within the culture of the interchange of theatre personnel and within the commercial ethic of large-scale design. The only effective demarcation between Shakespeare at the RSC and Shakespeare at the National is the comparative infrequency with which the latter produces Shakespeare: usually no more than one production a year. The RSC's Shakespeare style resonates far beyond its own work.

Since I have been and will be frequently praising simplicity over directorial excess it may appear perverse now to be praising Hytner's work over Warner's. But I have to record that, midway through the first half of the Stratford production, I found that I was shaking with fear, frightened by the action on stage, and that, going to the National Theatre with high expectations, I found myself often bored, engaged more often in thinking about the production than absorbed by it, able to stay serenely indifferent to the events on stage. Emotional effect is not everything but Warner's method seeks to make the actor into the generator of emotional power. When it does not happen, the production appears to have failed by its own intents. Hytner's work, operatically opulent and inventive, succeeded because the invention cohered, local effects growing into dramatic architecture.

The problem is less the intrinsic adequacy of a view of the play than the theatrical adequacy of the representation of the drama. Hytner's *King Lear* depended on theatricality, often of baroque extremes, for a dramatic argument. It was at times deliberately – almost too deliberately – controversial. Of course there were ideas that did not work. But if the local effects and sustained theatricality seemed to many nothing more than a display of artifice, overlaying the action, I found them the means to create a powerful emotional and intellectual force.

Hytner's productions have always been marked by a fresh rereading of the play. Nothing is assumed simply through tradition, theatrical rights of memory; nothing can evade sharp rethinking. Here the rethinking began with the nature of the text. For the first time in England a major production of *King Lear* took full account of recent textual scholarship. Hytner used a Folio text, though there were a few small additions from Quarto, lines actors could not quite be persuaded to part with but nothing that substantially affected the logic of the Folio text. Hytner's use of the Folio text was entirely convincing, providing a slightly leaner, more purposive form than the conflated text allows for. The energy of the third quarter of the play never flagged, not only because of the authority of Norman Rodway's Gloucester but also because of the clarifying drive of the text itself.

The only major incursion from Quarto was the mock-trial scene. Hytner argued that Folio 3.6 is weak dramatically, the scene seeming to lack shape and purpose. Given the possibility of censorship as the reason for excision, the dramatic and theatrical argument for including Q13.16–51 was convincing. If it affected the textual consistency of the production it did so for sound theatrical reasons. The scene became a pivotal moment of transition and recapitulation. Set in a room full of piles of chairs, effectively the lumber-room of Gloucester's house, the mock-trial set up two stools and two chairs in a deliberate echo of the arrangement of chairs for the daughters and for Lear himself in the love-test of the opening scene, with the 'throne' covered in broken-down blue velvet to echo the blue cloth over the throne at the start. Lear's moves and gestures again and again repeated and distorted his actions at the start, a nightmarish reworking of the opening. With the placing of the bodies at the end of the play again made carefully to echo the opening scene – and why else does Shakespeare bring the corpses of Regan and Goneril on stage? – the mock-trial became a crucial mark of dramatic shaping, the mid-point of the play's journey, a sign of the distance traversed and that yet to come.

In a two-text edition of *King Lear*, paralleling the Quarto and Folio versions, René Weis complained that Hytner's inclusion of the mock-trial scene made the production

> no purer in imaginative conception than any other text of Shakespeare cut and tailored to suit particular productions. Actual performances do not necessarily offer the best way of assessing the degree of adequacy of textual theories, even if the theories are formulated partly with imagined productions in mind.[10]

Weis's argument would only make sense if the aim of Hytner's interest in the textual problems of the play had been to validate textual arguments. But Hytner's concern was only to test the possibilities of using a substantially Folio text within the context of an aggressively late twentieth-century production. His aims were not scholarly and the viability of the Folio text was only tested within the particular cultural context of a large-scale, spectacularly designed RSC production. Yet the comparative rigour of the production's text, analogous to the textual purity tested out by Peter Hall in a number of productions in the 1980s and 1990s, assisted by Roger Warren, the academic as textual dramaturg, had significantly fewer arbitrary textual choices than most productions, which cut the text to suit themselves.

There were moments that Hytner's production failed totally to solve. The storm scene, for instance, was one of the moments when David Fielding's set proved inordinately constricting. The centre-piece of the set was a giant cube placed upstage and able to revolve. Scene changes were marked by quarter-turns of the cube, presenting alternately a metallic wall or an open space in which furniture could be set. At times, the effect was sharp: a 180-degree turn in 5.2 enabled a change from a green, flourishing, optimistic tree to one blackened and blasted by the cataclysm of the defeat of the Cordelia–Lear army. But placing Lear and Fool inside the cube as it turned continually for the storm, backed by a spinning vertical rectangle with storm clouds projected behind, failed to suggest substantive disorder, even if there was something unnerving in the way the half-turns of the cube always revealed Lear to be facing the audience.

But such rare misjudgements were offset by many other passages cast in a new and exciting light, physical action redefining the movement of the drama. The banishment of Kent will serve as an example. Kent's interruption disrupts the ceremonial formality of Lear's court. As Lear hurled Kent to the floor, Lear himself, as well as his courtiers, was appalled by his violence. Unable to admit to himself the destructive effect of disinheriting Cordelia, he could acknowledge what it meant to have stooped to a physical assault on a trusted councillor. John Wood's Lear was left beckoning to Kent (David Troughton) to rise, able to mitigate the brutal decree only by offering Kent five days' respite, stroking Kent's head as he did so. But he reacquired his awesome power as he moved upstage: 'Away! By Jupiter, / This shall not be revoked' (1.1.177–8) made emphatically clear that, while Kent may have demanded that Lear should change his mind, on this matter at least there was no possibility of change.

It was this intensity of local effect by Wood that most irritated many of the production's antagonists. Wood's voice is what used to be called 'a magnificent instrument' and he is unashamed to use it. The result was operatic in the extreme. Each speech was so full of detail, so richly filled with the possibilities of vocal colour that the result was for some simply excessive, language being burdened by the actor's attention. At times the colour seemed to be there for its own sake, a self-regarding display of technique. Wood demanded that we were seduced by his performance. We could only choose whether to be won over by it or to find it offensively indulgent. Its most extreme effects, as in the discovery of a new rich bass colouring on 'You do me wrong' (4.6.38), opened new ranges of emotional experience. What Wood could not allow for were the play's shattering moments of simplicity.

It would be wrong, though, ever to regard the vocal effects as thoughtless. When Wood's Lear put down the map which he had carried on to the stage in 1.1, seated himself in the throne and then realised that he could not reach the map, the line 'Give me the map *there*' (1.1.37, Wood's emphasis) became comic but it is not over-reading the moment to see his annoyance, as if it is someone else's fault that he cannot reach it rather than his own, as a small but indicative signpost to Lear's nature and the peremptory tone of the demand as the natural language for someone used to having every whim obeyed. Yet the pointing of the line and its relation to stage-business forced the audience's attention on to the line, as if each moment must be distinctive, a sweet to be savoured.

At their best, Wood and Hytner combined to take a familiar line and make it newly central. At Gloucester's castle, for instance, Lear's line to Goneril 'I prithee, daughter, do not make me mad' (2.2.391) became the key to a scene which was the most intense in the whole production. For the threat that Goneril brings with her was fixed visually by the two attendant nurses and the wheelchair she had in her train; she was not so much making him mad as recognising him as mad and treating him as such, certifying him insane in modern terms. He knew – and the awareness was excruciatingly painful, frightening and humiliating – that she probably was, for all her harshness, right. His earlier cry, 'O, let me not be mad, not mad, sweet heaven' (1.5.45), was uttered by a man who knew that he nearly was mad already, that the plea was already too late. Now the confrontation with his own insanity was extreme. What was unbearable here, both for him and for us, was the cold rationality of Goneril's action. Such moments anticipated Wood's playing of the madness later on. This Lear was quite the maddest I have seen, carefully charting the liberation that madness provided for him. By the time he met Edgar, Wood's Lear was a willing accomplice in Poor Tom's invented world, chasing across the stage to shoo away the imaginary devils.

Hytner can be a literal-minded director, overly faithful to the text: Gloucester no sooner said 'I shall not need spectacles' (1.2.36) than he took a pair out of his pocket and put them on. In the blinding of Gloucester, though, he made a small and highly indicative change. The Folio text marks an exit for Gloucester before Regan's line 'How is't, my lord?' (3.7.92), making the line clearly addressed to Cornwall. Instead Sally Dexter made the line a moment of concern for Gloucester himself, a tenderness entirely at odds with her brutality seconds earlier. It was of a piece with the production's whole approach to the sisters. If audiences have grown used to seeing Regan and Goneril as fairy-tale characters out of, say, *Cinderella*, Hytner argued for a different approach. This Goneril and Regan did love their father; they were driven to action against him by what he himself had revealed of his ungovernable rage in the first scene. The protestations of love in 1.1 may have been generated by greed, by fear and by fake rhetoric but they were not treated as insincere. Regan's language refers to her father continually; speaking to Gloucester, for instance, she identifies Edgar as 'my father's godson . . . / He whom my father named' before defining him as 'your Edgar' (2.1.90–1). When Gloucester was raised from his bed by the fight between Kent and Oswald she was tenderly solicitous, wrapping his blanket carefully around him, sitting him down while Cornwall dealt with the hubbub. Gloucester was clearly her substitute father, another example of a love that cannot be offered to the right object, that need to love that marked the production. The torture of the old man made her scream, releasing the violence of her hatred of her own father. Her concern for Gloucester in the redirected line represented her attempt to dissociate herself from the scene and her concern for a father in pain. There was a mixture here of incomprehension and appalled awareness of her own complicity. Everything Regan had done so far and everything that she would go on to do pivoted on this moment.[11]

I complained earlier about designers who seem not to have read the play they are working on. David Fielding clearly had and the

3. *King Lear* 4.5, RSC, 1990: Lear (John Wood) and Gloucester
(Norman Rodway)

detailing of the set was powerfully responsive to the play. For the
first time in my experience a designer took Cordelia's description
of her landscape as an accurate basis for the set: Lear has been
seen 'Crowned with . . . / . . . all the idle weeds that grow / In our
sustaining corn' and is to be found in 'the high-grown field'
(4.3.3–7). The sheaves of corn through which Wood's Lear made
his way were a bizarre vision of a perfect English summer, an
Arcadian idyll which made the pain all the more acute. The set's
beauty was no consolation, simply a disjunctive index of the inco-
herence of the play's world. At moments like these the production's trust in the play to make its meaning plain was richly
rewarded.

Deborah Warner's designer at the Royal National Theatre,
Hildegard Bechtler, created a minimalist set whose link to *King
Lear* was purely tangential, without leaving the stage bare enough.
Brian Cox's description, on first seeing the set during rehearsals,
was of

a large, empty white space on a slight rake, fractured by a series of cloths lowered to change locale and climate – a leaden sky, the white cliffs of Dover – and a white floorcloth which can be torn up at the beginning of the storm, leaving a vast muddy underlay. (*Lear Diaries*, p. 20)

But the meaning of the canvas hangings, dangling swathes of cloth and strips of floor covering were opaque to me. At the beginning of 1.2, for instance, Edmond removed a piece of gold drapery but it was never apparent whether this action belonged to the previous scene, arbitrarily carried out by a conveniently available actor, marking the ending of court opulence and formality, or identified the beginning of Edmond's own action.

It had been intended, according to Cox, that the set would be 'dominated by a long catwalk that will divide the floorspace' (p. 20) but in the event the catwalk, once built, proved far too heavy: Cox noted, in his rehearsal diary, 'we struggled again with the catwalk which no one can budge – a pity, because the stage is going to look mighty empty without it' (p. 59). Putting a few pieces of set into a space as large as the Lyttelton exposes both set and actors cruelly.

The only significant advantage the set gave the actors was a narrow gap in the middle of the back wall of the stage, an opening in the dirty canvas which focused attention for entrances and exits. Lear and Cordelia could walk slowly up the centre-line of the stage towards it at the end of 4.6 and Lear could enter through it, pushing the dead Cordelia in a wheelchair, her body lying grotesquely upside down with her red hair streaming, an entrance all the more powerful since it was a focus of attention for the audience but unseen by the other characters who were all facing downstage. This entry, indeed, showed the strengths of Deborah Warner's production. Where Wood's Lear howled his 'Howl's starting off stage, Brian Cox went quietly up to a number of the people on stage, quietly urging them to howl, speaking the word as if in some perplexity as to why they were not howling. Howling was, for him, the most natural action in the world and he looked for the others to participate, like a director who cannot quite see why the actors are not doing what they should so obviously be doing. Downbeat and simple, the playing revivified the line, making freshly painful an emotion which one thought one knew how to handle.

Cox, always a wildly dangerous actor, was, as if inverting Wood's work, most effective in such moments of quiet control. The meeting with Gloucester in 4.5 was filled with excess and coarseness, Lear, for instance, coming on with plastic carrier-bags or wiping his hand elaborately in his crotch before sniffing it on 'it smells of mortality' (129). Cox wanted such effects to 'heighten the humour and the fantastical. Much of the mechanics of *Lear* is in the humour and we need to exploit it to the full to keep up a buoyancy – a reflection of the madness – and suddenly switch and make people cry at the same time' (p.62). This was magnificently exemplified in the metamorphosis of the comic wry speaking to Gloucester of 'Ay, every inch a king' (107) into the calm dignity of 'I am a king. / Masters, know you that?' (195–6). Though dressed only in baggy combinations, a king humbled and humiliated, this Lear was still stating a simple fact, a fact painful precisely because true.

But at other times, director and actor combined to produce poor pieces of business. Red noses were back again, as they had been in the RSC's *As You Like It* the year before (see chapter 3, below). It made good sense for Fool to stick a red nose on Lear in 1.4 as a mark of the transfer of folly. But it was crass for Lear, cradling Cordelia's corpse, to fish around in his pockets, find the same red nose and try it first on himself and then on Cordelia to explain 'my poor fool is hanged' (5.3.281). Cox, who had proposed the idea, knew it was a risky piece of business. The response of others in the company was mixed but Jean Kalman, the lighting designer who worked with Peter Brook in Paris, and Hildegard Bechtler, 'loved the nose. It's a very unEnglish thing to do. David Bradley [who played Fool] thought it dangerous but exciting' (p. 65). It is far from clear why such an effect should be seen as 'unEnglish': English Shakespeare productions are as full of such visual devices as European ones and the danger of the business lay in its potential to distract from the actor's power to create desolate despair, leaving me wondering how it had been transferred through Lear's changes of costume.

The red nose was a spurious attempt to find coherence and connection across the expanse of the play. In the wheelchair, however, Warner found a linking motif. Where Hytner's Lear was threatened by the wheelchair Goneril brought with her, Warner's Lear entered in one. Careering wildly on to the stage with his daughters laughing around him, Lear was clearly celebrating his birthday, complete with paper hats and party favours for all the family. Gone was the solemnity of the moment, gone too was any suggestion that the division of the kingdom was a matter of state. Where John Wood's court was quite well populated with formally dressed courtiers who knelt at the entrance of the king, Cox's court had two or three people standing around while he indulged in his private party game. The idea of the wheelchair came to Cox even before rehearsals began:

The only image I have of Lear at the moment is of an old man in a wheelchair. The wheelchair could denote helplessness and also perhaps cunning. I got this idea from the amount of time I have spent in air terminals noticing the way the old are manoeuvred through passport queues or security checks: they arrive at the airport with loads of baggage, hale and hearty, and are transferred to a waiting wheelchair, which causes them to age twenty years. As soon as they arrive on board they are sprightly young things again. (p. 15)

In the course of rehearsals Cox found that the wheelchair paid unexpected dividends:

The big discovery of the afternoon was the tremendous advantages of the wheelchair. Unlike a throne fixed in the centre of the stage it is a shifting focal point which allows interesting staging variations. (p.27)

Lear's unexpected mobility, in a scene in which the actor often seems pinned into the throne, usually at least until the banishment of Kent, was satisfyingly disconcerting. The wheelchair came equipped with convenient holders for a rolled-up map and the scissors with which he carefully and playfully cut the map in three, 'showing the irony of something so huge as a country being reduced to the size of a school atlas, the irony reinforcing the edgy humour of the scene' (p. 27).

Lear teased his daughters as if they were still children but the teasing had become a repellent form of bullying; the game had gone on too long. Always ready to give Regan a kiss and a cuddle, Lear had tried to preserve her childhood, and Clare Higgins's Regan clearly found the old man's gropings a denial of her maturity, even though she had grown up conspiring in the flirtatious game. Higgins suggested and Cox resisted the idea that Regan had been sexually abused by her father but there was a strong current of sexuality in the relationship, leaving the hint of abuse.

The wheelchair was in 1.1 a sign of age but also of the resistance to being old. There was nothing restrictive about being confined to it; indeed, like the crutches used by Antony Sher as Richard III in 1984, the wheelchair freed Cox's Lear from the problems of physical infirmity. Throughout the scene, this Lear had the gleeful irresponsibility of age, the only problem being its inappropriateness both for a king and for the father of two dangerous daughters.

If Lear in 1.1 seemed to be mocking the implications of the wheelchair, then, as he waited for his horses at Goneril's palace in 1.5, the demands of the wheelchair had become irrefutable. Bundled up with a rug over his knees, Lear looked old and vulnerable, a geriatric out-patient waiting for the ambulance to take him home. As Lear's world fragmented, so too did the chair: in the storm scenes, staged as brilliantly as Hytner's had been disappointing, Lear and Fool sheltered under a cymbal, taken, apparently, from the wheels of the chair, as torchlight shafted across the black stage and two timpanists, visible on either side of the stage, thundered a storm, against which Lear tried to compete, banging on the cymbal with a whip.

All of this must appear very promising but the energy and excitement of such moments were far too intermittent. Warner's commitment to a full, conflated text seemed, after the triumphant justification of the Folio by Hytner, to generate diffusion and a lack of energy, magnifying the difficulty of making the production coherent. It was not helped by a series of lack-lustre performances: Ian McKellen's despairingly loyal Kent and David Bradley's Fool apart, Cox had painfully little support. Good Fools are dangerous individuals: the brilliance of Sher's Fool destroyed Michael Gambon's chances of success as Lear in Adrian Noble's production for the RSC in 1982. David Bradley's Fool posed no such problem, working with great generosity and harmony with Cox. This Fool was clearly an old pro, wearing an old flying-helmet, and bare-chested under a suit with trousers too short for him. Lean and pinched, he manifested an anger born of frustration at Lear and a self-deprecatory embarrassment born of an awareness of his hackneyed old jokes. But both the anger and the self-dismissiveness were part of his concern for Lear, recognised by his master who could kiss his hand and slap it away immediately after. As Lear moved further and further away from Fool's counsel, Fool became angrier and angrier, doggedly trying to make Lear listen. Once

Lear had met Edgar there was no longer a point of contact with Fool. Organising the mock-trial, Lear, almost without noticing him, casually tipped Fool out of the wheelbarrow in which he was resting. Fool became an unwilling participant, mocking Lear's fantasies with his dry 'I took you for a joint-stool' (Q13.47). The storm had exhausted him and he was left dying, stretched out on the floor, shivering uncontrollably, by the end of the scene, his weak attempts to get up to follow Lear useless. The interval, taken at this point, left the audience with the sight of Fool's corpse alone on stage.

Warner's *King Lear* lasted well over four hours; Hytner's *King Lear* little short of the same length. Reports of European Shakespeare productions lasting six or seven hours have always been received with incredulity in England; now English audiences were expected to have similar stamina. Performances of *King Lear* should be exhausting experiences but it takes sustained energy and drive to justify such a performing length. Warner simply could not. It was not helped by the strong feeling that the Lyttelton stage was too large for her. Warner's Shakespeare work for the RSC had been in small spaces. Actors in *King Lear* moved limply to fill spaces, unwilling to accept the vacuums around them. It seemed a studio production awkwardly metamorphosed.

In tandem with Warner's *King Lear*, performed by the same cast and toured with it, the National mounted Richard Eyre's production of *Richard III*, with McKellen as Richard. Where Warner's work effectively left the play to speak for itself, Eyre's was a grandly operatic production. The contrasts between the two were as provocative as anything in contemporary Shakespeare production. Eyre's *Richard III* would later be transformed into the 1996 film, directed by Richard Loncraine with a screenplay by McKellen and Loncraine, but my concern here is solely with the stage production, not with the differences between stage and film versions.[12]

Eyre identifies the especial need to 'present the plays in a way that is true to their own terms, and at the same time bring[s] them alive for a contemporary audience' but he also sees a peculiar difficulty in achieving this in a large theatre for an audience that no longer listens: 'nowadays we see before we hear.'[13] In such a context, the collaboration with the designer becomes of especial importance and Eyre writes eloquently of how 'you advance slowly, day by day, in a kind of amiable dialectic' (p. 163). Eyre, the designer Bob Crowley and McKellen did not begin with the concept of a precise analogy, a redefinition of *Richard III* through the choice of period for the setting, but none the less one emerged.

On a black curtain a huge projection announced 'Edward IV'. As it was whisked away, the noise of horses, trumpets and warfare accompanied a thick pall of smoke which cleared as a soldier moved slowly downstage: a First World War officer in full uniform, cap and greatcoat, one arm in his pocket, limping slightly. The voice, when he started speaking, was clipped Sandhurst. The impression, if one didn't listen to what he was saying, was of someone who had returned from the Front with a Blighty wound. The clash of two histories, the authoritative announcement of the projection defining the reign and the scrupulously precise dating of the costumes, recurred throughout the production. The curtain descending for the interval had 'Richard III' projected on to it but the figure caught by the spotlight alone high above the stage was in Fascist blackshirt uniform with his arm raised in a disturbing amalgam of a cheery wave and Hitler's version of a Nazi salute.

Eyre's production had carefully considered and then rejected a number of possible ways of playing. Divorced from the *Henry VI* plays, *Richard III* cannot easily appear the outcome of a long process of early modern history. After Antony Sher's 1984 Richard on crutches, there must have been little to tempt McKellen into a physically virtuosic performance. Instead the production saw in Richard's rise an analogy for an alternative history of Britain between the wars, a successful coup by a leader who adroitly perceived and utilised the efficacy of Fascist militarism, overthrowing an atrophied aristocracy by the energy of populist thuggery. As Ian McKellen wrote later, '[Shakespeare] was creating history-which-never-happened. Our production was properly in the realm of "what might have been".'[14]

Crowley's design emphasised the developing use of Nazi iconology. The early images showed the members of Edward IV's court dressed either in full white-tie evening dress with sashes and decorations or British military uniform. As Richard moved towards taking power, the production began to explore the threatening qualities of the new blackshirt uniform: Richard's entry to the council scene (3.4.20) startlingly revealed him to have discarded the codes of British costume for his new brutalist style, accompanied by guards from some private army, dressed in the same threatening uniforms. Crowley used the more recent English Fascist right's annexation of British nationalism with Richard's triumphant use of armbands and banners, mixing the red cross of St George with a Gloucester-derived boar-motif.

At its best the production used the insidious takeover of the black costumes to mark the growth of Richard's power. The Brackenbury who accompanied Clarence to the Tower in 1.1 was dressed as an English officer; by the time he refused the Queens entry to the Princes in 4.1 he had taken on the black uniform, defining himself as one of Richard's men. Richard's wooing of Anne (1.2) was played on an almost deserted stage with bored hospital orderlies waiting on the side to find out what to do with the body on the stretcher-trolley. Richard's wooing of Elizabeth for her daughter (4.4.197ff.) took place in front of a long, menacing line of his soldiers, silent until Richard's final comment ('Relenting fool, and shallow, changing woman', 4.4.362) elicited a huge guffaw, echoing with male barrack-room mockery of all women.

Controlled use of the armband motif marked the progress of tyranny. Buckingham's realisation of his need to escape (4.2.122–5) was pinpointed by his discarding the Richard armband. Stanley, present on stage when Buckingham engineered the assent of the citizens to Richard's coronation (3.7), manifested his reluctance to be there but still wore one of Richard's armbands. The whole scene became a Shakespearean version of a Nuremberg rally (or was it rather more like a piece of Brecht's *Arturo Ui*?) with Buckingham using the technology of thirties propaganda, microphones and all, to converse with Richard who loomed threateningly on the raised platform of an elevating truck. Richard's acceptance speech (3.7.217–26) was spoken in the rich fruity tones of popular oratory and the crowd's response of 'Amen' (3.7.231) was picked up by amplified offstage chanting with distinct overtones of 'Sieg Heil'.

The production's argument, followed with powerful dramatic logic in the first half, had the knack of throwing small segments of the play into prominence through their link to Richard's rise. The tiny scene of the Scrivener (3.6) details, exactly and disturbingly, the failure of those who can see what is happening to speak out against Richard's cynical manipulation of political process. At the end of the scene the speech itself proved to have marked the dangerous transition from seeing 'such ill dealing . . . in thought' (3.6.14) to revealing oneself as a target for Richard's men, as the Scrivener, the perfect exemplar of the weak middle-class liberal, was hauled away by two of the blackshirt guards.

The processes of politics in such a world became eerily dangerous. The fall of Hastings (David Bradley), for instance, became an unstoppable process through the simple device of moving the action away from Hastings' house after the conversation with the Messenger (3.2.1–31). Catesby and Hastings instead conversed at the council table as Catesby laid out the agenda papers and Hastings worked at a red dispatch-box. The conversations with the priest and with Buckingham were held as the meeting assembled. The executions of Rivers, Gray and Vaughan – brutally graphic garottings – were played out downstage in front of the board-meeting, specifying what was looming for Hastings. The arrival of the now-blackshirted Richard and his guards left no doubt about the threat to the other council members if they resisted his will – indeed, the whole fabricated story of the withered arm was obviously irrelevant to the real reason for the rapidity of the others' acceptance of Hastings' arrest: Richard's unchallengeable military power. As Eyre comments, 'at this point self-preservation takes over from courage, morality, or political expediency' (p. 166). If it might be easy for an audience to patronise such ready capitulation that is, for Eyre, a product of the audience's being 'comfortably insulated in our unchallenged, liberal, all-too-English assumptions' (p. 167). As a challenge to the audience's own constructions of individual action in a context of military tyranny, the production included its own doubts about the virtues of Englishness.

Such uses of rituals as contexts within which power-games are played out – here the ritual of the boardroom – were effective and sustained. For instance, 1.3 was played as a long formal dinner-table scene with everyone in evening-dress, a scene disrupted by the irruption of Queen Margaret as a religious fanatic, festooned with rosaries and crucifixes. Edward IV's reconciliation of the warring factions (2.1) was defined by the slow setting-up of a group photograph, complete with a flash-gun, immediately before Richard disrupted the assembly with the news of Clarence's death (2.1.78), the others previously having failed to notice Richard's black armband.

If the analogy with an imaginary history gave the play a threatening drive it exacted two heavy penalties. The first was that there was little room for a language of comedy. McKellen is, in any case, not at his best in comedy, even at its most sardonic. His Richard had nothing of the charm of the comic villain, defining himself instead simply as a wounded soldier. His deformities – hand, leg, merest hint of a hump and a massive piece of facial plastic surgery – always appeared more likely to be the result of active service in the trenches than birth. The adroit way in which he one-handedly extracted a cigarette from his silver cigarette-case and lit it or did up the complicated buckles on his uniform belt suggested a soldier who had had intensive rehabilitation therapy. The drive for power, as a result, seemed generated by the displacement of the soldier in peacetime. With nothing charmingly demonic about him the focus was on the disturbing ease with which he could seize power.

Such a process accounts for the second penalty: a loss of direction in the second half. There was, quite simply, nowhere for the production to go once Richard was crowned. The coronation itself was, however, magnificent, with lords in scarlet and ermine, Richard in full medieval costume and the stage backed by a massive example of triumphal Fascist art showing marching soldiers, a rearing horse (White Surrey?) and a naked Richard with raised-arm salute, his body healed and perfect as an example of an Aryan ideal. The clash of histories became complete here, a complex intermingling of the two periods: the scene effectively combined the pseudo-medievalism of Fascist art and the submerged historical moment of Richard's reign. Richard, like Hitler, exemplifies the self-creating mythologies of tyranny, and the production explored the medievalising rituals with which power tries to enforce our perception of its historical depth and inevitability.

But Richard's collapse, for all the technical virtuosity of McKellen's fighting soldier at Bosworth with his leg twitching in uncontrollable spasms, came from nowhere and went nowhere. The ghost scene, staged as a series of nightmarish echoes of gestures and moves in earlier scenes, stage-managed by a gold-crowned, beaming Queen Margaret, had an inventiveness that the second half largely lacked but it was also overblown in a way that the first half's tight control had not been. The arrival of Richmond was heralded by a new back-cloth, a chocolate-box depiction of the English countryside, a rural idyll of everything Richmond is fighting for. I wanted to see this vision as ironic but the production left no space for such a reading. Eyre's later account of the production revealed all too clearly his own sentimentalised vision which the image was meant to bear:

> I set [Richmond's] first entrance against a backdrop of a peaceful country village, in Devon in fact, near where I was born, the England of 'summer fields and fruitful vines'. If I was asked what I thought Richmond was fighting for, it would be this idealised picture of England. It was more than a metaphor for me; it was a heartland. (p. 167)

In the mourning of the queens (4.4) another note was heard, their candles making them echoes of Argentinian 'Mothers of the Disappeared', the survivors grieving the victims of the totalitarian state. If the model was an easy one to reach for – Eyre calls it 'only too obvious' – that does not diminish its power. In the rich dignity of the scene a lamenting estimate of the cost of Richard's rule was defined. As Eyre argued, 'The play is called *The Tragedy of Richard III*, and it is the tragedy of the women that is being told' (p. 166). Eyre's exploration of that tragedy grew directly out of his confrontation with the play, not a generalised sense of male guilt about the representation of women. What had appeared imposed and unproductive in Kyle's *All's Well That Ends Well* now grew boldly and successfully out of the collaboration between director and play.

CHAPTER 3

1989–1990: popular Shakespeare and the Swan Theatre

As You Like It, *The Comedy of Errors* (RSC, Royal Shakespeare Theatre); *Pericles*, *Troilus and Cressida* (RSC, Swan Theatre)

The RSC productions in the Royal Shakespeare Theatre that I considered in the previous chapter shared their characteristics as serious, intelligent productions of plays in the large-scale space. Whatever their varying degrees of success, they sought to accomplish their production almost without reference to the distinctive nature of the audience. But some of the RSC's main-house work seems to assume the audience to be tourists whose interest in Shakespeare is marginal and who therefore need energetically to be incorporated into the activity of the production, its visual rather than verbal energies. At the opposite extreme of the company's work lie productions in the Swan Theatre or The Other Place where a different form of interconnection with the audience is demanded. The populism of the former group contrasts with the achievement of popularity of the latter; where one group patronises its audiences, the other respects them while allowing that the audience needs accommodating within the performance, not least in terms of the communication of narrative. This chapter looks at productions that exemplify both tendencies.

The populist productions are often excoriated by the critics as 'feelgood Shakespeare'. In an attack in 1994 on Adrian Noble's reign at the RSC, Rupert Christiansen complained that Noble 'gives off a whiff of playing safe and the sharp radical edge that characterised the company in its heroic early days has been blunted . . . There are too many sugar-coated shows, over-designed and over-ingratiating.' But, Christiansen claimed, to balance his argument, [the RSC's] audiences are happy. Sit in the RST almost any night – if you can get a ticket – and you will be with rich and poor, young and old, gripped and moved and excited by Shakespeare, a living dramatist whose plays still speak to people. The RSC's Shakespeare may be glamorous to a fault, but it is never poncey or rarefied.[1]

The same doubts and the same response were true in earlier seasons.

After the popular success of John Caird's production of *A Midsummer Night's Dream* earlier in the split season of 1989, the RSC must have felt confident of repeating it with his production of *As You Like It*. Caird was expected simply to repeat the trick. Reviewing Caird's *A Midsummer Night's Dream*, Stanley Wells suggested that the brilliance of the comic invention, the frenetic cleverness of the production 'held the play at arm's length'.[2] This incipient problem is exacerbated when the comic invention dries up and the freneticism is unsupported by the play. Gags and comic business are no adequate substitute when they are vainly trying to cover up a lack of intelligent thinking about the play itself, and they are positively embarrassing when they become a succession of cheap theatrical clichés. Caird's *As You Like It* was an object-lesson in this respect, its tired ideas desperately trying to invest the production with excitement and popular appeal.

The wrestling scene revealed much, blown up, as usual, into a farrago with all the theatrical showiness of the television variety. Duke Frederick's entry was accompanied by the playing of a fake national anthem with the audience encouraged to stand respectfully. Most of the audience meekly did what they were told and I was made to feel curmudgeonly for sitting firmly in my place. For the fight itself some of the cast joined the audience in the stalls and shouted encouraging suggestions like 'Give him a good kicking' or 'Go on, Charlie-boy', suggestions designed to encourage not the wrestlers but the audience. It is not the adding of the odd extra line to Shakespeare that matters but the unbalancing of the play: the scene brought the play's momentum to a complete halt. Theatricality and dramatic rhythm were hopelessly at odds. Afterwards Orlando signed autographs, posed for photographs and received a huge trophy. There was no hope that his act of naming his father would push the play back towards any intelligent seriousness: it generated the sudden appearance of bodyguards drawing pistols, putting on sunglasses and effectively turning

Frederick into a comic mafioso surrounded by a gang of protective stereotyped thugs. When the lure of the momentary effect takes such extreme precedence over any sense of the place of the moment in the architecture of the play, when the energy of the moment has to be faked because nothing in the production's dynamic is generating it, and when the effects are neither particularly funny nor particularly well done, then everything that might give the play a reason for having started and a reason to continue is excruciatingly difficult to maintain.

There was an obviousness here, a confusion of novelty with creative originality. 'Novelties' is the word for the bad jokes and plastic trinkets found in Christmas crackers; 'originality' is what is needed for a complex play in a major production. It may be difficult to show the social and economic status of Phoebe and Silvius but nothing is gained by having them dressed instead as peasants in their underwear, Silvius in vest and y-fronts wearing a garland and carrying a green chiffon scarf. Britain may have had a 'red nose day' that year but Touchstone's liberal distribution of red noses throughout the play did not provide a definition of the spread of his view of the comic world of the play; it was one thing to encumber Joanna Mays' large and ungainly Audrey with one, a fair indication of her touching pride in him, but when everyone ends up with one the production seems only to have failed to understand that Touchstone's image of the world is not shared by the play as a whole.

Few actors could survive such competition. Sophie Thompson's Rosalind was gamely gamine. Gillian Bevan's Celia, once she had discarded the tiara and hostess manners of the opening scene, demonstrated a powerful sense of isolation and loneliness, finding nothing in Arden for her. Only Hugh Ross's Jaques, very much the act*or* in black coat with astrakhan collar, fedora, flower in his buttonhole and carrying a cane, offered something substantial. The whole world seemed a show put on for his benefit; indeed, at times he took a seat in the front of the stalls to watch the parade of folly, leaping back on to the stage, for instance, to help Touchstone get married. The bitterness of his out-of-place dignity turned his report on Touchstone into a brutal language that this Touchstone would not have used: there was no ambiguity here in the transition from 'from hour to hour we ripe and ripe' to 'And then from whore to whore we rot and rot' (2.7.26–7). 'Seven ages', marred only by the need to turn it even more explicitly into a party piece with an exit on 'They have their exits' and a prolonged pause before a re-entrance on 'and their entrances' (2.7.141), was painful in its acerbity. His final comments to Touchstone ('And you to wrangling, for thy loving voyage / Is but for two months vict-ualled', 5.4.189–90) were inordinately vicious, provoking a response of genuine distress from Touchstone himself. But his final exit, on a darkened stage through a lighted door suggesting a close encounter of the third kind, was empty, yet another moment of characteristic excess, the play's vision of the impossibil-ity of even a temporary Arcadia appealing to all buried under a cheap stagey device.

Caird's *A Midsummer Night's Dream*, its wry revisionary glitter pro-ducing an entertaining mockery of the traditions of the play, could only have been a one-off. His *As You Like It* suggested a lack of inter-est in the play, a dutiful piece of work, a typical product of the RSC as factory.

Caird's difficulties with *As You Like It* showed a director trying to tap into dried-up resources of comic energy. But Ian Judge's pro-duction of *The Comedy of Errors* exemplified the consequence of matching a director whose interest in the text was less than his interest in pleasing the audience.

In *The Conversations with Drummond of Hawthornden*, Ben Jonson talked about his plans for various plays. Drummond records: 'he had ane intention to have made a play like Plaut[us'] Amphitrio but left it of, for that he could never find two so like others that he could persuade the spectators they were one'.[3] Jonson, never one to place small demands on theatre companies, wanted two pairs of identical twins. For the twin Antipholuses and the twin Dromios of *The Comedy of Errors* modern technology can appear to provide an answer: the BBC Shakespeare series' production had each pair of twins played by one actor. Ian Judge decided to try the same on stage. But television is not the stage: Desmond Barrit (both Antipholuses) and Graham Turner (both Dromios), fine actors though they are, lack the paranormal skill of bilocation, necessary without cameras and editing.

Since the idea cannot possibly work in the theatre, I shall be wondering what is lost in the process. But I also wonder whether it would be worth doing even if it could be done. One of the great pleasures for the audience watching *The Comedy of Errors* is that we know the answer. We know, because Egeon has told us, that there are two pairs of twins; we know why Antipholus of Syracuse is recognised by the inhabitants of Ephesus and that the reason has nothing to do with Ephesus' reputation for sorcery nor is it a dream. But we also find that the overweening confidence with which we begin, knowing the answers, is shaken in the course of the play. Every time I watch the play, I end up forgetting which Dromio has been sent on which errand by which Antipholus, which one is locked up with Pinch, which one has ended up in the priory. We know how the play will end, in that moment when the Antipholuses and Dromios will all be on stage together, but along the way we are nearly as confused as the characters. When both Dromios are played by the same actor the audience's ability to be confused, a confusion that the play wants us to undergo, is simply evaded, evaded because the audience comes to follow actor, not role, Graham Turner not Dromio.

The two Dromios were differentiated by the colour of their waistcoats but the audience, rather than trying to remember which Dromio was wearing the green one, abandoned its interest in the confusions, comforted by its recognition of the actor, not the role. When, finally, the character had to face his *doppelgänger* on stage for the last scene, we came to see not two Dromios but two actors, one whom we knew and another whom we did not. The history of the characters is replaced by the history of the performance.

It was the emotional force of the ending that was especially harmed. For Shakespeare's ending teeters gloriously on the edge of sentimentality. As brother finds brother at last there is an emotional release for the characters and for the audience. When it works – and it usually does – there is something tearful about the reunions, the reconstitution of the family. Even the inevitably funny rediscovery of the missing mother does not prevent our joy, prefiguring something of the force of the families re-formed at the end of the late plays. By doubling the Antipholuses the force is diluted. The audience watched how the *doppelgänger* still tried to keep his back to them, following the theatrical technique, the actor's skill, not the play's argument. Even more unfortunately, Ian Judge's production misjudged Shakespeare's carefully downbeat ending. As the stage empties the two Dromios are left alone, their tentative awareness of their equality deliberately low-key yet

4. *The Comedy of Errors* 5.1, RSC, 1990: Antipholus (Desmond Barrit) and Dromio (Graham Turner) meet their *doppelgängers*

moving: 'We came into the world like brother and brother, / And now let's go hand in hand, not one before another' (5.1.429–30). The play denies the full-stage ending and ends up with two servants, beaten and mocked throughout the play, now finding a dignity in what they have in common, their brotherhood. Their exit in Judge's production, into the rays of the setting sun, was pure Hollywood schmaltz; it encouraged the audience to find the moment ludicrous, missing completely its simplicity and innocence.

Once past a sombre prison set for the first scene, the design, by Mark Thompson, was unrelentingly excessive, nine garishly coloured doors surrounding a rectangular playing-area. The games played with surrealism, the echoes of Escher and Magritte and the Beatles' *Yellow Submarine*, became in the playing of Pinch a grotesque parody of Dali turned into a cheap stage-conjuror. Dali, the great modern example of artist as showman, would perhaps have been amused. The magic was a perfect example of the production's obsessive busy-ness: as Dromio was sawn in two and Antipholus vanished from a cabinet skewered with swords, Pinch-Dali's aides rushed around the stage in a frenzy of activity not generated by a response to the action.

But the set's extravagances also transformed Ephesus into the world that the Syracusan twins wrongly perceive it to be, for Ephesus is not a place of irrationality and dream. The play charts the passage of a day, the day that threatens Egeon's execution, but, apart from the inhabitants of Ephesus appearing from behind their front doors to take in the morning milk, there was nothing in the production that recognised that fundamental diurnal rhythm in the text. The play's action suggests a single place, with houses on a street and, all the time, the beckoning possibility of that road to the harbour, the route by which the Syracusans might escape the perils of Ephesus. But this set could do nothing with this. Its only gestures to place, large objects hanging over the stage representing the Centaur, the Phoenix and the other places the text refers to, were empty gestures; indeed, on both the occasions I saw the production, I heard bemused members of the audience wondering what the hedgehog was, unable to connect it with any of the play's five references to the Porcupine.

In such a context the actors were driven to unremitting excess. Desmond Barrit's largely undifferentiated Antipholuses were an exercise in high camp, only becoming effective in the quiet wooing of Luciana in 3.2. David Killick seemed embarrassed by the leopard-skin drape jacket, tight black leggings and six-inch plat-form shoes of Doctor Pinch – as well he might – and sought to hide behind a Spanish lisp. Only David Waller's Egeon, narrating his history with dignity and drawing helpful diagrams of the distribu-tion of his family on the mast, showed that comedy is not neces-sarily or desirably hyperactive.

But the most serious problem with the production was that it simply was not funny enough. Let me take one example. Antipholus of Ephesus, locked out of his house, was confronted by a voice down an entryphone. The device is, of course, a fine solu-tion to the problem of having only one Dromio where two are needed; it was 'derived' from an earlier RSC production, the bril-liant musical version directed by Trevor Nunn in 1977. But watch-ing on video Mike Gwilym in that version, sheltering under an umbrella as defence against the indoor Dromio's assault, tearing the entryphone off the wall only to find that the damned thing still went on answering him back, I found a comic energy, a theatrical inventiveness and dramatic pace that I missed this time. It was sad to see a production borrowing jokes and gags and business and not learning how to copy the energy and style.

Judge's *The Comedy of Errors* was a hugely popular production, taken on an extended tour after its London performances. My dislike was not shared by most of its audiences and there is a risk that it is simply a form of academic patronising to disapprove of its treatment of the play. The Shakespeare text can rightfully be the basis for theatrical fun, offering the audience all the pleasures of the good night out. The attitude that demands of an RSC production that it explore and develop from the play's complexities may be a form of cultural elitism. Yet it does not necessarily follow that the production that recognises more of *The Comedy of Errors* than Judge's would be less popular or less funny. It is not the dark seriousness that the play contains within its farce that I was disappointed Judge excluded. Rather, the production's unremitting jollity became wearing. The surprises were tricks of theatre – like the adroit switches between Barrit and his double to allow an apparently impossible immediate re-entry on one side of the stage a fraction of a second after he seemed to have left on the other – but the audience's gasps of pleasure at such spectacularly successful *trompe-l'oeil* devices could not feed back into the play's concerns. The production skittered over the play, using it as pretext. The RSC has to be popular, for the economics of its functioning depend on its deriving a high percentage of its income from the box-office. It has regularly found *The Comedy of Errors* to be a box-office banker and it proved so again. But the production, in its conspicuous lack of interest in the text, seemed generated more by a capitulation to the RSC's perennial funding crisis than by a wish to see what the play could offer. In that, it might be seen as a representative moment in the company's history, a transition to a style of work in the main house that, occasionally visible before, was to become increasingly apparent.

By comparison with the stresses and strains of the work in the Royal Shakespeare Theatre, its oscillations between imaginative and provocative productions and popularised Shakespeare, the work of the company in the Swan Theatre seemed to bear a charmed life. The Swan Theatre, designed by Michael Reardon and Tim Furby, opened in 1986.[4] It created a space resonant with the forms of Renaissance theatres without ever being antiquarian in its explorations of the possibilities of audience configuration or actor–audience relations. Demanding in its stage design, with a long narrow thrust keeping the audience in a horseshoe of seating around it both in the stalls and its two galleries, it has consistently been experienced by actors (if not always by directors and rarely by designers) as a theatre of exhilarating energy, but its demands are also considerable for actors unsure how to respond to the fluidities its shape requires.

From its opening in 1932 onwards, actors playing the Royal Shakespeare Theatre felt distant from their audience. Baliol Holloway commented in 1934, 'On a clear day . . . you can just about see the boiled shirts in the first row. It is like acting to Calais from the cliffs of Dover.'[5] Repeated attempts to adjust the patterns of seating in the theatre have never resolved the problems, even in the extreme experiment in 1976 of placing audience seating behind the stage to create an effect of playing in the round.

At the Swan Theatre the connection between audience and actor is immediate and automatic. Ideal for comedy, where asides to individual members of the audience are easier than in any other theatre in the country, the Swan is much more difficult for tragedy, where distance and symbolic image are harder to achieve. The Swan, like the even smaller chamber space of The Other Place, makes the actor's body especially visible and dominant.[6] As early as 1970, Trevor Nunn had denied a broader political relevance for the company's work, arguing that 'we are concerned with the human personalities of a king or queen rather than with their public roles'.[7] 'Chamber' settings for Nunn's productions in 1969 had been designed to 'work within the scale of the individual actor – to make his words, thoughts, fantasies and language seem important'.[8] Tragedy in the Swan is from one perspective weakened and limited by this concentration on the individual over the social and political role but, from the RSC's perspective, with its increasing reluctance to allow the political dimensions of a play to dominate, the Swan was the ideal space.

The Swan is a space that, whatever its particular provocations, connects directly with most actors' experience. If the main house is dauntingly large, then the Swan is comfortingly small, the back

row of the top gallery apparently closer to the stage than the
middle of the stalls in the Royal Shakespeare Theatre, let alone the
vast expanses of the RST's balcony where one-third of the total
theatre audience can only see the stage well through opera-glasses.
Actors at Stratford seem visibly to relax on the Swan stage.

Though the first ever production in the Swan was
Shakespearean, Barry Kyle's *Two Noble Kinsmen*, the Swan was not
initially intended to be a theatre-space for exploring the
Shakespeare canon. However, just as commercial pressures have
come to limit the repertory for the main house, so the pattern
began to emerge of including one Shakespeare play in the Swan
repertory. The Swan makes possible both the production of the
margins of the canon and a reinvestigation of central texts in a different theatre-space. David Thacker's 1989 production of *Pericles*
belongs to the former category, Sam Mendes's 1990 *Troilus and
Cressida* to the latter. Thacker chose a play that the company had
rarely performed; Mendes chose one that the company had made
peculiarly its own. Each transformed perceptions of the text
through their confident negotiation with the possibilities both of
text and of theatre.

Some productions seem almost deliberately to set out to offer
projects for future academic research. Any production of *Pericles* is
bound to lure textual scholars like a swarm in search of academic
honey. The advance publicity for David Thacker's announced that
the rehearsal process had treated the text as a set of open possibilities for experimentation and I duly prepared myself carefully to
be able to report on the relative quantities of Shakespeare, Wilkins
and Gary Taylor in the final result. It is a clear indication of the
brilliance of Thacker's distinguished work that all my careful
preparation proved unavailing: the verve and energy of the performance simply stopped me noting textual variants.

What the production exuded through every pore was sheer
delight in the possibility of telling a story in the theatre. Much of
the best recent small-scale theatre, by Shared Experience for
example, has been rediscovery of the pleasures of narrative in performance, a development which fed into the RSC's *Nicholas
Nickleby*. But the company's Shakespeare work has rarely seemed
to be interested in the delights of a theatre of story-telling. *Pericles*
is a play that demands such treatment and Thacker responded.

The tone was set at once by Rudolph Walker's Gower. The

5. *Pericles* sc. 6, RSC, Swan Theatre, 1989: The knights at Simonides' court;
Gower (Rudolph Walker) is seated on the right

description of Gower in *Greene's Vision* (1592) suggests a figure to
match Shakespeare's Gower's archaic language and verse-rhythms,
a man with the 'wan . . . look' of 'they that plyen their book' and
with a minutely enumerated costume that justifies a summary of
him as 'Quaint attired'.[9] But Walker's Gower was a genial
author–narrator, reading from a book, watching the action from a
comfortable armchair, a figure closer perhaps to the traditions of
television story-telling, as if the stage of the Swan were no different
from the set for BBC's *Jackanory* and the audience an avid group
of children, eager to know what happened next. In place of
Greene's 'visage grave, stern and grim' was a broad grin and,
instead of the 'surcoat of a tawny dye / Hung in pleats over his
thigh', he wore a modern corduroy suit, the epitome of casual
style.

Thoroughly convincing, he engaged the audience immediately
in the pleasures of his tale. Avoiding the beat of couplets like
dangerous infection and minimising the oddities of lexis to
produce a conversational easiness, his performance was accessible

not mysterious, charming not distancing, modern not medievalising. This charm of narrative was shared within the play's own
action later, Pericles, for instance, finding a responsive audience
from the mariners for his account of his story in scene 5. But it was
also a basis for another transition on which the production rightly
harped: the transition from narrative to action. Gower's promise
is that 'Your ears unto your eyes I'll reconcile' (18.22) and the production justified the transformation promised by his next line: '*See
how belief may suffer by foul show*' (18.23, my emphasis). The sen-
timents indeed were contested by the production which never produced foul show to make belief suffer, whatever may happen to
Pericles. The same linking of ears and eyes is repeated later when
Gower promises 'Where what is done in action, more if might, /
Shall be discovered. Please you sit and hark' (20.23–4). Gower's
account is both listened to and seen, the sound always accompanied by sight, the statement proved by the stage-image and the
image proved by the narrative, a continuing interchange of narrative and enactment.

  The production's theatrical inventiveness was to be entirely at
the service of the story. In place of the row of heads which the
Oxford edition offers as the explanation for 'yon grim looks'
(1.40), Thacker showed a line of actors on the gallery at the back
of the stage, near-naked corpses which swayed gently as if in a
breeze, a perfect theatricalisation of the image, defining the audience's gaze on their bodies as an image to be observed and finding
its theatrical strength in a mixture of realism and stylisation. Again
and again the production offered such striking pictures as
accompaniments and symbolic embodiments of the meaning or
context of a scene but always with a delicate delight in making
theatre the resource for the story's enactment. The repeated
framing of Pericles at the top of the central stairs from gallery to
stage, for instance, served to pinpoint the stages of his journeyings.

  There was a similar pleasure in filling the stage, something necessarily easier in the Swan than in the Royal Shakespeare Theatre.
The parade of knights (scene 6) was something Simonides shared
in with a great deal of giggling and clapping, an almost child-like
joy in spectacle but one the audience was fully prepared to share.
The joust at Simonides' court was an ancient pentathlon of
combats, wrestling, spears and swords, all taking place simultaneously, a demonstration of Pericles as the all-round athlete and

increasingly isolating him in our attention. The dance of the knights (7.102) filled the stage and served gently to develop the relationship of Pericles and Thaisa, moving from an initial strong eye-contact and a manifestation of her genuine but also embarrassed delight in dancing with him, into a close embrace, responding to the rhythms of the music (by Mark Vibrans), ending finally with a kiss that left the other dancers, now halted in their dance, awkward observers of two so completely wrapped up in each other. Simonides' wry but firm instruction to 'unclasp' (7.110) became a necessary instruction to end the embrace. At such moments the potential of the stage to be both spectacular and focused on individuals was perfectly realised.

For each demand of the play the production found the theatrical form it needed. The exhilarating storm in scene 11 showed a man struggling with the ship's tiller in doing nothing more than trying to keep a piece of wood on the ground with others slipping and sliding around him, accompanied by more of the production's extensive score, but with this active chaos in ideal balance with the still figure of Pericles on a platform suspended over the stage. Never interfering with the play's action, the storm action could stop and restart, allowing a moving stillness for 'A terrible childbed hast thou had' (11.55) and restarting with the urgent haste of the sailors to be rid of the corpse, forcing Pericles to act with a speed he would do anything to resist.

The virtuosity of the production was at its best in the simple effects that movingly ended the first half in the revival of Thaisa. Cerimon, a female proto-Paulina here, created a stage magic of delicate beauty, accompanied by onstage assistants making 'still and woeful music' (12.86) from a vibrating bronze bell and other strange sources. Thaisa, reappearing from her coffin, arm first, slowly came back to life with a wide-eyed and panic-stricken terror, made to read Pericles' letter while still seated in her coffin (scenes 12 and 14 were run together). The mixture of stylisation and realism was never in conflict; instead the performance underlined Thaisa's fear, set off by Pericles on the gallery, handing over the baby Marina to Lychorida, Cleon and Dionyza and speaking with touching simplicity the last lines of Scene 13:

O, no tears, Lychorida, no tears.
Look to your little mistress, on whose grace
You may depend hereafter.—Come, my lord. (13.39–41)

Thaisa, Cerimon and the others still occupied the main stage, a silent commentary on Pericles' temporary loss.

There was here a remarkable ability both to uncover the theatrical possibilities of a scene that usually seems weak and to demonstrate the play's architecture. For this scene of theatre magic and rebirth was perfectly complemented at the end of the performance by the reunion of Thaisa and Pericles. If there was no attempt to claim theatrical power in the language of the last scene (scene 22), there was convincing proof of the theatrical power of its action. Diana (Sally Edwards) was doubled with Thaisa or, rather, Diana became a vision of a transformed Thaisa so that, as she spoke to Pericles (21.225–35), who slept with his head cradled in her lap, the vision anticipated the close family group of the final reunion. The music offered a version of the music for Thaisa's resurrection and in the strange lighting of this vision, the wish-fulfilment world of the final moments was complete with its reunion of a lost family, embracing closely and comfortingly, with the total assent of the audience; this was everything, indeed, that the final family reunion of Barry Kyle's production of *All's Well That Ends Well* was not, a theatrical moment generated by the text and fulfilling its demands, recognising its problems but solving them.

Plays as extravagant and wheeling as *Pericles* place massive demands on designers. For the most part the open stage and fluid range of eclectically historical costumes were allowed to flow with the text. Only in the brothel scene did something approximating to a substantial set and firm sense of historical period emerge, with lines of washing mostly in a filthy carmine colour which dominated the costumes of whores and bawd. The scene was consciously Hogarthian, full of unkempt and scabby whores vomiting, sleeping, snoring. Helen Blatch's Bawd, in huge and wild wig, wore a decayed crinoline. Marina, who alone seemed to be able to attend to her personal hygiene, was transformed from the electric blue of her first costume to a cleaned-up version of the whores' crimson costumes.

As Marina, Suzan Sylvester was triumphant. She has a rare and extremely important skill for Shakespeare: she can speak lines as if they have just been thought, turning the verse with a sensitivity to its rhythm and an understanding of its complex syntax until the whole becomes freshly infused with an interaction of thought and feeling. Her recognition of the emotional power and sensuousness of the language created a Marina with an unusually tactile and sensuous predisposition. Playing with Leonine it seemed only natural for her to jump on his very preoccupied back and then to be dumped unceremoniously on her backside, but also to caress him as she pleaded for her life.

Her virtue and innocence here (as in her Diana in *All's Well*) were unquestioned but they were manifest in a physicality that was both endearing and, in confrontation with male desire, deeply threatening. In the brothel scene, for instance, she persuaded Lysimachus by being close to him, making the proximity itself a means of enforcing his attention to her words. This was no distant vision of virtue but instead immediate and powerful in its vigour. When he gave her money (19.132–3) to ease her conscience she held on to his hand to thank him and the gesture made him weep. Brilliantly this proximity was turned on her when Boult, threatening in his closeness to her for the attempted rape, stayed close as he repented, the brutality of his desire (as in Pander's harsh 'Crack the ice of her virginity', 19.167) transformed into an enigmatically disturbing question about what else he might do (19.195–8). For the first time, she now pulled away from him to argue 'Do anything but this thou dost' (199) but the scene ended almost affectionately ('Come your ways', 223).

Challenged by the sight of Pericles, curled up foetally as if asleep, Marina was warmly benign and smiling. Her warmth found a response in him, an eagerness to hear her story (yet another aspect of the play's and the production's easy emphasis on story-telling). All went smoothly in the progress of the scene until she said 'My name, sir, is Marina' (21.131), the name provoking him to a frightening roar as he twisted to escape. Characteristically she comforted his weeping, keeping close to him as the reunion unfolded.

Throughout, Suzan Sylvester found a delight that was infectious and a clarity that was revelatory. It was precisely the humanising of the character that Thacker's reading of the play demanded, a rejection of assumptions about the play's weaknesses of characterisation in favour of a triumphant demonstration of their theatricality. It was the logical centrepiece for David Thacker's richly sensitive production.

Thacker's *Pericles* was followed in 1990 by Sam Mendes's *Troilus and Cressida*, his debut production for the company. For a director in his early twenties to achieve so much with a play that the RSC has staged often and well was a major accomplishment. The production's success was, even more surprisingly and gratifyingly, based less on the imposition of directorial concept than in allowing the play and the actors space in which to work as well as allowing the space of the Swan to work its effects on play and cast, precisely the qualities of accepting the text and the theatre that made for the success of Thacker's *Pericles*.

As soon as Pandarus (Norman Rodway) stepped out as Prologue the production made clear its confidence. Rodway fixed a cultured and wryly witty attitude to the Trojan war, pinpointed as he flicked the medal pinned to his blazer to define himself as the 'Prologue armed' (23). The decision to have Pandarus as Prologue was a tidy one, economically linking the beginning, the middle and the end of the play together, making the diseased Pandarus of the epilogue a distorted image of the dapper figure at the start.

Though this *Troilus and Cressida* was framed by Pandarus and the power of his urbane wit, its Troy was not defined by him. Throughout, the production realised the play's multivocality, its refusal to hierarchise the competing tonalities. As the Trojans returned from battle in 1.2 Pandarus and Cressida were displaced from the centre of the stage to one of the Swan's side galleries. Instead of the procession of warriors being mediated for the audience by Pandarus's dominance, Pandarus was forced to compete for the audience's attention with the silent entries, a conflict between what is seen and how it is interpreted that epitomises much of the play's method as in Thacker's *Pericles*.

Pandarus's wit was allowed its full weight of humour but our interest was focused as much on the ritual of washing which the returning soldiers went through centrestage, using the pool of water in which Pandarus and Cressida had previously been paddling. Even here there were jokes to echo Pandarus's mockery: Paris slicking his hair back, Helenus nearly forgetting his sword, Troilus slouching in so that even Pandarus could be excused for not recognising him. But there were others who, in effect, fought with Pandarus's wit for the right to behave with dignity, to make a ritual of purification out of the serious fact of their having survived a day's battle as they washed the blood from their swords and then washed themselves. The ceremony acquired the importance invested in it by the participants, an importance that Pandarus could not really dent.

Amanda Root's lightweight Cressida was not helped by Ralph Fiennes' Troilus, for Fiennes is unlike any other actor in the company, an actor who is like a throwback to an earlier world of classical emotional performance, expressing that emotion through his separation from the other actors on stage, a quality that would be especially marked in his Hamlet in 1995. This Troilus was unable to touch Cressida, either before their love-making or after it, and while there was a full-throated freedom in his violent response to seeing her with Diomedes, there was also a sense in which the actor was happier here, freed of the need to respond to any other prompting than his own. But a Troilus who has not made manifest the sexual excitement of the character has nothing on which to build the distress.

The Troy scenes stand or fall on the appearance of Helen. Like the wrestling scene in *As You Like It*, it has become a way of defining productions. Paris's servant describes Helen as 'the mortal Venus, the heart-blood of beauty, love's visible soul' (3.1.31–3) but then his hands, pushing out the front of his vest, turned the word 'attributes' ('Could not you find out that by her attributes?', 3.1.35–6) into a substitute for 'tits', registering the play's ambivalence about Paris's 'Nell'; Pandarus's uneasy response to this wit anticipated his difficulties in dealing with Helen and Paris themselves.

A version of Helen had been apparent from the play's opening. Anthony Ward's set included a massive stone Grecian female mask, one side perfect, the other decayed. When the Prologue referred to 'the ravished Helen', Rodway gestured towards the mask. But it did not prepare for the appearance of the real Helen. Helen's entrance was another ritual, a gold-wrapped figure carried in high on a dish and then unveiled. What was revealed was neither a piece of statuary nor a traditional image of blonde beauty but a buxom Hollywood vamp, a scarlet woman or at least a woman in a garish red dress, wearing a gold collar whose extravagance was perfectly tasteless as well as suggestive of a slave-collar, marking her out as Paris's property. Sally Dexter, acting with remarkable selflessness in her willingness to mock her own appearance, seemed a ghastly parody of Elizabeth Taylor.

But the scene allowed her a transformation. Left alone with

6. *Troilus and Cressida* 3.1, RSC, Swan Theatre, 1990: Pandarus
(Norman Rodway) and Helen (Sally Dexter)

Paris at the end, she was genuinely willing to help Hector unarm,
''Twill make us proud to be his servant' (3.1.152), and deeply
aware of her own shaming responsibility for the war. What was
missing in Root's Cressida was fully achieved here: Helen became
a space both of male objectification and of female resistance, her
action circumscribed both by the limits of her presence in the text
and by the ambivalences in her representation, visually objectified
but verbally released from that objectification.

Where the differing responses to and from Norman Rodway's
Pandarus served to define Troy, in the Greek camp all else paled
into insignificance beside Simon Russell Beale's Thersites.[10] I
found it easy to ignore Ulysses, Nestor and even Agamemnon for
few performances could survive such competition. Richard Ridings
managed it: his Ajax, bullish and magnificently stupid, with an
inflated physique to match his ego, fully deserved Ulysses' barbed
praise of his 'spacious and dilated parts' (2.3.245) but retained a
threat of violence in his bullying. Ciaran Hinds' supercool

bikeman Achilles was all leather, viciousness and designer stubble, a languid cross between poseur and introvert; Paterson Joseph's excellent Patroclus was a match for Thersites in the 'pageant of Ajax' (3.3.263ff.) but also deeply moving in his love for Achilles as he registered his pain at Achilles' comments on Polyxena.

But Thersites was always dominant. From his first entrance as he slowly and deliberately set up Ajax's dinner and then equally slowly and deliberately drooled into the platter, his denial of value, his reduction of everything below the lowest possible worth, was repulsively unquestioned. White-faced with eyes red with rheum, his hands covered in surgical gloves to hide his eczema, and hunchbacked, Beale's Thersites oozed physical exclusion and emotional resentment. He fed his loathing, encouraging Ajax to beat him, even seeming at first to enjoy his schoolboy whipping. Though he proudly announced that he 'serve[s] here voluntary' (2.1.96), he soon turned up at Achilles' tent with his belongings in carrier-bags with a fool's bauble sticking out, searching for employment, desperately ingratiating. While Thersites displayed the skills of alternative stand-up comic, it was also characteristic that the scene-setting for Hector's arrival at Achilles' tent, with Achilles and Patroclus languidly posed on the ladders, should be undercut by the awkwardness of his attempt to hang on to his ladder while holding a ghetto-blaster playing a sensual song. The song's title was itself a deliberate joke, a number called 'Lover man, where can you be?'.

Only at one moment was his perception of the world, his reduction of human behaviour into his grid of reference, defeated. After the double watchings of 5.2, Thersites picked up Cressida's discarded scarf. It looked for a moment as though he was going to sniff it like some fetishist fascinated by women's knickers but instead he contemplated it in genuine amazement. The object which had been invested with such value by Cressida and Troilus was simply beyond his comprehension. He could make nothing of their passion.

Mendes both enabled and was helped by such performances in creating a bleakly comic version of the play. Time and again he worked with remarkable economy. The addition of the moment of the exchange of Antenor for Cressida, for instance, became another ritual, familiar from spy-films perhaps but still powerful, particularly in the warm welcome Antenor received, neatly defining the unimportance of Cressida for the Trojans, even though it altered Shakespeare's sequence in which Antenor arrives back in Troy before Cressida is handed over.[11]

The handling of the battle scenes of Act 5 was simple and adroit, quickly creating multiple perspectives. Most of the cast were lined across the stage facing upstage, backlit so that they became a still frieze, with Thersites in top-hat as Master of Ceremonies, compering the war, but with the whole scene regarded by Ulysses, Agamemnon and Thersites from the upper gallery. As characters were required to fight they turned and moved downstage before reassuming their position in the line. Throughout there was a refusal to deny the adequacy of the text, an acceptance that the play works best when it is respected.

Mendes's *Troilus and Cressida* shared virtues of clarity, simplicity, and pleasure in the narrative with Thacker's *Pericles*. Both directors had no difficulty working within the Swan Theatre. No theatre-space is easy to work in and the Swan has its own intrinsic difficulties, its demands which must be respected, but its scale and immediacy make it so naturally suited to Shakespeare that it obviously helps directors, like Mendes and Thacker, who are comparatively inexperienced in working in the vaster space of the Royal Shakespeare Theatre. It is the transition that is so fraught with danger, as Mendes and Thacker would subsequently discover.

CHAPTER 4

1991: a new taxonomy

Richard II, Romeo and Juliet, Julius Caesar (RSC, Royal Shakespeare Theatre); *Twelfth Night* (the Peter Hall Company); *Twelfth Night, Love's Labour's Lost* (RSC, Royal Shakespeare Theatre); *The Two Gentlemen of Verona* (RSC, Swan Theatre); *As You Like It* (Cheek by Jowl); *The Merchant of Venice, Coriolanus* (English Shakespeare Company); *Timon of Athens* (Young Vic); *Measure for Measure* (RSC, The Other Place); *Henry IV Part 1, Henry IV Part 2* (RSC, Royal Shakespeare Theatre)

Critics often complain about the taxonomic systems used for Shakespeare. Dissatisfied with the Folio's 'comedies, histories, tragedies', bored with divisions like 'the major tragedies', 'the problem plays' or 'the romances', we try to find new and invigorating subdivisions of the canon, new juxtapositions to illuminate the plays' relationships. My major discovery from 1991's stint of reviewing was a new system for grouping Shakespeare plays. I have grouped the fourteen productions in this chapter into five new categories: the dark tragedies, the unproblematic comedies, the analogue plays, the materialist dramas and the triumphant histories.

THE DARK TRAGEDIES

What grouped together Ron Daniels' *Richard II*, David Leveaux's *Romeo and Juliet* and Stephen Pimlott's *Julius Caesar* (all in the Royal Shakespeare Theatre) had nothing to do with darkly cynical readings of the plays. Instead they shared a literal darkness, a lighting plot so gloomy that by the interval in each my eyes were strained with the effort of peering into the murk to see what the actors were doing. When Coleridge described Kean's acting as 'like reading Shakspeare by flashes of lightning'[1] he was not being terribly

75

complimentary. At the most extreme moment of darkness in these productions, Stephen Pimlott left Cassius and Casca playing out their scene in 1.3 on a pitch-dark stage with occasional flashes of stage lightning. Though they are meeting during a supernatural storm, there must be ways of suggesting it without forcing actors to deliver long speeches in circumstances which turn them into disembodied voices. The Royal Shakespeare Theatre is not the place to try out Shakespeare on radio.

In *Richard II* the effect of the low level of lighting was intensified by the costumes to create a world of blacks and dull greys. Only Richard himself in red velvets and blue cape had a showy extravagance. The costume aptly matched Alex Jennings' ostentatious physical presence: an extremely tall man, his head topped with cascading golden curls, there was no tinge of camp in his fiercely authoritative presence. This court of whisperers and muttered threats was in awe of their dictator whose presence at the lists in 1.3 was accompanied by sinister guards armed with crossbows ceaselessly scanning the stage for armed terrorists. There was no space here for intimating a lyrical, poetic Richard, only for the dictator's splendour and power. Throughout Mowbray's speech of accusation (1.1.47ff.) Richard did not take his eyes off Bolingbroke, trying to probe his face for a sign of weakness. It was of a piece with Richard's arrogant confidence in his tyranny that Jennings could deliver the council's decisions on banishment (1.3.123ff.) standing far downstage but facing upstage, turning his back on the audience.

This tyrant made no journey towards discovery of the poetry of Richard's language later. Jennings pursued his line rigorously to the end. Always a threat to Bolingbroke, as much by virtue of his vocal authority and physical power, as Jennings towered over Anton Lesser, Richard could burst disruptively into scenes that Bolingbroke was trying to control, introducing a mocking tone that denied Bolingbroke any authority (for example, at Flint Castle, 3.3).

This extremely unlyrical Richard was opposed by a strikingly unambitious Bolingbroke. There was nothing subtextually hidden about this Bolingbroke's denial of desire for the throne; Bolingbroke nervously put off the decision as long as possible and regretted it as soon as it was taken. The Duchess of York's praise of him as a 'god on earth' (5.3.134), praise Richard would have taken as his due, found King Henry extremely harsh in response out of sheer embarrassment. The pardon to the Bishop of Carlisle (5.6.24ff.) was a weary response to so much killing and, when he replied to Exton's news of Richard's murder ('thou hast wrought / A deed of slander with thy fatal hand / Upon my head and all this famous land', 5.6.34–6), Lesser's sharp emphasis on '*my* head' made clear how much this king realised where responsibility would be seen as lying. Indeed so many of Lesser's most striking effects seemed to be reactions to others' lines that it marked this Bolingbroke as a passive pawn, pushed unwillingly into power, particularly by Paul Jesson's vicious Northumberland.

Through the murky devious world of this production's politics wandered the central tragic figure, not Richard so much as Linus Roache's Aumerle, the political innocent destroyed. His touching concern for Richard in 3.2 was met only by being violently pushed aside. In the glove scene (4.1) the intervention of the Duke of Surrey made abundantly clear that Aumerle was being set up, the victim of an orchestrated campaign to smear him. By the time he returned to his parents in 5.2 Aumerle was traumatised into a state of near-catatonic shock, needing to be slapped hard into awareness by his father.

Antony McDonald's design was as unafraid of large gestures as the production's whole concept. As England's political system began to fall apart the steel walls were replaced by piles of industrial scrap and the back wall of an empty warehouse with grimy windows. The massive painting of Atalanta by Guido Reni that had backed the princely domesticity of 1.4 was now to be seen in tattered decaying heaps on the floor. Such a production style carries its own predictability: inevitably Richard in prison was to be found in grey prison garb, with a shaven head, curled up foetally on a bare iron bed. Yet the production was capable of small gestures of simple effectiveness: in 2.1, York's bedside dialogue with the dying Gaunt hinting at a hospital visit; Richard's genuine affection for his wife in 1.4 marked by caresses; the sight of the Welsh departing across the back of the stage in 2.4 as Richard's power ebbs away.

Clear, consistent and as bleak as it could be, Daniels' production almost justified the eye-strain, even if it left the ear straining for a touch of Richard's imagination. Where Daniels made the darkness part of his argument about the play, David Leveaux's transformation of the sharp Italian sunlight into a gloomy shadowy world for

Romeo and Juliet rejected the advantages of realism with no significant gain.

Where Daniels nearly managed to compensate for the loss of poetry, Leveaux could not hope to compensate for the loss of passion. For this *Romeo* was the least passionate imaginable: these lovers seemed unable to touch each other, certainly incapable of desire. Leveaux's interest was clearly much more in the macho world of young males who were more interested in each other's bodies than in any women. This homosocial world of schoolboy sexuality had Mercutio trying to grab another young man by the balls but could not begin to suggest the fantastical world of his imagination, 'Queen Mab' becoming an unstoppable but uninteresting outpouring. Tybalt's fight with Mercutio was balletic and dancingly choreographed; Romeo's killing of Tybalt was the other side of the coin as he stabbed the unarmed man and then kicked him to death, the game of macho preening turned into a brutal street murder. Leveaux, whose production of *'Tis Pity She's a Whore* in the Swan Theatre earlier in the season showed him to be a talented and sensitive director, was left floundering on the mainhouse stage.

Alison Chitty's design for Leveaux bisected the stage with a screen of quattrocento fragments, raised and lowered in panels as needed. I noted in chapter 1, above, the problems posed by Tobias Hoheisel's set for Stephen Pimlott's *Julius Caesar*. It was of a piece with the awkwardness of Pimlott's operatic effects which often worked against the play. Staging the forum scene with a crowd staring out at the audience on stage left while Mark Antony spoke straight out to the audience on stage right makes good enough sense if both groups are singing and need to see the conductor but denies them any dramatic relationship; the sudden switch, midway through the sequence, to having Antony mobbed by a heaving mass of plebeians was unmotivated. Such switches were echoed in the costuming: as soon as Brutus instructed the conspirators to 'look fresh and merrily' as the Ides of March dawned (2.1.223), the conspirators promptly turned their gowns inside out to reveal their alternative red colour. Similarly the strong colour coding of the second half, with Octavius and Mark Antony associated with red while Brutus and Cassius were linked to blue, was simplistically emphatic.

Robert Smallwood found himself 'often aware of the deliberation with which the production's effects had been studied' so that, in the end, 'It was a production in which the actors, and with them the play, were sacrificed to the scenic schemes of director, designer, and lighting designer.'[2] It was not so much the artfulness and artificiality of the effects as the self-consciousness with which they were placed within the visual and aural structure of the production that was marked. European actors often comment enviously on the freedom and authority wielded by English actors. Even if it is often thought that the English style of classical theatre, whatever exactly that might be, has become director-dominated or over-designed, the actor's power and imagination are still the central feature of the audience's response. The RSC's work is predominantly actor-centred, even when its designs can be overbearing. The litany of complaints about Stratford verse-speaking, for instance, are based on an expectation that the actor must generate lyrical poetry, that the word or what is conceived of as the music of the poetic line must be dominant.

It is always tempting to believe that the Anglophone tendency to see non-Anglophone Shakespeare production as exactly one in which actors are 'sacrificed to the scenic schemes of director, designer, and lighting designer' results solely from the exclusion from the linguistic basis of the performance, a topic I shall return to in my final chapter. If one does not understand the words, then what else is there to do but react to what one sees? But the dictatorship of the director has often been more extreme outside England. In such a context of making theatre the actors are servants – or slaves – to the overall conception arrived at without their help. While English Shakespeare actors complain of the indignities they are put through, their collaboration is sought and needed rather than their complicity demanded. The volumes of *Players of Shakespeare*,[3] accounts by individual actors of their work on roles in recent RSC productions, belong firmly to a tradition in which the individual actor's account might be an interesting voice that one wants to hear. In some other traditions, for example the dramaturg-culture of German theatre, the actor's voice is almost completely suppressed. What the cast of Pimlott's *Julius Caesar* complained of was that the production left them no space in which to develop their own performances, a space for their own creativity, a space for them to make theatre.

Pimlott began the evening with a joke on the audience's

expectations, placing on centrestage an enigmatic cloaked figure who was revealed to be not the Soothsayer, as the audience had been lured into believing, but Mark Antony, leaping up when Caesar called his name (1.2.6) ready for his race in leather cycling shorts. The device at least gave a momentum to the scene. But when from 5.2 onwards the stage slowly filled up with soldiers arranged around the walls like a frieze of death or exhaustion the effect was distracting, never interesting enough to justify its demand for a visual attention over an aural awareness, a diversion away from the play towards the director.

Lighting – or its absence – was still the overall authority. The gloom that left Cassius and Casca in the dark could be magnificently effective (as Brutus had to strike a match on a pitch-black stage to find Caesar's ghost confronting him) but was more often perverse: the quarrel scene, lit by a single overhead light, left Jonathan Hyde and David Bradley straining for vocal effects, Brutus's orotund language contrasted with a nasal, mannered monotone for Cassius. Such visual tricks make life difficult for actors. I would have liked to have seen Bradley's neurotic Cassius or Hyde's intelligent Brutus properly but the lighting made it impossible. Only Robert Stephens' elderly Caesar, conspicuously deaf and physically frail, was consistently visible; I admired the controlled way in which he accompanied 'Et tu, Brute' by spitting into Brutus's face.

As with Leveaux's *Romeo*, the keynote was the stage's exploration of violence. Caesar was stabbed over and over and over again until the blood ran over the stage floor and the conspirators were left weak and exhausted and hysterical. They really did 'bathe our hands in Caesar's blood / Up to the elbows' (3.1.107–8). The murder of Cinna the Poet was an exercise in stage violence of such extreme brutality and such graphic detail that I felt physically sick. The confrontation of the two armies (5.1) seemed like rival hordes of football fans facing each other on the terraces, rhythmically chanting and beating their spears' ends on the ground. This violence, the production argued, was what lay all too near the surface of urbane or devious politics, a coarse brutality that denied political morality or individual dignity. In this setting, Owen Teale's beaming, open Antony, genuinely affectionate in his attachment to Caesar, came over, like Roache's Aumerle in Daniels' *Richard II*, as the innocent unable to cope with the demands of politics. At the end, as Octavius and Messala were sorting things out, Antony's final speech burst out, without preparation, across their distinctly unemotional dialogue. His praise of Brutus made no contact with Octavius's world. Discarding his sword he did not wait for a response but strode off stage, leaving Octavius enthroned on Caesar's golden chair. At such a moment the production's argument was both intriguing and justifiable but too often it had left its actors floundering in an operatic darkness.

THE UNPROBLEMATIC COMEDIES

If the dark tragedies left the audience straining to see what was happening, then the unproblematic comedies have the reverse effect, making everything blindingly clear. This group of productions is made up of two contradictory subgroups. The first contains productions that simply ignore any problems in the text. Where scholars and previous productions alike have found complexity, doubt or irresolution, such productions find radiant joy and ease. Where others have found darkness, these find pure, clear light. The second subgroup is made up of productions that recognise but surmount the problems, clarifying what had often seemed too obscure in production, renewing the texts as plays for the theatre through the consistent application of a theatrical and critical intelligence.

Two very different *Twelfth Night* productions belong firmly in the category of the bland refusal to recognise the problems. When Michael Billington transcribed the conversations of recent RSC directors of *Twelfth Night* about its difficulty, the four (Alexander, Barton, Caird and Hands) would probably have agreed with Billington's own assessment that Peter Hall's production of 1958 'solved many of the play's problems'.[4] The delicacy and intelligence that have so often been ascribed to that production were invisible in Hall's return to the play with his own company at the Playhouse Theatre in London. Many critics found in it all the virtues of that mythic ideal of 'Shakespeare done straight', of 'traditional Shakespeare', of the director's humility before the wonders of Shakespeare's genius, but I found only ordinariness and banality. It was also desperately unfunny, with barely a titter from the audience as the characters laughed away on stage to make up for our respectful silence. It was a warning that one cannot and should not return to the scene of past triumphs. The piercing intelligence of 1958 had become either cliché, like the sea noises heard at various moments throughout the evening, or oddity, like the Watteauesque swing on which Olivia sat in 1.5, denying her own mourning. The performances were mostly polished but they circumvented anything that might be worth confronting. Martin Jarvis is too intelligent an actor to miss the opportunities of Sir Andrew but he is also not a natural comic fool, with the result that he offered not a fool but the performance of a fool, the actor's self-consciousness substituted for the character's self-confidence. Sir Toby (Dinsdale Landen) became a rather decrepit aristocrat, needing his walking-stick, but a relative neither endearing nor troublesome.

Of course there were nice touches, some already present in the 1958 production: Malvolio, for instance, entering for 2.2 as Sebastian was leaving at the end of 2.1, had a neat double take as Viola entered from the 'wrong' side; the Priest in 4.3 was clearly the Sir Topas of Feste's disguise in 4.2. But such moments could not cover the perfunctory nature of 'doing it straight'.

With this production I was, I must admit, out of line with many of the reviewers. With Griff Rhys Jones's production in Stratford the horror was more equally shared. The director, a gifted comic actor himself, would have been brilliant in any one of half a dozen different roles in the play but he seemed unable to conjure good performances from his actors. Only Tim McInnerny's Sir Andrew, his physique beautifully described by Peter Porter (*TLS*, 10 May 1991) as 'like a much-loved bendy toy', created a performance of density and thoughtfulness as well as fine comedy. If there was a distinct view of the play, perhaps what Peter Porter described as the discovery that 'love is not moody but the occasion for a release of sexual energy', then it was comprehensively masked by the staging.

The problem was not entirely Jones's fault for most of the blame lay with Ultz's set. I do not think it matters greatly where or when one sets the play; almost any analogy can be made to work. If Illyria is the perfect romantic no-place, then the Gilbert and Sullivan style adopted by Ultz is a perfectly valid choice. It is not that much of a leap from *HMS Pinafore* to Shakespeare: Orsino's court has lost contact with its function just as surely as Gilbert's sailors have never been to sea and Orsino in velvet knee-breeches was a love-sick Bunthorne from *Patience*. Robert Smallwood suggested that the earlier sight of Orsino in the uniform of an admiral was 'a rank to which, one felt sure, his position as head of state, rather than the faintest possibility of naval competence, entitled . . . him'.[5] But the Orsino who remembers the last time he saw Antonio, 'besmeared / As black as Vulcan in the smoke of war' (5.1.48–9), has surely been in the middle of the fight. It is the peacetime sailor who is out of his element as surely as the sailor turned romantic lover. Orsino is no longer running the country and his court of uniformed naval officers are left frustrated, aiding and abetting their lovestruck ruler. The prettiness and artificiality of the set's allusions to Gilbert and Sullivan argued for exactly that displacement, of a society which, from the top down, has lost its purpose, just as Gilbert's libretti wickedly transform Victorian ideals into bathetic idiocies.

It was not the analogy but the scale of the set that caused the trouble; it was both overblown and flattening, its steps and levels forcing the actors into awkward lateral patterns that made interaction difficult or pushed the action far too far upstage. Actors were dwarfed by the William Morris sliding panels of Olivia's garden or lost on the flat planes of the stage. *Twelfth Night* is a tale of two households just as surely as *Romeo and Juliet* but the set militated against creating those households by putting characters into rooms in which they had never lived. Orsino and Cesario listened to Feste's song 'Come away, come away death' in 2.4 while seated at a mess-table but the table was a device for the scene, not part of the daily rhythm of Orsino's court. When Malvolio came down to quell the late-night revelling he entered a set with a fireplace defined by a red footlight and vast hanging pots and pans but there was no sense that he came from somewhere else in the house, that there were other rooms contiguous in which the rest of the household were trying to sleep.

What was left was more a reminder of pantomime, with emotions simplified and gags broad, less the satiric mockery of the first performances of Gilbert and Sullivan than the comfortable cosiness of the modern amateur local G and S. Characteristically, in the letter scene, the antics of the three watchers were far more interesting than anything offered by Freddie Jones's Malvolio, as they crawled from one piece of scenery to another, leaving Sir Andrew at one point forced to pretend to be a statue in full sight of Malvolio and fainting from shock when he got away with it. Such gags have an honourable history but here they only obscured the social tensions of Malvolio's ambitions. Interest in character was replaced by the stock devices of comedy; the text was rendered unproblematic by the easy availability of comic business.

Griff Rhys Jones, comic actor turned director, was entrusted with a difficult play. Terry Hands' last production as artistic director was *Love's Labour's Lost*, an odd choice for a director who has never found comedy an easy option. This production marks the mid-point between my two contradictory subgroups of unproblematic comedies, by turns flattening and illuminating. If some of the problems were ignored, others were carefully laid out but the care was always a little too evident, our attention directed towards the production's hard work.

Hands managed to create a production that took no pleasure in the play's language, an unexpected parallel to Daniels' *Richard II*. When Dull replied to Holofernes' comment 'Thou hast spoken no word all this while' with 'Nor understood none neither, sir' (5.1.142–4), he raised the biggest laugh of the evening. The reason lay partly in Richard Ridings' fine Dull who moved with such preternatural slowness that, when playing boules, even the bowls themselves seemed to hang in mid-air. But I suspect that the audience shared too readily Dull's incomprehension. Long speeches were scampered through in double-quick time, tossed off as so much verbiage. Biron's 'O, 'tis more than need' (4.3.287ff.) was a prime candidate with the rattling delivery brought to a sudden halt for portentous intensity at 'It adds a precious seeing to the eye' (309). By the third night of the run the production was twenty minutes faster than on the first and it may well be that the slow relishing of language had been quickly rejected in a search to keep the audience's attention. But *Love's Labour's Lost* is not a play that any audience is going to enjoy for the pleasures of its plot. Only in the relishing of puns (e.g. Armado's swain/swine at 3.1.47 or Jaquenetta's grace/grease at 4.3.191) and in the language of Don Armado and Holofernes was the language savoured for its own sake.

Timothy O'Brien's set was French impressionism turned three-dimensional, its trees and hedges vivid splashes of colour. The lords sat for the first scene picnicking, reading and sketching, in a tableau carefully arranged to remind the audience of Manet's *Déjeuner sur l'herbe*, though here with Manet's naked women conspicuous by their absence. By 2.1 the garden had been cordoned off with a sign 'Interdit aux femmes'. At 1.1.158, once the men had all signed to their oath, there was a long pause as the four realised they could think of nothing to do. A buzzing fly distracted them, eventually crushed by Longueville in his book, but Biron's enquiry 'But is there no quick recreation granted?' (1.1.159) was a welcome relief from the prospect of three years of unending tedium.

This heavy underlining of the men's naivety in signing the oath in the first place contrasted with the confident sharpness and maturity of the Princess and her women. Gender confrontation was followed through to the end of the evening where the women were clearly embarrassed and ashamed of the men's vicious cynicism at the Pageant of the Nine Worthies, Simon Russell Beale's King sharing the women's distress. But such differentiation contrasted sharply with the clichéd treatment of Jaquenetta as a woman of rustic lasciviousness, close to orgasm as she listens to Nathaniel's dignified and sensitive reading of Biron's poem in 4.2 and so excited by the presence of Biron himself in 4.3 that, oblivious of what is going on around her, she unbuttons his shirt and starts nuzzling his stomach.

The production seemed more at ease with Armado and company. John Wood's fascination with the possibilities of voice was ideal for a very Spanish Don. From his first entrance, collapsing on to a heap of cushions, Wood's Armado was madly illogical with a grasshopper mind. Yet his devotion to Jaquenetta was affectingly obsessive, passionately excited by her easy display of sexuality, as he crawled around after her exit at 1.2.158, kissing the carpet wherever she had trodden. By 5.1 the audience was in the presence of a mad gallery of eccentrics, each marked by odd tics: Armado's twitching, Dull's infinite slowness, Nathaniel's odd Japanese parasol and Holofernes' curious high giggle. The Pageant was a logical outcome of such idiosyncrasies, but viewed so sympathetically that the hurt was all the more acute when, for instance, Nathaniel was reduced to tears. Only Don Armado's Hector, a performance unstoppably big, shamed the mockers with his panache and power.

By this point in the production the effort of the evening had been transformed into ease and confidence, the play doing what it wanted. As the final song ended with Dull's basso profundo suddenly and surprisingly hitting a note at least three octaves higher than anything he had managed before, a note of poignant sweetness and beauty, the touching pleasures of art were complete. Armado's last lines were straight to the audience with a shrug: 'You that way, we this way', marking the division of the stage-world from us but also emphasising unportentously that that is how life and art are. As the stage cleared, Jaquenetta came on into the light previously occupied by Mercadé, and Don Armado, happily ready for his three years' vow as a ploughman, kissed her, a tender act that the other nobles would never approach. As the production moved from its effortful opening to its effortless conclusion, a rhythm that it might reasonably be seen as sharing with the play, so it moved from a blandness to a delicate recognition of the play's sensitivities, from one type of unproblematic comedy to the other.

The three comedies I have so far looked at also divide across two forms of Shakespeare production. Hall and Hands are part of a different RSC generation from the invitation to Griff Rhys Jones to direct. It is not simply the division by age nor the fact that the tight control of the list of directors in previous reigns would have left no space for Jones, essentially an amateur, to be invited. It is rather that the concept of the experience needed to create Shakespearean comedy for the RSC was changing emphatically. Hall and Hands directed a wide range of Shakespeare, tragical-comical-historical-pastoral, allowing the work in one area to inform and support the work elsewhere. The interconnectedness of an attitude to structure, language, style and design across genres is repeatedly marked. To understand a Shakespeare comedy sufficiently to direct it was seen as necessitating the prolonged study, in the library and rehearsal room, of Shakespearean dramaturgy. If the result could be dark and troubling, a bleak view of the comic world, then it could also be joyous. It is no accident that Terry Hands established his reputation at the RSC with a production of *The Merry Wives of Windsor* in 1968 marked for its energy and celebration as well as for its creation of Windsor, a precise socio-historical imagining of the play's world; the production could be revived in 1975 to take its place in a Falstaff cycle alongside both parts of *Henry IV*.[6]

If, under Hands' artistic control, the RSC occasionally produced Shakespearean comedy with a resolutely populist feel, refusing to be concerned with the possibility of the text in favour of a broader, more reliably guaranteed box-office appeal, these productions seemed like temporary aberrations. With Noble's assumption of artistic control the balance shifted substantially: *Twelfth Night* was entrusted to someone whose interests lay in comedy rather than Shakespeare and to a performer who could attract audiences even though he was not himself on stage. It took a step further the process begun with Ian Judge's *The Comedy of Errors* in the previous season.

Hands' disappointing *Love's Labour's Lost* was hamstrung by its weighty awareness of what it means to direct Shakespearean comedy. Griff Rhys Jones's *Twelfth Night* was panned by the critics but played to full houses and huge ovations throughout the season, leaving the actors perplexed by their popular success in a critical catastrophe. David Thacker's production of *The Two Gentlemen of Verona* in the Swan Theatre was that rare experience, a production both hugely popular and admired by Stratford's scholarly visitors.

In David Lodge's novel *Small World* (1984), Persse McGarrigle proposes to write a book on the influence of T. S. Eliot on Shakespeare; Thacker's production was surely about the influence of Dennis Potter on Shakespeare. But where in Potter's work the thirties songs mark the gap between the sordid and painful action of *Pennies from Heaven* and the language of sentimental song, in Thacker's *Two Gentlemen* the songs were a reassurance, translating the action to a thirties context in which the characters' obsession with love was validated. The audience needed to have no anxiety, for the songs guaranteed that the characters' sharp pains could and would be resolved within the terms of this romance world. Gershwin and Cole Porter inhabited the same world as the play, sharing the same perceptions of love as an uncontrollable anthropomorphised force which the characters so often voice; Valentine could have said with Gershwin 'Love walked in.' The play matched our yearning, that yearning that Potter's salesman so unavailingly voiced, that the songs should turn out to be true. As the opening and closing song reminded us, 'Love is the sweetest thing.'

The songs were also there as part of the play's visual – as well as aural – design. The band and chanteuse, placed upstage, made sure the audience could enjoy the scene changes, making an entertainment of the fairly laborious process of moving rather too much furniture. But they also belonged with the spring blossom that decorated the stage, sharing with it the visual language of romantic springtime, the belief in the painful seriousness as well as the joyful immaturity of the play's view of love. One might want to say, with the wisdom supposedly born of age, that there is a great deal in the world that is more important than the concerns of this play but the production, with unflagging charm, denied the space for such cynicism. One had to be feeling really curmudgeonly to dislike this production.

Only at one point did Thacker misjudge the play: in the final company song that sentimentalised an ending that, up to that point, he had carefully and successfully refused to see as sentimental at all. Elsewhere the production proved capable of harsh pain and hard thinking. It was, in particular, remarkably successful at showing a character reconsidering himself or herself. Proteus's shift of tenses after first seeing Silvia was part of this: 'She is fair, and so is Julia that I love— / That I did love' (2.4.197–8), Barry Lynch's pause after 'that I love' creating the space for the character's oleaginous awareness of the need to redefine the time of that emotion.

When the Duke banished Valentine in 3.1, Richard Bonneville found in Valentine's soliloquy (3.1.170–87) a newly serious and wondering comprehension of the depth of Valentine's love for Silvia, showing Valentine puzzling out the ramifications of a love that was proving to be far more profound than he had yet considered it to be. From being a string of romantic clichés the speech moved the character into a new realm of feeling. I am not entirely convinced that the speech will quite do all that; the language still seems to be caught up in the narrowness of feeling possible in the range of romantic simile: 'Except I be by Silvia in the night / There is no music in the nightingale' (178–9). But I respected the actor's attempt here, the ability to discard the Woosterish silly-ass style of Valentine earlier in the play, a style made possible both by his gullibility and by the way the thirties setting allowed for a tinge of P. G. Wodehouse.

Certainly the Duke's tricking of Valentine into a revelation of his elopement plot was beautifully handled, as the Duke prepared a picnic with malign intent; I had never before taken the instruction in recipes to remove the seeds from a melon as an encouragement to mimic disembowelling. The audience was way ahead of Valentine here and could be heard registering with a certain glee how innocently he strode into the trap. This was the Valentine that had become familiar in the production: young, handsome, good and very stupid. But the new access of the pain of love immediately afterwards, in the soliloquy, refused the audience the right to patronise Valentine and forced them to re-evaluate their view of the rather naive emotions and very naive confidence that had driven the character thus far.

Something similar happened in the fine playing of the scene between Silvia (Saskia Reeves) and Julia (Clare Holman) over Proteus's ring (4.4.106ff.). Again there was the transition between the audience's superiority to the action and its being surprised by the movement of the play. The audience's pain and sympathy for Julia when Proteus handed over the ring earlier in the scene was transformed into Silvia's pain and sympathy, a pain which was a precise expression of the women's similar positions, both vulnerable to the duplicity of Proteus. This scene, above all, managed to question and nearly to shatter the limits of romance, making of the women's vulnerability and the oppressive power of the man something that cut through the limited terms in which we are usually prepared to consider action in such a play. The transition was marked by the difference between Julia's comic tearing of Proteus's letter at 1.2.100s.d. and the harsh truths that lay behind Silvia's pained tearing of another letter from him here (4.4.128s.d.).

All problems in the play pale into insignificance beside Valentine's handing over of the nearly raped Silvia to the rapist: 'All that was mine in Silvia I give thee' (5.4.83). Thacker's production, while not making the line unproblematic, offered it as a problem squarely confronted and tentatively solved. The production had, slowly and thoughtfully, allowed the significance of the women to grow as the play progressed, accepting their rights to decide what happens to them, their ability to initiate action and to actualise a form of friendship that the men talk of but cannot carry through into action. It seemed only logical and fully justifiable therefore to see Silvia resolving the play's crux. Anne Barton has argued that the moment is 'Shakespeare's blunder . . . when without warning he gives ideal friendship precedence over love', seeing the 'gift of Silvia to his friend' as 'an intolerable clumsiness' which 'has the effect here of negating the whole previous development of the comedy'.[7] Thacker's modest and highly intelligent solution reintegrated the moment into the development of the comedy as this production had explored it. After Proteus's 'My shame and guilt confounds me' (5.4.73) Barry Lynch left a colossal pause, showing Proteus considering the possibility of conning Valentine again, before finally resolving on genuine repentance. If the audience hesitated slightly as to the genuineness of the repentance – and Lynch's smirk was so beguiling that one had to have a moment's pause – it was Silvia's silent intercession, a calm gesture of moving towards Proteus, that reassured them. Her judgement that this man was worth forgiveness justified Valentine's generosity, a symbolic act of love and respect for Silvia as much as of friendship for Proteus. Such work, accepting the play's difficulty, was as honest and intelligent as one could wish for.

Robert Smallwood, while applauding the subtlety of this revisionist treatment, had a moment's hesitation:

It was a daring and in many ways brilliant solution to what has so often been regarded, on the page, as an intractable problem: from seeming to many readers merely a property, a chattel, in the scene, the silent Silvia was made its motor, and comic form was thus preserved. One could argue, of course, that from the character being the chattel of the dramatist's chauvinist vision the actress had become the chattel of the director's sentimental inversion.[8]

At such intractable moments of text, directors are confronted by three choices: to abandon the production completely, to attempt to recreate a Renaissance context for understanding the event or to redefine the moment in a way that, while the text may inadequately support it, at least allows the moment to be transformingly and intriguingly playable. Unwilling to take the first option, some directors attempt the second as academic critics often now demand that such authenticity of referential meaning should be achieved or at least attempted.

It would be possible to play this climactic moment of *The Two Gentlemen of Verona* in terms of Renaissance concepts of friendship, though audiences probably would not be able to follow it; it is certainly possible to play it as a moment of male oppression that denies Silvia any of the space and power she has slowly started to achieve in the course of the play, but that would be to make the ending's mechanisms a bleak vision of the inevitable reassertion of patriarchal control. Thacker's version, a fellow-travelling male vision of female strength and generosity, allowed the play to reach its ending, through an exploration of silence, the text's 'failure' to mark Silvia's reaction allowing an open space for her approval, rejection or, as here, intervention, in the reconciliation of Valentine and Proteus.

The finest production of comedy in the year, however, was well away from the RSC. Cheek by Jowl celebrated its tenth anniversary with *As You Like It*, directed, as usual, by Declan Donellan. The production proved so successful that, at a time of financial anxiety, the company could revive the production in 1994 in time to catch the Christmas audience. Cheek by Jowl's Shakespeare productions had often been emptily radical but this was like watching a much-loved picture restored, the colours bright and shining, unnoticed details newly apparent, the brilliance of the whole pristine and exhilarating. After the tired revivals of the play by the RSC (e.g. by John Caird in 1989, see chapter 3, above) this *As You Like It* was a revelation.

Donellan used an all-male cast, defining his point by opening the evening with the beginning of 'All the world's a stage' with the whole cast on stage, using 'all the men and women' (2.7.140) as a means of dividing them into their gender roles for the performance. The gender of character was thus sometimes disconnected from the gender of actor and sometimes not. A male actor performing a female role was not therefore more performative than a male actor playing a male role; instead the production allowed character to exist dissociated from performer.

Where Clifford Williams' 1967 all-male production for the National Theatre had been at times coy and camp, Donellan rigorously resisted the trap. Gender became a construct of performance, and sexuality was placed within the control of character, not actor. Adrian Lester's astonishing performance as Rosalind, sensuous and winning, was never simply a pretext for exploring the play's homosexuality, even though it enabled a subtle consideration of it. The play-acting of Rosalind-Ganymede was both more intriguing and simpler than it is when a woman plays Rosalind but the tremendous erotic charge between Rosalind and Orlando had nothing glibly homoerotic about it. Instead, performing gender became a game, as when Orlando playfully punched Ganymede's arm and Rosalind awkwardly returned the male gesture, though the actor could easily have punched him back. But such moments never dominated, never unbalanced the investigation of love.

The problem of love and desire was defined here as lying

beyond gender, simply coming into being, irresistibly and unaccountably. As John Peter argued in the *Sunday Times* (8 December 1991), 'Declan Donellan's production reveals that *As You Like It* is not about sexuality – hetero-, homo-, bi- or trans- – but about love, which both transcends sexuality and includes it.' Yet the production's politics were argued over. In the continuing debate over how modern Shakespeare production might represent women, the Cheek by Jowl *As You Like It* could be seen as an extreme form of male colonialism by completely eliminating women from the practice of representation, so that they became characters, not performers, figures able to be voiced only by men.

This silencing of women in performance would then extend into an argument about precisely that quality of non-gendered desire which John Peter (and I) admired: for the rejection of the female voice could be seen as the rejection of the particularities of female desire, its separateness absorbed within a dominant male discourse, the discourse of Shakespeare, of Donellan and of the male cast, and by extension the discourse of a patriarchal society. Certainly, the production turned Arden into a paradisal world in which the normal, socially constructed constraints on sexuality could be ignored (rather than transgressed), just as it was not interested in the economic structures of ownership of land with which the play is intriguingly concerned. But in its positing of an alternative vision, while it could not accommodate the tensions in current social formulations of desire, it offered a refreshingly new green world through which the characters made their way.

Celia, for instance, irritated by the treachery of her friend in having fallen in love, wandered through the play waiting for Mr Right to come along, as he duly did in the person of Oliver. If Tom Hollander's Celia was inclined to the petulant flounce this was less a male comment on female behaviour, a gesture of camp creeping into the performance, than an ungendered response to the character's exceptionally long periods of time silently on stage, excluded by the rapt attention of Rosalind and Orlando in each other. Richard Cant's cheerily sexy Audrey, always ready to yodel summoning her goats, was innocently desirable without being mocked for it, unlike Jaquenetta in the RSC's *Love's Labour's Lost*.

Where Donellan at his worst (as in *The Tempest* in 1988) is excessive and mannered, this production was clear and controlled. Nick Ormerod's set of bare boards with hanging green strips of paper

7. *As You Like It* 5.4, Cheek by Jowl, 1991: Orlando (Patrick Toomey)
dances with Rosalind (Adrian Lester)

for Arden was all that was needed, a space on which the actors could work. The comic invention was always driven by the language, not by business. Mike Afford as Corin spoke so slowly, as if it took ages for messages from his brain to reach his mouth, that he drove a frustrated Touchstone to extremes of agony. As Oliver Reynolds commented (*TLS*, 20 December 1991), 'A pipe-smoking ruminant, he pauses constantly, to singular effect. Each. Word. Becomes. A. Sentence. (Almost.) This is carried off so well that the word "and" looms horrifyingly large.' Only Joe Dixon's Jaques, played as a repressed homosexual, had difficulty avoiding being mannered, partly the consequence of the repressed sexuality suggesting too neatly a rationale for his tense misanthropy.

The rethinking of the production allowed a sustained realism of reaction. When Rosalind lifted her bridal veil and offered herself to Orlando (5.4.115), Orlando turned on his heel and stormed to the back of the stage, shocked at the trick and shamed at his failure to have recognised her. It took time, covered with other action, before he could come downstage again, now back in control, fully accepting Rosalind, unashamed and more in love than ever. This has a truth that far transcends the conventions of happy endings, finding an answer for the character in a realism of lived experience rather than the norms of comedy, and making the discovery all the more Shakespearean. Even the Epilogue, so often an awkwardness where the text's comments of gender are not matched by the performer's ('If I were a woman' (16–17) is gibberish when spoken by a woman), came over with simple charm, Lester's natural easiness creating an exquisite engagement with the audience.

In such a production there were no problems unresolved and no problems avoided, the play's joyousness fully accepted and expressed by the company. Unproblematic comedy needed no stronger advocate.

THE ANALOGUE PLAYS

Empires grow; success breeds expansionist policies. The English Shakespeare Company, after their extraordinary triumphs with the Histories, decided that more meant better, subdivided the company into two and sent both out on tour. One, looking suspiciously like the B team, offered *The Merchant of Venice* and Jonson's *Volpone,* both directed by Tim Luscombe, to damning reviews; the other, with Bogdanov directing and Pennington in the cast, offered *Coriolanus* and *The Winter's Tale* to reviews as excited as the others were despondent. I sampled one of each.

Both *The Merchant of Venice* and *Coriolanus* responded to the lure of the analogue, the precise analogy in recent history to serve to explicate the Shakespearean text as if the play had no function in relation to its own time and, more significantly, could only be made popular by the recreation of the play as modern parable. The English Shakespeare Company was addicted to its own popularity, feeding off its own box-office figures as the justification for its existence. But at its worst its policy of trying to make Shakespeare popular made the productions weakly populist, offering simple answers where the text is complex, failing to follow through the implications of analogy. Bogdanov is horrified by academic approaches to Shakespeare, what he describes as 'the gelatinous blancmange of academia'. The loathing is fuelled by an anxiety that 'the language will be lost to all but a fortunate few within the span of my own children's lifetime' and the compensating drive to 'give contemporary audiences some kind of folk memory as to what the stories are about'.[9] Bogdanov wants to share the pleasures of live Shakespeare with a younger audience, finding the answer most frequently in modern-dress productions.

Luscombe's *Merchant*, however, found its analogy in the rise of fascism in Italy in the 1930s. Pinpointing the production's date as 1938, the programme offered a helpful history lesson, documenting fascist anti-semitism. Venice, the city that invented the ghetto, has regularly been seen in recent productions of the play as structured on anti-semitism. Hence Luscombe could show more and more Venetians wearing fascist uniforms as the play progressed, and could follow Lorenzo's flight with Jessica (2.6) with a scene of an elderly jew beaten up by blackshirted thugs.

The problem was that the more the production underlined the viciousness of the Christian community as equivalent to modern fascism, the more Shylock was consequently shorn of any villainy, standing only as the dignified representative of a beleaguered community. After arranging for Antonio's arrest with Tubal,[10] Shylock (John Woodvine) did indeed head to 'our synagogue' (3.1.121) where he donned prayer-shawl and lit candles, joined by other jews frightened by the growing fascist threat. As moving as such a moment was for the audience it denied any mercantilist motive for Shylock's pursuit of Antonio ('for were he out of Venice I can make what merchandise I will', 3.1.118–19), replacing it with the horror of threatened genocide. The modern anxiety of presenting a bad jew was soothed: Shylock became a decent chap, a businessman with barely a hint of a jewish accent, seen at first working efficiently at his desk (1.3). In so far as the audience was anxious about Shylock's aims, they were excusable as the response of a desperate man to a vicious situation: his actions were nothing like as bad as those that the Venetian fascists had in store for his 'tribe', his 'sacred nation' (1.3.49, 46).

But this both narrowed the play and made nonsense of the chosen analogy. As Jonathan Steinberg has shown in *All or Nothing* (1990), Italian fascism was decisively lacking in anti-semitism and its government resisted Nazi pressure to hand over its jewish community. If the analogy is not historically true it serves no purpose. It will not even work within the play. It is hardly credible that in 1938 Shylock could have got a fair hearing or that the rule of law was such that the blackshirted guards would hold Antonio down for Shylock rather than taking the plaintiff out and beating him up. Even worse, the production could not defeat the inevitable rhythm of the scene so that, in spite of the fascist banners, uniforms and salutes, the audience still could be felt wishing that an answer to Shylock could be found, that this act of butchery, intensified by the sheer size of Shylock's carving-knife, could be prevented. The audience found itself siding with the fascists.

Nothing in the production gave me any confidence that these paradoxes were within the director's awareness: too much else was equally inconsistent. Nerissa, told by Graziano to 'cheer yon stranger' (3.2.235), made much too much of her refusal to help a jew; Belmont was as anti-semitic as Venice. To play Morocco in 2.7 as a parody of a westernised Arab was either risky or ignorant. In any case, the pleasures of Belmont were dulled by playing Portia (Lois Harvey) as a Jean Harlow look-alike addicted to her wind-up gramophone and a large heart-shaped box of chocolates; it was impossible to see what a Bassanio as sensible as Laurence Kennedy's could see in her. At the end, with marital harmony comfortably restored and not the slightest hint of a problem left over Antonio, the couples danced out as an offstage crowd could be heard roaring as if at a Nuremberg rally. The play's fascination with the antithesis of place went for nothing.

8. *Coriolanus* 1.1, English Shakespeare Company, 1991: The plebeians perform
an uprising

If this analogue over-reached itself, Bogdanov's *Coriolanus*
worked hard at a parallel with Eastern Europe. I suggested in
chapter 2, above, in analysing Hands' *Coriolanus* for the RSC, that
the collapse of the Soviet bloc seemed to lie behind the audience's
perception if not the director's intentions. Bogdanov made the
analogy specific and explicit, exploring the tensions and potentials
of popular movements overthrowing communist patricians. The
plebeians' discovery of the power of the people was, in this production, the creation of a party, analogous to Solidarity of course but
here called 'Democratie', identified by a large banner unfurled
across the stage for the opening demonstration. The crowd, chanting 'Give us this day our daily bread', was broken up by sirens, tear
gas, riot police and beatings – the weapons of the state – before
reforming to be addressed by Bernard Lloyd's Menenius, a party
apparatchik in an astrakhan hat, the sweetly reasonable face of
Sovietism.

It is no disrespect to Michael Pennington's subtle and powerful performance as Coriolanus to suggest that this production displaced Coriolanus by placing the people at its centre. In its highly sympathetic treatment of the people and its not unsympathetic treatment of the tribunes, the English Shakespeare Company's production achieved what Brecht had suspected when, in a note in July 1955, he commented 'I again make an analysis of _Coriolanus,_ and wonder if it would be possible to stage it without additions (made by me two years ago) or with very few, just by skilful production.'[11] This was, in effect, Brecht's _Coriolanus_ without Brecht's rewriting.

By intelligent individuating, the production turned the people into characters, not in terms of their trades and families but through identifying and sustaining a particular political position for each one, a marked contrast with Hands' inadequate crowd. This crowd's discussions (for example in 2.3 and 3.3) became intense and complex political debates, conducted with the house lights up and with the people spread through the auditorium as well as on stage, debating through a microphone, prompted where necessary by the tribunes who saw their role as the creation of the new party. In 2.3 the crowd's moderates attempted to oppose the direction in which the tribunes were taking the meeting but were soon silenced by the rational argument of the others, leaving a fairly united group to exit chanting 'Democratie'. This examination of the hijacking of a popular movement by ideologues whose personal ambition was balanced by their genuine belief in the role the people's party should play was consistently thoughtful, helped by the fine work of Michael Cronin (Sicinius) and Robert Demeger (Brutus). In this context of workers' politics, it was fitting that the gown of humility for Coriolanus should be a dirty boiler suit, a symbol of the plebeians' workclothes.

Bogdanov has often been accused of using cheap theatrical tricks but in _Coriolanus_ the logic of the production was consistent in its use of the apparatus of modern media. The news of Coriolanus's league with Aufidius arrived over the telephone in 4.6 in an office, obviously the editorial hub of the Democratie newspaper, where Sicinius was dictating to a worker-typist; the scene of the triumphant return of the 'ladies' (5.5) was watched on television by Sicinius and Menenius in the middle of 5.4. But the production was equally capable of achieving its effects by the simplest means: Volumnia's humiliation after Coriolanus's banishment was pinpointed by highlighting her extraordinary arrogance in the image of herself as 'Juno-like' (4.2.56), the phrase mockingly echoed by a woman in the crowd who could not this time be stared down by Volumnia's withering gaze.

This rebalancing of the play did not diminish the central struggle but made it more equal, Coriolanus never being allowed unquestioned dominance, the sharpness of his wit and his vocal brilliance always offset by the dogged reasonableness of the people and their politically astute tribunes. It did, however, marginalise Andrew Jarvis's Aufidius, an alien figure with his crossed bandoliers, *four* swords and headband, a man for whom the political realities of Rome could have no meaning. At the end Aufidius moved from standing triumphantly on Coriolanus's corpse to a horror at the strength of his own emotion, stroking the corpse with love and despair. Militarism dominated, evidenced in the soldier's kit-bag, which Coriolanus carried into exile, or the presentation of his son in 1.3 charging around playing soldiers, an ironic parody of his father.

In this context Volumnia's plea (5.3) was a serious attempt to reconcile two sides, a genuine argument for compromise but with a strong awareness, shared by Coriolanus, of the price he will have to pay. The silence of his acceding to her (5.3.183) was sad, almost tragic, precisely because his subsequent outlining of its danger ('Most dangerously you have with him prevailed, / If not most mortal to him', 5.3.189–90) only made explicit what both already knew.

It was part of the success of the production that it could turn theatrical clichés into potent meaning. Productions of the Roman plays have too often used statues on stage. Here the statue's decapitated head, wheeled forward in 3.1 and looking sufficiently like Coriolanus's, suggested Soviet representations of its deities. For an audience seeing the production when statues of Lenin were being decapitated throughout Eastern Europe the image had a genuine, unforced potency.

An English company's view of Eastern European politics cannot possibly have the same emotional charge as an Eastern European company's view. Bogdanov's work was not as charged as Alexandru Darie's *A Midsummer Night's Dream* for the Comedy Theatre of Bucharest, in London for the London International Festival of Theatre, with its wood full of security police. To claim, as Lachlan

MacKinnon did (*TLS*, 19 April 1991), that *Coriolanus* made 'a political nonsense of Shakespeare's most overtly political play' was grotesquely wide of the mark. This intelligent production made the analogue a means of redefining the play in ways that Brecht would certainly have approved but without going against the grain of the text.

THE MATERIALIST DRAMAS

Reviewing Trevor Nunn's production of *Othello* for the RSC in 1989, Stanley Wells commented on its 'wealth of social detail'. He identified its technique as 'rooted in naturalism; indeed, a fully written account of this production would read like a Victorian novel'.[12] In 1991 Nunn directed two Shakespeare productions, *Timon of Athens*[13] at the Young Vic in London and an RSC touring production of *Measure for Measure* which opened in the rebuilt Other Place in Stratford. What had seemed experimental in *Othello* was now becoming a recognisably fixed style for small spaces: emphatically naturalistic acting as if the plays were Ibsenite social dramas, consequently a phenomenal density of detail, a certain literalism with the text and above all a belief in the plays' explicability. Nothing now could be left enigmatic or inexplicit and the process of explication was doggedly rooted in the material reality of the design and the style – hence my label for this group. Pudovkin recognised that 'the playing of an actor which is connected with an object and is built around it . . . is always one of the strongest methods of cinematic construction'[14] but this proof that 'films can be an excellent means of materialistic representation'[15] will not necessarily hold true for theatre.

The opening of the two productions exemplified the approach. *Timon of Athens* began with the after-effects of an armed robbery. Two masked gunmen rushed on stage carrying the loot; one was shot by a plain-clothes policeman while the other escaped. I put this down as a symbol of a dangerous materialist world in which this very modern Timon lived, the violent underbelly of the Thatcherite consumer capitalism which the rest of the production delineated. But at the opening of the second half, with the whole stage now transformed into a scrap-yard with the wrecks of six cars and a heavy layer of sand and rubble, the escaped bank-robber reappeared, dug a hole in the sand and buried the loot so that, a few scenes later, it was conveniently in place for Timon (David Suchet) to uncover it (4.3.25). This is explication with a vengeance. It had never occurred to me that the gold was other than a symbolic entity, there because it was there, not something that needed its source exactly depicted. Such a narrative gave it a social reality and a history, drastically reducing its emblematic potency.

Measure for Measure opened to the strains of Strauss's Emperor Waltz and with the Duke (Philip Madoc) seated on a couch which deliberately looked like Freud's. He read from a well-thumbed book the first few lines of 'He who the sword of heaven would bear' (3.1.516ff. – the rest of the speech would be read at various other points during the performance). He also looked at and carefully pocketed some newspaper cuttings and a photograph. These, again, seemed easy to interpret as mementoes he wanted to carry with him; again, the explanation was shown to be inadequate. In 3.1, explaining the history of Mariana to Isabella, the Duke produced the cuttings as verification of his story; the photograph proved to be of Mariana. What in Shakespeare is troublingly discontinuous – when after all *does* the Duke know about Angelo's treatment of Mariana and should that have affected his decision to make Angelo his deputy? – was now in Nunn's version completely apparent. The entire feigned disappearance had no cause other than the need to test Angelo. In 1.3 none of the other reasons the Duke offered, least of all his own slack government, was remotely as important as the heavy emphasis placed on the last: 'Lord Angelo is precise' (1.3.50).

In both productions this careful placement of detailing functioned not only as novelistic realism but also to lay bare cause and reason for every line. Nunn's stuffing of the plays with material detail so emphatically underscored the lines that every word seemed to need its accompanying point, until the business justified the existence of the line rather than the line justifying the business. Out of dozens of examples I offer a few: the Duke could think of death as 'an after-dinner's sleep' (3.1.33) because the Provost could be seen asleep on a chair; the 'stuff' at which the Duke wonders ('oh heavens, what stuff is here?', 3.1.274) turned out to be a stock of dirty postcards, revealed when Pompey turned out his pockets on going to prison; Lucullus proved it was 'no time to lend money' (*Timon*, 3.1.40–1) by calling up some account

displays on his computer-screen; when the Poet and the Painter
came to 'offer you our service' (5.1.70), they offered Timon a
camping stove and toothbrush, gifts which they had brought in
their backpacks.

Sometimes this emphasis on the visible reality denied what the
play's language is clearly saying: Timon's comment on 'Twinned
brothers of one womb' became not a thought on sun and earth but
a comment on two halves of the parsnip he was eating. Sometimes
it was just too glib: Timon's jewels handed out at the first banquet
(1.2.166ff.) were car-keys, emphasised by the sound of the new
cars hooting off stage; Sempronius was found for 3.3 changing
after a game of squash, writing out a cheque and then tearing it up
– the change of mind cued by 'No' (19) – before grabbing his
shampoo and heading off for his shower.

While *Measure* was played almost unaltered, *Timon* was exten-
sively rewritten. At its simplest this tidied up the problems of the
talents so that 'five talents' (1.1.97) became 'fifty thousand' (suggesting pounds), 'A thousand talents' (2.2.195) became 'A
million'. But speeches and entire scenes were added wholesale to
make the movement of the action absolutely clear. To ensure that
no one in the audience could imagine that Timon was the friend
for whom Alcibiades was pleading in 3.6, Alcibiades asked for the
case to be delayed until Timon could arrive. A new scene between
a senator and one of Alcibiades' men, dressed as a motorcycle messenger, made explicit the progress of the strategic manoeuvring in
Act 4. Other sections were re-ordered: the scene with Apemantus
(Barry Foster in filthy raincoat, old boots, old school-tie knotted
over a string vest, and a woolly hat, making him a parodic labourer)
in 4.3 was moved to follow 5.1, a decision that made a natural dramatic progression from what is inconsequential in the text. Other
characters were substantially developed, particularly Timandra; far
from making only a brief appearance in 4.3, her role was built up
until she became a major figure. Starting as one of the Amazons in
1.2 (who changed midway through their routine from figures from
a baroque opera into frilly-knickered prostitutes), Timandra took
up with Alcibiades. By the end of the play she had become his
second-in-command and political adviser, negotiating with Athens
on his behalf in another series of newly added speeches.

Nunn is, of course, perfectly entitled to his view, in his programme-note, that the play is unfinished; he saw it as his task in the

production 'to clarify what is impossibly obscure, to expand what is impenetrably telescoped and to make dramatic what is inert in the story'. But he and I obviously have different views on what is obscure or inert. To have Timon tell Alcibiades at the climax of their dialogue in 4.3 'I despise myself' was to spell out what Shakespeare left vague, as well as crediting Timon with a degree of self-awareness hardly apparent in Shakespeare's text. To have the dying Timon – he had shot himself in the back of a van – brought back on to the stage so that the evening could close on a weeping Flavius kneeling beside the corpse while Apemantus stood behind it was to make the magnificent casualness of Shakespeare's perfunctory exit and offstage death ('Timon hath done his reign', 5.2.108) into a sentimentalised cliché, to turn what was unquestionably dramatic, a prime moment of the play's 'extraordinary originality and urgency' (Nunn's note again), into something inert, rather than the other way round.

There was never any doubt that one was watching the work of a virtuoso director but the virtuosity seemed misplaced. The materiality of this play-world seemed less a representation of a fiercely materialist culture than a slightly self-regarding tribute to the director's own imagination. I did not find that Lucullus's aside about what Flaminius might be bringing (3.1.5ff.) was sharper for being spoken over a telephone intercom to his secretary or that the Second Senator's offer of 'such heaps and sums of love and wealth' (5.2.37) was helped by his brandishing a blank cheque drawn on Coutts.

But equally there was never any doubt that whenever Nunn's largesse, which at times risked rivalling Timon's, was capable of being restrained the results could be extraordinary: the Apemantus–Timon scene (4.3.198ff.) took on the collocations of Beckett's tramps, the Shakespearean wasteland and inner-city decay in the 1990s, adding historical precision to what might otherwise have been a recapitulation of Peter Brook's treatment of Lear and Gloucester in 1960, and creating a precisely imaged social reality of desperate emptiness.

Nunn's *Measure for Measure* was more restrained than his *Timon* but for one highly visible quirk. Concerned to underline the time-sequence of the play, its rapid movement through day and night towards the moment fixed for Claudio's execution, Maria Bjornson fixed a large clock dominantly over the set. Walter

Benjamin warned that 'a clock that is working will always be a dis-
turbance on the stage'[16] but the warning was not heeded this time.
Sometimes the clock moved in real time but sometimes it had to
move faster so that it would, for instance, hit the time with
appropriate precision for the Justice's reply to Escalus's 'What's
o'clock, think you?': 'Eleven, sir' (2.1.264–5). It jumped hours
between scenes, forcing the audience to watch it: 8.45 p.m. for 4.1,
11.55 p.m. for 4.2, 4 a.m. for 4.3, 8 a.m. for 4.4 and 11 a.m. for
the Duke's arrival back in 4.5. What it never managed to manifest
was the play's temporal pressure: that is present in the play's language, not its material design.

Set in Freud's Vienna and touring in tandem with Pam Gems'
new version of *The Blue Angel, Measure* was bound to be about
sexuality and repression. Unlike the fascination in recent productions with the Duke, Nunn's interest was much more firmly
focused on Angelo (David Haig).[17] The Duke may judge Angelo as
someone who 'scarce confesses / That his blood flows' (1.3.51–2)
but here the blood became specific: Angelo's reaction to his first
meeting with Isabella ('What's this? What's this?', 2.2.168) was his
awareness that he had an erection, his body reacting without the
conscious control of his repressing mind. The physical response to
her – by 141 he had been close enough to find himself sniffing at
her hair – turned in 2.4 first into a quivering sexual fantasy as he
imaged her body lying over him during his opening soliloquy and
then a violence close to rape when she failed to fulfil the fantasy,
throwing her on the couch and, during 'Who will believe thee,
Isabel?' (2.4.154ff.) holding her firmly, almost viciously, from
behind with his hands clamped on her breasts. With an Isabella as
much the fair young English rose as the waif-like Claire Skinner
the vulnerability was intensified frighteningly. Haig pursued every
twist and turn of Angelo's psychology with intelligence and power.

Haig's Angelo, as a study in sexuality and repression, was
matched by parallel examples of neuroses and sudden emotional
excess: Isabella's hysterical outbreak when Angelo announces that
Claudio 'must die tomorrow' (2.2.84), Juliet's grief when the Duke
reveals his inadequacy as a psychologist in telling her the same news
(2.3.39) and Mariana, clad in her wedding-dress like a prototype
for Miss Havisham and the moated grange really Satis House.

I have suggested that Nunn's treatment of the end of *Timon of
Athens* was sentimental. He was certainly content in *Measure for*

9. *Measure for Measure* 5.1, RSC, The Other Place, 1991: Reunited under the clock, Isabella (Claire Skinner) kneels to embrace Juliet (Teresa Banham) and Claudio (Jason Durr), watched by the Duke (Philip Madoc, right)

Measure to see the play reaching a conclusively happy ending, with Claudio and Angelo shaking hands, Isabella accepting the Duke's proposal and all dancing off stage. Some critics found this fully achieved by the emotional intensity of the reunited family. I was much more struck by the naturalistic truth of Angelo's shocked faint when Claudio was brought in and the arrival on stage of a fat prostitute, presumably Kate Keepdown, to claim Lucio. Fairy-tale endings do not belong in materialist settings. Yet, if finally unsatisfying, Nunn's productions were a provocation to the traditions of English Shakespeare production. It would be a pity, though, if such a style became a new orthodoxy.

THE TRIUMPHANT HISTORIES

The last production at Stratford during Terry Hands' reign was *Richard II*; the first under the new king, Adrian Noble, was *Henry*

IV Part 1. One could, in the summer, see Anton Lesser's Bolingbroke being crowned King Henry IV at the Barbican while Julian Glover's King Henry IV ruled in Stratford. In some ways the disconnection symbolised the RSC change-over, a deliberate discontinuity, a touch of the new broom. It was hardly surprising that Noble should choose to begin his reign with the two parts of *Henry IV*: Trevor Nunn had directed them to open the Barbican. I have dubbed Noble's productions 'the triumphant histories' for the simplest of reasons, for they were a triumph, a coherent and jubilantly theatrical exploration of the plays.

In an interview in 1988, Ralph Berry, noting the 'exciting and vivid theatrical moments, which [Noble had] found for the characters and the world of the characters' in his *Macbeth*, asked 'Is that what you are consciously working for, much of the time, this eliciting of metaphors and vivid theatrical images?' Noble replied,

That's the easy bit of directing. I find it very stimulating to create exciting pictures on the stage. I can do that. The real grind of rehearsals takes place with the actors trying to make a text 400 years old alive with meaning, now, that it should have the right rate, the right phrasing, that it should penetrate our dull ears.[18]

Creating exciting stage pictures may be easy for Noble but I was exhilarated by the visual and theatrical imagination that created the battle of Shrewsbury in Part 1, when a backstage panel lifted to disclose a huge battery of percussion thundering away, and through the stage floor there came, rising further and further, a seething, writhing tableau, figures struggling in slow motion for the throne with a woman screaming silently at the horror of war to one side. It is not simply that battles are notoriously difficult to stage – Shakespeare knew that as well as any modern director – but that the icon complexly imaged the war, bringing together so much that the production had been exploring. The incorporation of the throne itself as the focus made manifest the ambitions of the rebellion, satisfyingly concretising the notion of kingship. The mass of bodies was terrifying but the woman, dissociated but reacting, brought together the production's thinking about the place of women in this society, connecting back, for instance, to 3.1, where Lady Percy and Mortimer's Welsh wife appeared with a female harpist behind a gauze scrim, plaintively separated from the political debate and masculine posing of the rebels at the front of the stage.

One of the major achievements of Noble and his designer, Bob Crowley, was precisely this sense of interconnectedness, forcing the audience to link together events across vast tracts of stage time through a visual device that echoed and resonated. The stage lift that rose threateningly for this emblem of war in Part 1 was used once again – and only once – for Part 2, 5.3, now bringing up not the perfect image of political disorder but the perfect emblem of English rusticity, Shallow's house, a world of peace and drinking and singing, its warm glowing reds and browns suggesting an idyllic utopian space, a world one might want to patronise but cannot for its charm is not sentimental, its comedy too gentle. The song that accompanied that scene fed back to the other songs in the production, the raucous songs of the Boar's Head Tavern, the violent urban sexy world of London, the other side of Englishness, and a different form of comedy, the energies of Albie Woodington's mad biker Pistol and Joanne Pearce's dangerous loving Doll. The songs encouraged comparison, the difference between rural and city England, the calmness of the one and the hysteria of the other but also the comedy of both.

But such echoes were everywhere. To take a much smaller but equally resonant example, Henry IV violently and mockingly crowned Prince Henry with a cushion and the crown during his tirade in Part 2 (4.3.221ff.), offering the audience an echo of the cushion Falstaff used as his crown in the play-acting of Part 1 (2.5.382), a similar mockery of kingship, part of the production's consideration of the two kings, Henry IV and Henry V, and the two fathers, Henry and Falstaff, and the same son. Did those cushions make their last appearance as the ones stuffed up Doll's dress to feign pregnancy in Part 2 (5.4.14), the plays' last visual image of the child?

Let me take a third, even smaller object, two ribbons in Part 1, the one taken by Lady Percy from her girdle to give to her husband as he left for the rebellion in 2.4, the other given by Mistress Quickly to Prince Henry when he arrived at the tavern in 3.3 in his magnificent armour on his way to Shrewsbury. That Prince Henry has no other woman, no wife, mother or lover to give him her favour was touching, a mark of his isolation in the play, and the simple sincerity behind Mistress Quickly's gesture was equally moving. But it became poignant when it was this ribbon that Prince Henry used at Shrewsbury to 'let my favours hide thy

mangled face' (5.4.95), inadequately covering the face of
Hotspur's corpse.

Noble's control over the architecture of the whole structure was
magnificently assured. I noted dozens of such links traversing the
expanse of the two plays, articulating the movement of the action,
the changing relationships of the characters, the development of
dramatic meaning. Noble added to it a rather different effect, what
I want to call cinematic theatricality. Elizabethan theatre thrived
on the fluidity of space, the empty stage metamorphosing with a
few words from one location to another. But Noble used a theatrical version of the dissolve in film, the slow fading from one scene
to another, to great effect.

When, for instance, King Henry entered on to the set of the
tavern in Part 2 at the end of 2.4, the space both was and was not
still there; the King was obviously not in the tavern but the tavern
was an echo of so much for him: a version of the England that he
rules, a representation of the anxiety focused on his son that was
preventing him sleeping and a commentary on the political concerns with a philosophy of history in 3.1, all of which justified the
simultaneity of space. This particular transition made for great difficulty for King Henry: after the boisterous energy in the pursuit
of Pistol across the set almost any actor delivering a long, agonised
speech would have struggled to keep the audience's attention, and
even Julian Glover, who spoke the verse with intensity and clarity,
had to work hard. But such a moment combines a vivid theatrical
image with an actor triumphant at finding what Noble had
described as that 'right rate' and 'right phrasing' to 'penetrate our
dull ears'.

There were some moments that did not animate the language
in that way: the dirty politics of Gaultree Forest in Part 2 (4.1) was
neither clear nor interesting. I had reservations too about
moments where animation was taken in the wrong sense, particularly Michael Maloney's restless Prince Henry. Maloney needed to
have learned the lesson Kenneth Tynan once offered: 'Don't just
do something – stand there.' I exempt from this stricture
Woodington's Pistol, a glorious performance that explained
exactly why the title-page of the 1600 Quarto made sure it
announced that this was the play with 'swaggering Pistol' in it.

In the same interview, Noble offered this view of Shakespeare's
method:

[He] worked in a theatre and explored an aesthetic in which each play created its own imaginative world, its own cosmology, if you like, its own earth, heaven and hell. Which are different from play to play. And which indeed are sometimes different within the plays themselves. For example, you will go on a journey in a Shakespeare play and you may well *en route* visit paradise, briefly. You may well visit Dante's purgatory. The world changes in the course of the evening and has its own rules.[19]

The *Henry IV* plays are clearly a journey, a strange and disconcerting one in which the heavens and hells are not quite what one would expect. A cinematic dissolve took Henry IV's funeral procession movingly through a ghostly Gloucestershire full of beekeepers, underlining the countryside activities that throughout the Shallow scenes were offered as emblems of rural cycles that continue irrespective of the activities of kings, and that are more important than kings' temporary and temporal concerns.

The religious side of this cosmology was fixed from the beginning of Part 1 by the church candles flickering in pillars on either side of the stage, the cross into which the massive mobile panels of the back wall had been arranged and by the reliquary, shaped like a model of a Jerusalem church, suspended over the stage throughout the performance. But it is an ironic religion: Henry's reaction to realising that the Jerusalem he will die in is a room, not a city, was mocking laughter (Part 2, 4.3.364).

Noble realised, as too few directors ever do, that stages are vertical as well as horizontal spaces. The tavern scenes had upstage rooms with musicians or prostitutes and their clients, adding new perspectives to the scenes' rich blend of the medieval, Hogarth and Brecht. But a play's cosmology has to be vertical. Noble used ladders often in the production, as the way down to the cellars of the inn in the cold dawn as the carriers prepared to make their journey in Part 1 (2.1), on the battlefield of Shrewsbury where Prince Harry perched on one to mock Falstaff (4.2), and for the apple-picking in Shallow's orchard (Part 2, 3.2), suggesting the complexity of Noble's view of the two plays' cosmology, the different English places on this journey.

Noble was able to allow for the ambiguities of these places, the delights as well as the stupidities of Gloucestershire, the viciousness and sleaziness as well as the energies of Eastcheap, the shallowness as well as the honesty of rebellion. It was there in the

10. *Henry IV Part 2* 2.4, RSC, 1991: Doll Tearsheet (Joanne Pearce) and Falstaff (Robert Stephens)

knife Doll kept concealed in her hair, in Owen Teale's naive Hotspur, by turns charming and brutal, in David Bradley's Shallow, an old fool but also a man at peace with himself and his community. Philip Voss's two roles marked the change between the two parts, from a wickedly machiavellian Worcester to a Lord Chief Justice benignly tolerant of Falstaff, epitomised in his final generous handshake with him as Falstaff and his companions were forced from the stage at 5.4.94.

It was there above all in Robert Stephens' Falstaff, the most intelligent of Falstaffs, witty and charming of course but also fastidious rather than gross and gluttonous. But the intelligence and perceptiveness induced melancholy. Falstaff's clear thinking, in, for instance, the cold, hard logic of the catechism on honour, only confirmed his belief that the end will be melancholy. Pained by his isolation and accompanying self-awareness, his goodbye to Doll split the conventional word, 'farewell' (2.4.385), into 'fare well', stating both his concern for her future and his sharp awareness that they will not meet again.

This awareness of his isolation meant that the whole of Part 1 seemed to hinge on the search for an embrace, the gesture that his Hal found it so difficult to give him, even as he lay asleep at the end of the tavern scene (2.5), just as Prince Henry so desperately wanted the same embrace from *his* father but was in turn refused it when Blunt entered (3.2.161). Falstaff's childlessness was an acute pain, there in the hollow boast of 'if I had a thousand sons' in Part 2 (4.2.118). But it was registered most powerfully at the end of Part 1 in Falstaff's lamenting embrace of the dead Hotspur, the man whose true father, Northumberland, had left him to his fate but also the man he had just stabbed in the groin. Only at such a moment, in the recognition of his own grief, could this Falstaff be surprised. Certainly King Henry V's rejection came as no surprise at all; he had read the signs clearly enough even before Henry's 'I do; I will' in Part 1 (2.5.486). Confronting the crowned Henry V, he knew what the response would be; everything he had learned about people had taught him to expect it.

If this clear-sighted Falstaff induced our sympathy – as well as that of the Lord Chief Justice – the intelligence revealed a callousness as well. It was funny before the battle of Shrewsbury when Bardolph waved a tatty banner after the swirling multiplying banners had thrillingly filled the back of the stage. But during the battle Falstaff was surrounded by corpses and wounded men, a visual reminder of the truth of his discourse on honour and of the practice to which he had put his theory, leading his men 'where they are peppered' (5.3.36), while Bardolph looted the corpses. In Part 2 the conning of Mistress Quickly out of yet more money was heartless. The mustering of men in Gloucestershire was plain nasty. Wart was humiliated by the drill, and Feeble, for all his courageous statements, was reduced to tears. There was a sneering contempt for people in Falstaff here as well as a cunning streak, a contempt that only mellowed as the good humour and good will of Shallow's world began to affect him. Falstaff's intelligence was cruel as well as melancholic. In the sharp and disturbing oscillations of audience response, the ambiguities of Falstaff's earth, heaven and hell were perfectly registered.[20]

After my earlier strictures on the gloomy work of other lighting designers – whose names I have left as covered in obscurity as their work left the plays – I end with praise for Alan Burrett's subtle lighting for these productions. Adrian Noble suggested that his understanding of the broader canvas of England in Part 2 was intensified by Burrett's perceptive comment that he could light Part 1 with two follow-spots but would need three for Part 2. But then the productions were consistently perceptive, a triumphant moment in the RSC's history.

CHAPTER 5

1992: productions and spaces, large and small

Hamlet Q1 (Medieval Players); *Richard III* (RSC, The Other Place); *All's Well That Ends Well* (RSC, Swan Theatre); *Much Ado About Nothing* (Oxford Stage Company); *The Winter's Tale* (Theatre de Complicite); *The Winter's Tale, The Taming of the Shrew, As You Like It, The Merry Wives of Windsor, Antony and Cleopatra* (RSC, Royal Shakespeare Theatre); *Coriolanus* (Chichester Festival Theatre and the Renaissance Theatre Company); *A Midsummer Night's Dream* (Royal National Theatre)

There seems to be a peculiar difficulty at present in fitting Shakespeare productions to the available theatre-spaces. I have commented earlier about the problems of the Swan and the Royal Shakespeare Theatre but the productions for 1992 can aptly be considered to exemplify the larger issue. Though the aim is an appropriateness of scale, productions are often over- or under-sized for their stages. Some productions take on the scale assumed to be required by a particular space only to find that assumptions about that scale have carried with them constricting assumptions about the appropriate style. As directors confront the often bewildering variety of spaces in which Shakespeare plays are now performed, their sense of scale often seems to go seriously awry.

There are, along this particular faultline, two modes of production which ensure that the tectonic plates of production and theatre do not grind together or split apart: productions which manage the perfect and comfortable fit and productions which make the space appear exhilaratingly barely able to contain them, the strain at the seams being a controlled part of the effect. Directors and companies are still attempting to come to terms with Buzz Goodbody's revolution of the 1970s[1] with its discovery that *Hamlet* will fit and will benefit from being fitted into the small tin hut called The Other Place, but they also confront the changing organisation of theatre in Britain at the end of the century, allowing and encouraging touring companies to explore new possibilities of Shakespeare production. I have divided this chapter according to the size of the productions.

SMALL

Through much of 1992 and in almost every conceivable corner of the United Kingdom (from Skye to Guernsey), the Medieval Players, a small professional company, could be found performing *Hamlet* in its Q1, 'bad' Quarto incarnation. With only seven actors in the company, their resources were even more straitened than the 1603 Quarto requires but there was very little pruning. Assuming for their purposes that the text represents the play 'adapted to the practical exigencies of touring, tailored to the tastes of an audience unused to the plentiful theatrical fare that London enjoyed',[2] the company sought a style that connected performance with a medieval and Renaissance tradition of travelling troupes. Whatever the scholarly opinion of such an assumption about the text, their decision led them to a mode of staging 'with fewer props and costumes, and with a far more direct story-line'. The company used a simple booth and trestle stage familiar from countless European illustrations; I saw it appropriately set up in Old Court, Corpus Christi College, Cambridge, within sight of the memorial to Marlowe and Fletcher.

But the company also sought to defamiliarise the play for the audience so that they would 'rediscover *Hamlet* – both Shakespeare's and the story itself – by having it placed before you anew'. While some members of the audience could be seen frantically checking through New Penguin texts in the fading light, others more readily left the Q1 text to have its own values, values which the production excellently represented. At no point did the company evince the slightest apology for the oddities of language or action; the text, even when it was making less than sense, was spoken with a confident acceptance of its own logic, not as some shadow of a far greater other, Q2 or F. There was no difficulty in accepting Corambis, Q1's name for Polonius, and I became used to Rosincraft, Guilderstone and Leartes (pronounced trisyllabically). Ben Benison's direction ensured a merciless pace that reconnected the audience to the pleasures of narrative rather than the different virtues of introspection. Patrick Knox's Hamlet, the only actor not to be doubling or quintupling roles, became an actively melancholic man in a fast-moving world. If his black hose and white shirt summoned up comforting shades of nineteenth-century tradition, his performance suggested something alien and distanced. Both Hamlet and *Hamlet* were intentionally and intriguingly uninvolving.

On the bare platform, gesture became simple and powerful: Leartes embraced warmly by Hamlet as he left the court, providing a neat bridge to Claudius's turning to his 'princely Sonne'[3] (and Hamlet's flinching from his step-father's touch) and a yawning chasm to their duel at the play's end, or Ofelia (Susannah Rickards) not playing her lute in the mad scene (though the original direction requires her entrance 'playing on a Lute, and her haire downe singing', sig. G4b) but using it as a threatening weapon or to represent, most movingly, her dead father's head.

It was especially shocking here to see Ofelia become coarse and crude, as if the veneer of nobility had been stripped away to reveal a stereotyped East End barmaid beneath. Similarly, Roy Weskin's Ghost, walking on stilts with a billowing cloak, making him tower over the others on stage, screamed in pain both from the murder itself and from the 'flaming fire' in which he was now 'Confinde' (sig. C3b). Such effects underlined a readiness for emotion that burst through the speed and thrills of melodrama.

Other scenes were allowed an unexpected prominence: Fortinbras's first scene, at only six lines even shorter than in the Folio, was intensified in importance both by Hamlet's absence and by its pointed brevity. Even the exigencies of doubling seemed not to obstruct: Corambis was forced to die unseen (though not unheard) because the actor would need to appear in the middle of the scene as the Ghost after a quick but not impossible costume change. Played with such conviction and energy before an appreciative audience, the Medieval Players' *Hamlet* Q1 never pretended to be more than a small play for small spaces, fitting neatly on to the tiny platform of their stage. Such unpretentiousness of scale deserves approval.

The opposite to 'unpretentiousness' is 'pretentious-ness', a word which Irving Wardle places on his critic's blacklist, in his brilliant, sane account of the activity of a theatre critic.[4] It is not the term I would wish to apply to Sam Mendes's *Richard III*, premiered at The Other Place before its tour. It was a production with clear pretensions and ambitions outstandingly realised. Above all, it sought to make the play coherent, to find for it a structural shapeliness that the chronicle history often appears to be evading in performance. This may be a form of directorial imposition, though far less extreme than the historical analogy in Eyre's 1990 production at the Royal National Theatre, but the gains in defining the play's architecture were ample compensation.

In Act 5 this shaping involved a little rearrangement, intercutting segments of scenes (5.3 to 5.6), to produce a balance between the two opposing powers of Richard and Richmond. Richmond was a worthy opponent, rather than a shallow nice guy, and Mark Lewis Jones's calm delivery of the long final speech of the play released the tensions of the evening, establishing a new dramatic rhythm opposite to Richard's, a rest from the whole long history of civil strife. The audience has been waiting for the necessary male antagonist to Richard. In the juxtaposition of the two tent scenes and the circling of the ghosts, or the paralleling of the two speeches to the armies, Shakespeare was already aiming at an intercutting effect. Mendes's cinematic switching simply intensified the effect already there in embryo. The splicing of the two orations to the armies, counterpointed with Richmond and Richard side by side on stage, was thrilling theatre, with the drumbeats, strongly thematised earlier as the accompaniment of Margaret's curse, now reaching a tumultuous climax. This both achieved dramatic effect with simple means and underlined the play's rhythm, its natural architecture.

Mendes shares with great directors the ability to uncover a play's rhythm for an audience. Realising that the fulfilment of Margaret's prophetic curses defines the play's progress, he allowed Margaret to reappear hauntingly, often framed by a doorway in the set's upper level, repeating part of her earlier speech as each character in turn justified her prediction and invoked her name as they realised their place in this line of death. Her curses in 1.3 and 4.4 became two strongly ritualised moments, as she sprinkled a circle with chalk dust and then chalked her face. In Act 5 her presence was marked as a kind of ticking clock, tapping on a pole from her upper vantage point, brooding over the final stages of her oracular truth. This exceptional prominence for Margaret elicited a per-

11. *Richard III* 4.2, RSC, The Other Place, 1992: 'Why, Buckingham, I say I would be king': Richard III (Simon Russell Beale), Queen Anne (Annabelle Apsion) and Buckingham (Stephen Boxer)

formance from Cherry Morris worthy to set beside memories of Peggy Ashcroft in *The Wars of the Roses* in 1964, a mad woman, of course, but also a woman of true vision.

But then all the women in this production were good. Kate Duchêne's Elizabeth, in particular, made the audience understand that this is the greatest of all English plays of female grief, the one play to be set beside Euripides' *Trojan Women*. With her eyes red-rimmed and staring, her hair unkempt and more like Margaret's than before, her confrontation with Richard in 4.4 became a pivotal moment, no recapitulation of the wooing of Lady Anne. Richard's comment as he slumped in his chair, harshly triumphant, 'Relenting fool, and shallow, changing woman' (4.4.362), only showed how completely he had failed to understand what she meant. It was the first moment at which this Richard was found to be imperceptive, deceived by Elizabeth. But the maturity of playing in the scene emphasised the horror of

Richard's calm promise of 'Death, desolation, ruin, and decay' (340) if the marriage does not take place. Simon Russell Beale's delivery of the following lines, 'It cannot be avoided but by this; / It will not be avoided but by this' (341–2), was quietly apocalyptic and absolutely confident.

A small-scale RSC tour, even with a company twice the size of the Medieval Players, necessitated doubling. But the result could be architectural: Simon Dormandy's Ratcliff became a multitude of linked executioners, an eerie presence teetering on the edge of caricature Gestapo with his wire-rimmed spectacles and thin hands, but saved by the sheer viciousness of the action as he did no more than delicately close each victim's eyes to mark the moment of death. This simple effect was terrifyingly brutal. Indeed the production found throughout a remarkable mode of theatrical brutality. I have never seen anything as brutal and callous as Richard's statement to Catesby, 'Rumour it abroad / That Anne, my wife, is very grievous sick' (4.2.52–3), spoken so calmly over Anne seated next to him and his casual explanation, not in an aside but directly to her, as if to a child, 'I must be married to my brother's daughter, / Or else my kingdom stands on brittle glass' (62–3). Her exit, turning to him dignified but weeping, was greeted by the equally stony matter-of-fact rejection, 'Tear-falling pity dwells not in *this* eye' (67, Beale's emphasis). The proximity of the actors in The Other Place and the open glasnost politics in which he can announce to the victim herself her own imminent death belong to a terrifying normality and rationality of evil.

Simon Russell Beale's Richard veered alarmingly from style to style but always with tremendous control, a mature actor knowing how to manage his effects, from the comic opening in which off-stage dogs really did 'bark at me as I halt by them' (1.1.23) to the frightening pause after York has climbed on to his back until he forced a squeaking laugh in the face of the dreadful humiliation. If Touchstone found 'Your "if" is the only peacemaker' (*As You Like It*, 5.4.100), Richard demonstrated the opposite: Hastings' 'If they have done this deed, my noble lord' (3.4.73) induced in him a bellow of rage, '"If"?' (74). This was the rage of a man unable to be crossed or doubted, a man who has constructed his own world. But it could modulate quickly as Richard took one of the Bishop's strawberries and crushed it on his own shaven head as a wound to mock the Lord Mayor (3.5) or as Hastings' head, brought on stage wrapped up as a neat brown-paper parcel, was first cuddled by Richard and then transfixed with his stick.

From the sweet younger brother of 1.1, head clasped to Clarence's belly as Clarence kissed the top of his head, this Richard grew in confidence and mania, a man alone because he refused help. His coronation entry in 4.2 to the sound of crashing cymbals led to his stumbling and falling, his bad leg caught up in his kingly robes; the fall automatically made the others on stage (except the already enthroned and numbed Anne) move to help him – for who would not help a fallen cripple? – eliciting again that rage, 'Stand all apart' (4.2.1), and the request for help from the one man he would always turn to, 'Cousin of Buckingham'. In the United States people who are disabled or handicapped are termed 'differently abled', a term that I find unbearably patronising. Beale's Richard *was* differently abled, his intellect at odds with his body.

This was not a 'definitive' production (another word Wardle damns[5]) but it was an extraordinarily good one. It had the virtues of the RSC's traditions of work in small spaces, particularly at The Other Place: freshness, energy, clarity. Above all it used the potential of the space for simple and strong effects. Quickly unrolling a map across the stage floor at 4.4.363, for instance, left Richard and Richmond standing on the kingdom they were struggling for, an exemplary piece of Tim Hatley's design. As an image it was powerful but unfussy, a grand effect in a small theatre, an apt epitome of the production as a whole.

MEDIUM

Sir Peter Hall has set himself the task of making Shakespeare clear, the most challenging version of 'doing Shakespeare straight'. His recent style of Shakespeare production, well spoken and working hard to realise what he believes the text to be saying, is an ambition I would not quarrel with, in spite of his disappointing *Twelfth Night* in 1991. It is an ambition exactly suited to the potentials of the Swan Theatre, where Hall first directed in 1992 with a production of *All's Well That Ends Well*.

All's Well That Ends Well is a precisely social play, deeply concerned with rank and status. Gunter's set failed to create a social context for the action, but his costumes, from the first scene onwards, clearly defined social difference: Bertram's huge ruff and extravagant shoe roses; Helen's servant-like restraint, echoed later in the uniform of the Countess's steward in 1.3. Indeed, the movement of the play was precisely charted by Helen's costume changes, to the white aristocratic dress she wore to dance with the King, back to her Roussillon black modesty, the cloak and kit-bag of the pilgrim, and finally a version of a wedding-dress for the last scene.

Hall's commitment to clarity is far from being a commitment to neutrality. When Helen outlined to the King her contract of cure, offering a guarantee for her treatment, 'The great'st grace lending grace' (2.1.160ff.), her invocation of God was accompanied by heavenly music and she spoke with divine inspiration, as if her statement was spoken through her, intensified by the introduction, for the first time, of an echo to surround her small voice: 'What is infirm from your sound parts shall fly, / Health shall live free, and sickness freely die' (167–8). This was a beautiful recognition of the new diction of the speech, its elaborate image of the 'horses of the sun', its single, massive, complex sentence stretching over more than eight lines. The understanding of the text informed the production decision, showing the audience what it had found. The moment had been prepared for by Helen's claim to the Countess that her father's 'good receipt / Shall for my legacy be *sanctified*' (1.3.243, my emphasis) and by the remarkable little catechism of faith that followed that claim: 'Dost thou believe't?' 'Ay, madam, knowingly' (248–9), lines that, in their disruption of the rhythm of whole verse-lines, warned of their weighty significance.

Hall continually attended to such detail. Helen's interview with the Countess disturbed me: where, in Barbara Jefford's fierce confrontation with her in 1.3, was the warm approval of Helen's right to love Bertram that I have so often seen? But it is not there in the Countess's language; instead Helen's long speech of love (187–213), spoken so helplessly, kneeling in the corner of the stage, was answered only by 'Had you not lately an intent—speak truly— / To go to Paris?' (1.3.214–15). Jefford, magnificent throughout, left the audience in no doubt that this *grande dame* had the measure of her son from the start, with her heavy emphasis on his need for manners: 'succeed thy father / In manners as in shape' (1.1.58–9). Her sense of shame late in the play was entirely a product of that grand style; Bertram's behaviour had shamed his family, and the Countess, by Act 5, was left in tears, unable to control herself in public, humiliated by her son's actions.

Touchstone finds 'much virtue in "if"' (*As You Like It*, 5.4.100–1). Hall's *All's Well* found much virtue in 'et cetera', as Helen spoke to Bertram in the final scene:

> And, look you, here's your letter. This it says:
> 'When from my finger you can get this ring,
> And are by me with child,' et cetera. This is done.
>
> (5.3.313–15)

Helen's refusal to read the rest of that dreadful letter, tearing it in pieces before she announced 'This is done' marked the possibility of change, the possibility of forgiveness. Paul Taylor, writing in the *Independent*, saw the tearing as 'a wonderfully double-edged gesture. On the one hand, it seems to be saying that all this can now be put behind them; but the thickened intensity of the action suggests that damage has been done that cannot be so easily forgotten and forgiven.' That full awareness that the past cannot be dismissed by saying 'This is done' was followed through into the tentative, nervous grouping of the Countess, Helen and Bertram that formed on the side of the stage, with Bertram still unable to look at Helen, as centrestage, to warm audience laughter, the King began the play's action replay, announcing to Diana, 'Choose thou thy husband' (5.3.329).

But the production's running sore was Anthony O'Donnell's brilliantly foul Lavatch, the clown as Mr Punch, with shaven head, sunken eyes and facial sores that anticipated the ones that may lie under Bertram's patch (4.5.93–7). The phallus he carried was an offensive weapon, the fool's bauble drained of all humour and now a threat of violence, not of comedy. It was difficult to see why the Countess kept on such a vicious, angry figure, a representation of everything that seethed under the play. Demonic, deeply troubling, this Lavatch was untameable, menacingly non-human.

As such, Lavatch counterpointed the sheer humanity of Michael Siberry's Paroles. Paroles' extravagance, from his first entry with piles of luggage including a case of hat-feathers, was only a cover. This Paroles was consistently more intelligent and wittier than any other I have seen. His intelligence led him to adopt a role as a means of surviving. His humiliation at the hands of the others in 4.3, his genuine fear of torture and death, was, as a result, more painful and extreme. It was his pain, even more than Helen's, that made the production veer from comedy to tragedy and made us shift uncomfortably in our seats. At the end of his ordeal, his speech of resilience, 'Simply the thing I am / Shall make me live' (4.3.335–6), was spoken from anger as much as hurt. His desperate pleas to Lafeu and his humiliating public appearance at court in the last scene showed a man trying to salvage dignity in the full consciousness of what he has lost.

If Paroles' plight was unequivocal, around Helen's there hovered a shade of something very disturbing indeed, the sense that Bertram, though snobbish, arrogant and foolish, does not deserve what happens to him. As the dance of the suitors was whittled down to a *pas de deux* and Bertram realised with mounting horror what was about to happen, the audience could share that horror with some sympathy. Sophie Thompson's Helen induced fear in Toby Stephens' Bertram here just as surely as her divine power had induced fear in Richard Johnson's King. But in addition the actress's physical appearance transformed the play. When Bertram's nemesis is played by someone like Harriet Walter (as in Trevor Nunn's famous production for the RSC in 1981), the audience cannot begin to understand why he should reject someone so intelligent and attractive. But Sophie Thompson's weeping Helen was a figure one could well appreciate Bertram trying to avoid. The play rebalanced itself, not in Bertram's favour but with understanding of his position.

Humane and tentative, vulnerable and hurt, the characters of Hall's *All's Well* stumbled towards the end, with only Diana exuding the confidence of innocence triumphant and inviolate. Hall's method paid rich dividends, demonstrating as clearly as possible its comprehension of the complexities of this nervy play, unlike Kyle's 1989 production.

In Wardle's glossary of damnable terms figures the word 'eclectic': 'a word suggesting that the artist has not found his own voice, and is parroting other voices which the reviewer finds himself unable to specify'.[6] Alexandru Darie, director of *A Midsummer Night's Dream* for the Comedy Theatre of Bucharest, seen in London in 1991, directed the Oxford Stage Company's touring production of *Much Ado About Nothing.* Darie's eclecticism was of a different type, a bewildering bricolage of materials; as Paul Taylor commented, in the *Independent*, of this 'ethnic and cultural hodge-podge', 'if, to the strains of a sitar, an eskimo had suddenly wandered on shaking a shillelagh, it would not have seemed unduly eccentric'. A wedding ritual from Transylvania was juxtaposed with an opening Yoruba chant from West Africa; this is eclecticism with a vengeance, supposedly justified by the director's perception of *Much Ado* as a play peopled 'with characters from a variety of civilisations' (programme-note).

The production opened with a card-game between Don John and a character dubbed 'Angel', who then played out their rivalry across the play's action, and with an extravagantly stylised[7] representation of war. The war between Don John and Don Pedro is disposed of at the opening of Shakespeare's text with almost perfunctory abruptness. Darie not only built it up into a full-scale battle on stage but altered the ending to turn the whole action of the play into a period of brief truce: the messenger's speech at the very end, 'My lord, your brother John is ta'en in flight, / And brought with armèd men back to Messina' (5.4.124–5) had been rewritten to say 'My lord, your brother John is *turned* in flight, / And *comes* with armèd men back to Messina', threatening a renewal of the war that had ended as the play began and providing a new gloom to hover conveniently over the end. The director may have wanted to 'evoke an unstable world precariously caught between two wars where the time for happiness is brief but lived to the full' (programme-note) but the play does not. The ending of *Much Ado About Nothing* is quite difficult enough without such assistance. Darie's revision made the action into a trivial interlude in the serious (male) business of war where, one might argue, the play is a serious outcome of the trivial business of war. After the refreshing excitements of his *A Midsummer Night's Dream*, this was a dull rag-bag of expectations unfulfilled.[8]

'Eclecticism' need not be a pejorative term. Theatre de Complicite is a collective company whose members are able to make their different backgrounds converge on a style of physical theatre that is distinctly alien to the English tradition. Many of the company were trained at the Jacques Lecoq school in Paris and the company's early work was devised rather than text-based. *The Winter's Tale* was their first attempt at Shakespeare. The resultant production, by Annabel Arden with Annie Castledine, had some misses, notably that perennial problem of representing rural festival in the sheep-shearing, but many more startling hits. The cumulative effect was exhilarating in its rapidly switching moods. It was a production in which anything was possible to match a play perceived as narrating the joys of possibility.

This *Winter's Tale* found the ending joyous, though not unequivocally so, for the pain so sharply created in the first half was deliberately recalled in a series of gestures (a handshaking ritual with Camillo, Leontes' stroking Hermione's belly) and in the reversal of Paulina's *pietà* cradling of Leontes in 3.2 into his cradling her, fixing her marriage to Camillo with tender love and concern. But the achievement of joy out of the pain of memory still allowed the production to end with a running, swirling parade of the characters round the stage and up a ladder to the sounds of the polonaise from Tchaikovsky's *Eugene Onegin* overlaid with the noise of crackling flames.

Again and again the cast took the full measure of the play's rhetorical moments: Simon McBurney's Leontes was almost hysterical at the statue's movement, twitching back, then moving tentatively towards her, hardly daring to touch before releasing the pent-up tension with a full-throated cry of 'O, she's warm!' (5.3.109), as magnificent as the descriptions of Macready at such a moment.[9] Such grandeur, achieved with simple means but a full acceptance of the actor's physical and vocal power, contrasted with the opening sequences. McBurney's Leontes was more neurotic and funnier than usual. In his dialogue with Camillo (1.2.212ff.), Camillo became a comic stooge, not following the argument, as Leontes made the images graphic and so made them comically exaggerated: 'slippery' (275), 'hobby-horse' (278), even 'inside lip' (288) were held up for Camillo's – and the audience's – regard but by being acted they became parodied. The jealousy was allowed a full quota of overtones of the comedy of cuckoldry. If this suggests Leontes as a comic figure, yet, in a single line, 'Why then the world and all that's in't is nothing' (295), the tone could become a tragically perverse vision.

The risk, treating Leontes as a trivially comic butt, was also offset by a violence predicated on his power as King, a power suggested in the robes of Polixenes and Leontes, strange coats made by stitching together half-a-dozen jackets so that the monarchs seemed to be trailing their subjects behind them. In 2.3, pouring

sweat in a T-shirt and track-suit bottoms and dousing himself liber-
ally with bottled water, Leontes attacked his lords with hideous
ferocity, clawing and scratching at them, close to gouging out their
eyes or chopping off an ear, in his rage. Antigonus, made to 'Swear
by this sword' (2.3.168), was forced to hold the blade and, the oath
made, Leontes deliberately drew the sword through Antigonus'
hands, cutting his palms. But all the time the violence could be
offset by comedy, a camp gesture for 'I am a feather for each wind
that blows' (154) or the successive shouts of 'bastard' (140, 155,
161) turned into 'brat' (163) with a pause after the initial 'b' to
tease us with 'bastard' again before coyly retreating from the word
into the tamer form. Brilliant and unnerving, McBurney's performance was impossible for the audience comfortably to pigeon-
hole. Unquestionably a tyrant, this Leontes could be turned by the
deaths of son and queen into a twitching heap with staring eyes,
demanding Paulina's tenderness as well as her ferocity, exiting to
great shouts of 'sorrows' (3.2.242), the word taken up and shouted
by the rest of the cast.

Unashamedly theatrical in its resources and achievements,
McBurney's Leontes was supported by the simpler dignity of
Gabrielle Reidy's Hermione, exhausted and barely post-natal in
the trial scene, wearing a shabby army greatcoat but with the
strength of voice to encompass the huge periods of her speeches.
He also established a remarkable relationship with Kathryn
Hunter's Paulina. Hunter, surely the first person ever to play
Mamillius, Paulina, Time and the Old Shepherd in the same production, displayed extraordinary virtuosity, allowing the roles to
move between the pain of the innocent child, the love of the
woman and the comedy of the old man, each with its own value,
none simply grist to her own brilliance.

Hunter's sudden entry as Old Shepherd, after the appearance
of a huge, vampiric bear from under the floorcloth, switched tones
with all the theatricality the moment needs, to the accompaniment
of the rest of the cast baa-ing away as lost sheep, pursued by a
human sheepdog. This prepared the way for Marcello Magni's
Autolycus, an Italian clown who elaborated his lines in Italian or
English (the two indistinguishable in his accent), so that 'three-
pile' (4.3.14) became 'an Armani suit'. Picking lecherously on
women in the audience, Magni tapped into a full tradition of *com-
media* styles, playing out the timeless *lazzi* of trickery.

The transition from 4.4 to 5.1, from Bohemia back to Sicilia, was accomplished by a remarkable procession, creating the journey by the cast's parade around the stage as they slowly transformed their costumes from one world's to the other's and took again the characters they had abandoned in the play's earlier shift of time and space, revealing Leontes crawling on his knees as if he really had spent the intervening years doing nothing else (and hence recalling Paulina on 'A thousand knees' at 3.2.209). Its move from pleasant comedy to myth provided the firm foundations for the richness of the production's ending.

LARGE

Complicite's *Winter's Tale* may have had rough edges but its virtuosity and passion spoke of a dangerous play. Such a production belongs in medium-sized theatres. Its ambitions would never have survived the unyielding scrutiny to which a large house, like the Royal Shakespeare Theatre (where all five of my 'large' productions were seen), subjects all work. It would simply be unfair of me to allow Annabel Arden's *Winter's Tale* to be compared and contrasted too directly with Adrian Noble's production for the RSC, a production designed to respond to that scrutiny.

Noble's *Winter's Tale*, a production much praised by many critics, left me unmoved (which might be thought allowable) and unconcerned (which is not). The production's unquestioned triumph was the sheep-shearing where Noble created an exuberance that was unforced. It was partly the setting, partly the energy Richard McCabe's Autolycus imparted to every scene he was in. I could almost forgive him the fact that he is tone-deaf, though an Autolycus who cannot sing a single note does seem slightly odd casting. He was always in inventive control whether gulling Graham Turner's Young Shepherd of item after item (including his watch, a condom and his bicycle) in 4.3 or in his realisation that the change of clothes with Florizel (4.4.635–48) meant that he would lose every penny he had stolen at the sheep-shearing (neatly offsetting the harsh efficiency with which he went through purse after purse at 4.4.611, never letting the audience simply be amused at his theft). Only Autolycus's reformation at the end of 5.2 – stealing the Young Shepherd's watch again, and then, overcome with remorse, dropping it back into the Young Shepherd's carrier-bag – was incredible. A lecherous, down-at-heel spiv in a loud suit, arriving on stage from the flies lowered on an enormous clutch of green balloons, 'out of service' (4.3.14) because, as the headline of the copy of *The Bohemian Gazette* that he held up made clear, 'Servant Guilty', he had been caught with his hand in the princely till, McCabe milked his performance for all it was worth like any music-hall comic, a Bohemian Max Miller.

But the success of Bohemia was due as much to its familiarity. There was in this very English, Edwardian village fete something comfortably and nostalgically recognisable, a myth of England past, jellies and trifles, small boys in short-trousered suits and the town band, far more successful than Complicite's Mediterranean ethnicity. Noble suggested resonances of Stanley Spencer's Cookham paintings. Like them, the production portrayed a world that is familiar and yet completely fictional. The villagers belonged in this uncomplicated world, a golden age of a recent past, stripped of the real rigours and poverty of a village community, an idyll of paradisal innocence. I could almost forgive the cheap gag for the dance of satyrs (4.4.340), performed by men each holding two red balloons as testicles of various sizes and an erect mop.

The problems were not in Bohemia but acute in Sicilia. Here Noble allowed himself one piece of excess in a hugely extravagant storm to accompany Apollo's anger (3.2.145), thunder and high winds flattening the courtiers, umbrellas skidding across the stage, leaving the language lost in the theatrical tempest. Otherwise, Noble created a clear space for actors to work in, marked only by Anthony Ward's large gauze box. The box functioned, if I read it aright, as a representation of another world, a different perception co-existing with the rest of the stage and always offering to burst on to it. Sometimes the box's world seemed conjured into exis-tence, as when Mamillius's shaking of a snow-storm toy brought the rest of the court, frozen in tableau in the box, into play at the start, or his whispering of the sad tale of sprites and goblins made Leontes suddenly appear in an echoing world within the box, a greater terror than his son's attempts to 'fright' Hermione. In the statue scene the mass of the court was crammed into the box facing downstage, gazing at the single figure outside it, Hermione, iso-lated at the front of the stage, until they tumbled out towards her. The cast and the audience, divided physically by the enigma of her silent presence (so powerful when she is placed with her back to the audience), were unified by their gaze at her, and then unified by her reanimation, for both groups needed the miracle of her return.

Noble has always sought to tie a play together through a visual language. Here it was balloons. They functioned in three ways: marking the green world of Autolycus (ambiguously balloon or tree), divine intervention (Time) and parties. Mamillius's birthday party opened the play, its balloons echoed by those brought on for Mamillius's sister's party, the sheep-shearing over which Perdita presides. Rain, the dominant weather of Sicilia, reappeared at the end of the sheep-shearing, prompting the clearing of the trestles and beginning the play's journey back to Sicilia.

But, balloons and box apart, Noble's Sicilia was a place for actors. Leontes' language, clotted and incomprehensible, reveals only the density of his imaginings. Noble trimmed the role of some of its difficulty, cutting the 'Affection' passage (1.2.140–8), for instance, to barely two lines. But trimming the text of the first scenes is a mistake if it tries to make things clearer. Even with this directorial help, John Nettles, back with the RSC after a long break, showed his lack of technique for such a task. From the first guttural sounds of 'Too hot, too hot', he tried every trick but they stayed as tricks, his voice strangely dissociated from his body, the lines chopped meaninglessly into fragments (an old RSC device to suggest emotional extremes). Try as Nettles might, Leontes steadfastly refused to appear on stage, especially after McBurney's performance.

And if Leontes is not there the drive and dynamic of the first half of the play goes for nothing. Samantha Bond's calm, warm, loving dignity as Hermione was unavailing. As she tried to patch this terribly public matrimonial squabble, going close to him even in the trial scene, trying to calm him and silence him, her hand over his mouth, she seemed more than usually isolated because the two actors seemed unable to connect their performances.

The danger of Complicite's production was missing and the play became merely a pleasing but undisturbing story. One moment of directorial invention demonstrated Noble's difficulties: the appearance of Hermione's ghost to preserve her daughter, encouraging the bear to miss out on its hors-d'oeuvre and go straight to the main course. Bringing on a ghostly Hermione, floating inside the box, to protect Perdita, who at her mother's appearance cries for the first time, only muddles things – it made me mutter pedantically that if Shakespeare had intended Hermione's ghost to appear he would have written the scene that way.

I had always thought that *The Taming of the Shrew* was a play about gender-conflict. Bill Alexander's production nearly convinced me that the play is instead about class and that male subjugation of women is only an example of masters' oppression of servants. The play's punning on 'gentlewoman', Kate as aristocrat and Kate as gentled by her treatment, tied the two firmly together. Anton Lesser's Petruccio found delight in calling Amanda Harris's Kate, after the sun/moon scene, 'my wife, this gentlewoman' (4.6.63), splitting the socially accurate last word into two, now true through her transformation, 'gentle woman'.

Alexander's extensive rewriting of the Induction was not only about updating to the 1990s, turning all the characters into young aristocrats; it was also an attempt to see the frame as an exercise in class mockery. As 'Lady Sarah Ormsby' warned 'Lord Simon Llewellyn' (alias a Huntsman and the Lord) at the sight of Sly, 'Leave him alone, Simon. Don't touch him. He's disgusting; probably working-class', her contempt seemed to drive the play forward. But for 'Simon', in addition, 'The drunk needs teaching a lesson, so we'll mess around with his mind for a bit.' Language like this is not exactly Shakespeare and it is a little disingenuous to call it 'adapted from the 1594 Quarto text' as Alexander's programme-note suggested. But at least it made explicit what the production had in mind. Anything designed to humiliate Sly of course fails. Maxwell Hutcheon's Sly was too kindly, too little affected by the class-assumptions of the young Sloaneys, too normal compared with the neurotic anger and power-games of the Lord, a man brutally coercing his brother (not his page in this production) to play Sly's Lady. As Sly intervened to try to break up the fight in 5.1 with a broken bottle[10] or as he offered the starving Katherine food, Sly reacted with a natural goodwill that was alien to the noble world of his hosts.

The players at Llewellyn's house, servants of their aristocratic patrons, were as humiliated as, say, Grumio in the play. But revenge is sweet: the actors cast the aristos as extra servants at Petruccio's house, giving the troupe the pretext to embarrass their masters, as their reluctant amateur actors were left helpless when Grumio walked off stage and joined the audience with 'Tell thou

12. *The Taming of the Shrew* 5.1, RSC, 1992: 'It's alright; it's only a play': Sly
(Maxwell Hutcheon), clutching a broken bottle, is reassured by
Petruccio (Anton Lesser)

the tale' (4.1.64). The interval placed midway through a scene,
before Petruccio's 'Thus have I politicly begun my reign'
(4.1.174), underlined the point, closing the first half on the
humiliation of the unwilling extras ordered around by Petruccio
with the same arrogance that the Lord had exercised in his vicious
mind-game with Sly.

Such Pirandellian devices were balanced within the play by
Petruccio's fury with Grumio and by Richard McCabe's excellent
Tranio, the servant humiliating his master as he sustained the disguise far longer than Lucentio wished. The play cohered but at the
expense of dramatic energy: humiliating the onstage audience
stopped the forward movement of the play in its tracks. An
amateur stumbling over his or her script may be an object of
ridicule but it here suspended the action while the awkwardness
was played out.

By the final scenes of the play, inner and outer mixed. Kate and
Petruccio's rapt and prolonged kiss at 5.1.139 caused not only a
change in lighting but an outbreak of kissing among the onstage
audience, with Sly shyly taking his 'lady's' hand. Kate's pleasure at

the lesson she has learned from Petruccio, the sheer delight in game-playing, was also now shared by the Sloane playing the Widow in 5.2 who could confidently discard her script and improvise. The disaster of Bianca's marriage to Lucentio, with Bianca now making eyes at Tranio, and Lucentio embittered in melancholic gloom on the side of the stage, was mirrored by the Lord's being rejected by his girlfriend as they finally left the stage. The solution of *The Shrew* became a rather visible lesson for the young aristocrats who had watched it. Game, its pleasures and perils, now ruled the stage.

Though the frame's presence finally paid off, it had been an intrusive presence, the seven actors immured upstage being a distraction as they wandered around to refill their glasses at suitable gaps in the action. The size of the Royal Shakespeare Theatre stage allowed for a double stage: a full-scale grand drawing-room for the onstage watchers as well as a substantial space downstage of them for the acting troupe to play out *Shrew* to them (or rather to the theatre audience with their backs to the group that had ostensibly commanded and paid for their performance). The play became a pedagogic device, changing the onstage audience. Substantial in its exploration of this change, Alexander's *The Taming of the Shrew* clearly placed a high value on the worth of theatre as mirroring experience, a confrontation between play and onstage audience intended, I presume, to suggest the effect of the play on its paying public. Alexander took the Induction seriously as a response to the inner play, for all the excesses of the rewriting.

I suggested before that this Katherine had learned from Petruccio the pleasures of game-playing but she had also come to appreciate that agreeing with someone was not always submissive. Her apology for her 'mistaking eyes' (4.6.46) became an apology to Petruccio rather than to Vincentio; in this new world in which compliance seemed a positive possibility rather than another humiliation, 'everything' she now looked on 'seemeth green', fresh and new. Her 'mad mistaking' had been an error of perception, an assumption that everyone had only her worst interests at heart. Amanda Harris had clearly been to the same school as Lewis Carroll's Mock Turtle where she too had learned Uglification and Derision. The jutting jaw and dishevelled hair, the screwed-up eyes and furrowed brow softened by the end of the play as the rage went. But it took courage for an actress to spend so long distorting her features into such twisted shapes, while she derided the sweet prettiness of Rebecca Saire's Bianca. Characteristically, this Bianca was perfectly content – indeed positively keen – to hear Gremio's recital of his wealth and Tranio's capping of it (3.1). Kate, I assume, would find money only another aspect of her subjugation.

By contrast with the endless pacing of Harris's Kate, Lesser's Petruccio exuded calm confidence, seated while she flailed around him in 2.1 before using his chair like a lion-tamer dealing with a large and recalcitrant cat. His witty assumption of her agreement to the marriage (2.1.298ff.) reduced her to foot-stamping fury, shocked and speechless as he circumscribed the space in which she could express her will. At the same time this Kate clearly fancied Petruccio from the first time she clapped eyes on him and her tears before the wedding were as much at the thought of not getting him as at the public humiliation she was undergoing.

Alexander's *The Taming of the Shrew* denied our assumption that this is nothing more than the Katherine–Petruccio play, finding a new balance in the text's materials. If it tried at times too hard to produce a theatrical solution, its occasional lurching rhythms served to underline the play's difficult architecture.

David Thacker's productions of *As You Like It* and *The Merry Wives of Windsor* had not the slightest interest in anything so revisionary. After his fine productions of *Pericles* and *The Two Gentlemen of Verona*, I was expecting much and was disappointed. *As You Like It* had none of the freshness of Cheek by Jowl's and was even duller than John Caird's 1989 RSC production. As Robert Smallwood commented,

this production was well intentioned and well spoken, careful, earnest, and very lavishly packaged in terms of scenic and musical accompaniment ... audiences often seemed to be enjoying it hugely, so that one felt mean-spirited for finding it essentially empty. It thus provides a very pertinent example, worth contemplating, of a certain kind of skilful, highly professional Shakespeare production, satisfying audiences' expectations of a big 'show,' full of sound and fury, signifying ... not a great deal.[11]

I found myself sharing with Anthony O'Donnell's fine Touchstone – a man memorably described by Michael Billington in the *Guardian* as 'a stubby little Napoleon endlessly confined to St Helena' – the sense that life in this Arden was 'tedious' (3.2.18). There was a dull inevitability in Arden, in the way that sooner or later someone, Touchstone pushed by William in 5.1 as it happens, had to fall into the onstage pond – for there is no point having a pond on stage, it seems, unless someone falls in it.

After the intelligent investigation of gender by Adrian Lester in Cheek by Jowl's production, Samantha Bond's Rosalind belonged to the tradition aptly defined by Lindsay Duguid: '[She] is wholesome and pert with her slightly husky actress's voice and her gamine gestures (legs apart, arms akimbo, hands in pockets, and so on). The English actress playing Rosalind is a gender all her own' (*TLS*, 8 May 1992). If this was Rosalind in a limbo of gender, it was also Rosalind without sexuality. For in a play so full of sexual desire the production saw only clichéd romance, epitomised by the long hard look between Celia and Oliver at the end of 4.3 or their rapt attention to each other in 5.4.

As You Like It had some redeeming features; *The Merry Wives of Windsor* had none. The play, so often a glittering success for the RSC, became an inglorious catastrophe, devoid of charm or interest. No one had the courage to suggest that the play's prose is a comic achievement. The only line that raised a laugh was, with dreadful predictability, Doctor Caius's 'If there be one or two, I shall make-a the turd' (3.3.225). Even the comic business was tired. Anton Lesser's Ford, bowler-hatted and brief-cased like a suburban commuter in Elizabethan dress, suffered the required paroxysms of agony but was also reduced to gnawing his handkerchief, punching holes in the furniture, stepping in bowls of dirty water, pulling his hat so far down over his eyes that he bumped into a bench, and tearing off his false moustache with a delayed yelp of pain. That he was made to do the last twice was only too indicative of the poverty of comic invention; as Paul Taylor commented, 'To see that gag once might have been considered nostalgic, to see it twice . . .' (his ellipsis).

Such productions would look bad in any theatre and at their very worst on the pitiless main stage at Stratford. John Caird's *Antony and Cleopatra*, whatever its other limitations, at least exuded confidence about the scale of play and stage, the necessity to represent the large scale grandly. If the opening and closing images of Antony and Cleopatra standing side by side at the back of the stage contemplating the Nile smacked of a strenuously romantic cliché, at least it made abundantly clear the full-blown emotion the play was seen as embodying.

This unequivocal view of the lovers was supported by firm

cutting. It is one thing to cut the Parthian scene (3.1) in favour of a more single-minded concentration on the central action (for all that it shrinks the play's geography), but cutting Seleucus's and Cleopatra's games over her wealth in 5.2 disambiguates the movement of the scene, making it too easy for Cleopatra to achieve a formal tragic emotion for her death. Clare Higgins did not seem to need help but such simplification was strongly characteristic of the production style.

Caird made much of the Soothsayer (Jasper Britton). Determined to find a determinism in the play, he built up his appearance in 1.2 into a strange black-clothed figure daubed with white dust whose telling of Iras's and Charmian's fortunes involved sending them off into a genuine trance. In 2.3 his make-up now included eyes painted on to the palms of his hands. Octavius's description of Antony and Cleopatra and their children in the market-place (3.6.1–19) was played out on stage as the last action before the interval: as the family group processed downstage and exited, the Soothsayer was revealed behind them. He was to be found on stage again watching Enobarbus's death in 4.10. Antony's invective at 4.13.30, 'Ah, thou spell!' was taken literally: Cleopatra appeared as a vision dressed as Isis brought on by the Soothsayer and protected from Antony's fury by his eye-hands. That he should appear yet again as the Clown in 5.2 was inevitable, carrying the basket that, then enigmatically, he had balanced on his head on his exit in 1.2,[12] but the choice of such patterning also neatly excised the scene's comedy in favour of an eerie supernaturalism, with his forcing Cleopatra to look into the basket and, without harm to himself, holding up one of the asps.

There was, throughout the last scenes, a sense of cavernous desolation in the monument. When Octavius's troops abseiled in like a Roman SAS brigade, they left Charmian and Iras huddled scared in the corner and Cleopatra, now in a black wig rather than her earlier red one, also curled up on the ground. Mournful despair, intensified by the frequent recurrence of the music that defined Hercules' leaving Antony in 4.3, was unremittingly accomplished, typified by the queen's shuddering wails through her realisation that 'there is nothing left remarkable / Beneath the visiting moon' (4.16.69–70).

Such emotional monochrome did not do justice to Clare Higgins's earlier achievements, moody anger giving way so quickly to laughter that it almost justified Paul Jesson's Enobarbus in his description of her 'infinite variety'. Cleopatra's skills as performer became also the pleasures of play-acting so that the bored waiting of 1.5 found Cleopatra dressed as Isis with flail and sceptre, anticipating the performance in 3.6. Tossing the Roman messenger's papers in the air in 1.1 or throwing Antony to the ground and kicking him hard in the ribs as 'the greatest liar' (1.3.38) typified her restless activity. It also produced brilliant playing of the two-part scene with her own messenger (2.5 and 3.3), aided by Alan Cox as the terrified servant, desperately trying to work out what could possibly placate this unpredictable tormentor and unerringly putting his foot in it with his eagerness to report 'I do think she's thirty' (3.3.28).

Higgins was helped by an alteration during the production's run. Early on, the change of wigs from red to black was, sensibly, abandoned. Thereafter Cleopatra wore the same wig throughout but, tellingly and powerfully, stripped it away in the final moments, showing it to be a wig, revealing the theatricality of the hair-piece as Cleopatra's rather than the production's, and, as it deconstructed the theatrical effect, replacing it with a new theatricality in the revelation of the 'genuine', unornamented Cleopatra underneath.

Returning to the role which he had played at Stratford in 1972 (opposite Janet Suzman), Richard Johnson as Antony was quite simply too old and wearied – or so his performance seemed at first. While a production might reasonably have wanted to explore an age-gap between the lovers, it cannot dispense with a sexual charisma around Antony. If Antony is not attractive, even in an elderly, grizzled way, the play's argument will be unbalanced and Johnson could do nothing to project a reason for Cleopatra's fascination with him to match his justifiable obsession with her. When Antony's callous laughter at announcing Fulvia's death (1.3.59) was met by this Cleopatra's serious and anxious comparison with her own future ('Now I see, I see, / In Fulvia's death how mine received shall be', 1.3.64–5), Johnson was left throwing his hands up in the air in mock-desperation at the difficulty of dealing with women, failing to take on the powerful question Higgins had thrown him. But, returning to see the production some months later, I found Antony's weary echo of an earlier heroic self much more fully achieved. If the performance still did not match his

Cleopatra's, it argued quite movingly for the tired elderly man's yearning to be again what he had once been and was all too painfully aware of no longer being.

What Johnson may have lacked in grandeur Sue Blane's set amply provided, its four pairs of massive shutters like sections of walls and monuments, rough stone on audience left, rendered brick on its right, drawn back for the Egyptian scenes and closing in for the Roman scenes to push their action right downstage. Simple and small-scale devices spoke as eloquently as the grand tableaux: Lepidus and Octavius conversing in 1.4 at a table designed for three triumvirs but with one seat conspicuously empty; Antony's courteous concern for Lepidus at 2.2.175–7 while Octavius pointedly ignores the old man; Antony, wishing Octavia (Phyllida Hancock) goodnight (2.3.7) by trying to kiss her lips as she formally turned her cheek to him, though she left the stage laughing easily with her brother; Thidias's whipped back being anointed while Octavius read Antony's letter in 4.1; Octavius quietly directing his explanation of the war (5.1.73–7) confidentially to Decretas, needing to explain himself to Antony's man. But the production could also rise to the play's heights; with drummers on the two corners of the forestage for Ilona Sekacz's thunderous battle music, it looked and sounded properly operatic.

If 'operatic' is a term I have occasionally used to mark a visual over-elaboration in a production, it is a term unquestionably necessary for a production of *Antony and Cleopatra* on the main-house stage, even though the RSC had found quite a different chamber-play in Adrian Noble's version in 1982 in The Other Place. The play's demands change with its performing space: Peter Brook's production on the main stage in 1977 had been deliberately cramped in its reluctance to explore the scale of its playing area, crying out for a smaller theatre than the one to which it was committed.

Caird's direct style was also reflected in the willingness to have characters unequivocally address speeches to the audience. Philo, at the very start of the play, had no Demetrius to speak to and instead offered his angry comments straight to us, describing something discrepant from the image of the lovers we could see; it was for the audience to 'Look where they come' (1.1.10) as they entered hopping ('forty paces through the public street' (2.2.236) perhaps). Octavius spoke to the audience of the tableau of Antony and Cleopatra in the market-place, his language again to be judged by our sight of what he described. The play's argument was presented and imaged, its gaps and discrepancies left for the audience to mark. The production unquestionably had the measure of the play.

XXXL

If Caird's *Antony and Cleopatra* was 'large', then the T-shirt size 'XXXL' is the only possible label for something of the scale of Tim Supple's production of *Coriolanus* at the Chichester Festival Theatre, a co-production with the Renaissance Theatre Company. This, the third major *Coriolanus* within three years, was without any doubt the biggest; indeed it had the largest cast I have ever seen in any professional Shakespeare production. Given permission by Equity to recruit local amateur actors, something he had previously done for *Oh, What A Lovely War!* at the Haymarket in Leicester, Supple marshalled a crowd of over fifty on to the vast expanses of the Chichester stage.

For the first time in my experience the crowd looked like a crowd, not the little huddle of most productions nor the sheepish group of members of the audience in Hall's 1984 *Coriolanus* at the National Theatre. Superbly drilled, this embodiment of the Roman and Volscian people was not strongly individualised, without the detail of Granville-Barker's crowd of over 300 in *Julius Caesar* in 1911 ('"X 186 groans heavily and moves up stage, where he joins a doleful group consisting of Ys 48–54 and Zs 201–10", or something of that sort'[13]). Men, women and children moved quickly and comfortably across the stage or scrambled on to the set's upper levels, filling the spaces or clearing them to leave, for example, a large area for Menenius (Richard Briers) to exert his aristocratic control in the fable of the belly in 1.1, or hurtling off the stage completely into the area on the edge of the stalls at the first appearance of Coriolanus (Kenneth Branagh). Anonymous and amorphous they may have been, but the crowd was unremittingly human, a mass of humanity that could be despised by Coriolanus but called forth our humanity in sympathy. There was an exciting tension between the sense of the operatic chorus under directorial control and the realism of these people, their lack of professional skills producing an unactorish normality on stage; as soldiers, the men looked like a conscript army, tall and short, overweight and thin, but their sheer weight of numbers had its own exhilaration. Defending Coriolanus from the onslaught of the people in 3.1, the patricians became a tiny group, surrounded and hopelessly outnumbered, albeit better armed.

Above everything else, the production revealed why Shakespeare might have used the speech-prefix '*All*', a mark that usually produces a rather embarrassing effect. Incited by Sicinius, 'What is the city but the people?' (3.1.199), fifty voices thundered back in unison 'True, / The people are the city' (199–200), a memorable sound in its volume and precision. Coriolanus whirled his sword back in response but it was no longer a threat, only a memory of the battlefield; the plebeian sound was far more threatening and powerful. This quantitative effect was not some after-echo of nineteenth-century production styles. For *Coriolanus* above any other Shakespeare play, the numbers matter; the play's argument and its structure of oppositions depend on producing a central balance. Supple's device simply worked.

Of course, colossal effects are not only achieved by numbers. Volumnia announces, hearing the trumpets of Coriolanus's victorious return to Rome, 'These are the ushers of Martius. Before him he carries noise, and behind him he leaves tears' (2.1.155–6). Judi Dench's voice at this point, ice-cold and mysterious, was devastating in its confidence, totally uncompromising in its pitiless approval of her son's effect on the world. Dench was the Volumnia I have always hoped to see, one of the great Shakespeare performances of recent years. Almost normal in her first scene (1.3) as she played games with Young Martius, teaching him to fight and arming him through the scene, Dench's Volumnia was perhaps little more than a rather objectionable mother-in-law, marking her triumph over Virgilia by taking her grandson with her 'out of doors' (1.3.73). The portrait built carefully from that foundation. Her statement to Menenius after Coriolanus's banishment, 'Anger's my meat, I sup upon myself' (4.2.53), was terrifying because of its matter-of-factness, its simple truth for this driven character. By the climax of 5.3, cleverly blocked with Coriolanus seated at the furthermost downstage point facing upstage so that Volumnia could play the entire scene out to the audience as well as to her son, Dench was crushed and humiliated, a woman who has never knelt before now kneeling to her son, a woman who has

13. *Coriolanus* 3.1, Chichester Festival Theatre and the Renaissance Theatre Company, 1992: Coriolanus (Kenneth Branagh) turns his back on the plebeians and their tribunes

never had to plead for anything in her life now humbled before the figure she had moulded. As he tried to leave, 'I have sat too long' (132), her attempt at authority, 'Nay, go not from us thus', made it possible for him to move to strike her, something unimaginable in their relationship earlier. Now, slowly, she started to find again her anger and control; nothing else mattered to her but regaining her control over him, exerting her will single-mindedly. And the result was that she had never envisaged the consequence: Coriolanus's perception that 'Most dangerously you have with him prevailed, / If not most mortal to him' (5.3.189–90) was a complete shock. For the first time he had proved wiser than she and that in the prediction of his death. Her face pulled suddenly into a mask of grief as she recognised the truth of his statement and her reappearance in the 'triumphal' entry of 5.5 was as a mourning statue of horror, a ghost, herself destroyed by her destruction of her son, the mother guilty of filicide through her absolute belief in the necessity of proving her own power.

Such great acting was not matched by Branagh's Coriolanus. His 'O' in reply to her final speech (5.3.183), slumped as a crying mummy's boy, was drawn out forever, not because the pressure of the emotion forced an unending wail but because the actor wanted to demonstrate the size of his lungs. A vocal trick, put firmly in its place by Aufidius's mocking mimicry of it to the Volscians ('He whined and roared away your victory', 5.6.100), it indicated Branagh's difficulty with the character as hero, offering not a representation of the play's paradoxes over the meaning of the word but an attempt to represent by device something his skill did not allow him to create.

Like Dance for the RSC in 1989, Branagh was at his most comfortable in finding the part's comedy, the embarrassed laughter at 'I will go wash' (1.10.67) or shuffling out on his knees at 'Look, I am going' (3.2.134), the naughty little boy mocking his mother though doing what she wants. By the end, entering perched on a single ladder carried by soldiers (a deliberate echo of his entry in 1.4), waving a piece of paper like some Roman Neville Chamberlain and clearly ripe for a fall from his vulnerable perch, Branagh had proved to have lacked the vocal range and depth, the imagination and power of Dench.

Among a fairly weak supporting cast, Briers' Menenius was an honourable exception, particularly in his argument with the Volscian guards in 5.2 where the mask of geniality slipped and the underlying cold patrician contempt was sharply revealed. But elsewhere the old bluffer of tradition became a man of considerable political nous, a match for Jimmy Yuill and Gerard Horan as decent tribunes, men conspicuously out of place in the circle of cushions on which the patricians lolled for meetings. The production was hardly notable for its sophisticated political reading of the play but, for all its limitations, Supple's *Coriolanus*, with Dench and such a crowd, burst the bounds of normal Shakespeare production.

Nothing in the year burst those bounds quite as completely as the Royal National Theatre's *A Midsummer Night's Dream*.[14] Robert Lepage, the French-Canadian director, had only been known in England for his work in experimental theatre (*The Dragons' Trilogy*, *Tectonic Plates* and his brutal one-man show, *Needles and Opium*), though he had often directed Shakespeare, including *A Midsummer Night's Dream*, in Quebec. Inviting him to direct on the huge expanses of the Olivier stage was deliberately to propose something radically different. Different is not better and the result, visually magnificent, vocally catastrophic, was a production in which the play-text was not even a pretext, only a curious encumbrance to the theatrical poetics of the director's imagination. Take, for instance, the moment at which the lovers made their way along a line of five chairs, with, as Hermia reached the front one, Philostrate taking the rear one, now empty, and running to the front of the line with it over and over again as they made their slow progress across the back of the stage. As a stage-image (of the repetitive type familiar from much performance art) the move was mesmerising and beautiful, but at the front of the stage Allan Mitchell's Theseus (who seemed for some reason to be blind) was trying to speak of lunatics, lovers and poets, a speech which neither had any perceptible link to the upstage action nor could compete with the hypnotic power of the visual image. It would be perfectly possible to argue that the importance of Theseus's speech has been grossly overrated but Mitchell's delivery suggested weight while the image denied it. The result was confusion rather than cohesion, the elements of the theatrical performance breaking into their constituent parts.

At least in the case of Mitchell's Theseus the language was comprehensible. Lepage cast as Robin a French-Canadian actress-contortionist, Angela Laurier. Wearing tight red leggings and with one breast bare (as if she, not Hippolyta, were the play's Amazon), she made her first entrance, at the opening of the performance, crab-like, walking on her hands with her legs outside her arms. Laurier proceeded in the course of the evening to reveal that the human body is capable of remarkable distortions, ending the epilogue by lying on her front, raising her legs slowly behind her and bringing her feet forward over her head to tuck them under her armpits. This is, of course, an astonishing feat, a physical metamorphosis of the body that might be argued aptly to represent Robin's transforming powers. Other tricks, particularly a dizzying high-speed spin on a cable for what seemed many minutes to represent Robin's travels round the world (from 2.1.176), were similarly extreme and dazzling. But the glare of physical malleability shone sharply on vocal constriction. Wardle quotes critics' attempts to represent the phonetics of Eugenie Leontovich's notorious Cleopatra for Komisarjevsky in 1936 ('O weederdee degarlano devar'[15]) but my skills do not include trying to transcribe Ms Laurier's pronunciation. Even if I could, her voice was so under-projected that I doubt whether anyone beyond the first few rows realised that there was anything vaguely incomprehensible being spoken. The director's imaginative choice of a performer capable of extraordinary physical feats foundered on the failure to offer anything even barely adequate vocally. It only served to throw into unmitigated relief how crucial Robin's language is to making even the most basic narrative sense of the play.

Such circus tricks, especially ones far beyond anything in Brook's *A Midsummer Night's Dream* (RSC, 1970), are guaranteed to be distracting. Sally Dexter as Titania was hung up by her ankles for her sleep like some large bat (an image intensified by her black costume). For some of the time she was hidden and the audience could not know whether she was still hanging upside down; from 2.2.30 to 3.1.122, a long period of stage time, the audience could think of nothing else but the blood rushing to Dexter's head – not the best way to ensure attention to the intervening action.

Michael Levine's set complemented the extreme nature of Lepage's view of the play. The stage was covered with an enormous shallow pond surrounded by grey earth that muddied throughout the course of the evening as the characters slithered and splashed their way across the central expanse of water. Not for nothing were the front rows of the audience provided with plastic macs to protect their clothes from the flying mud. Occasionally the light reflected off the water threw beautiful images on to the back walls, accompanying, for instance, Oberon's image of the 'mermaid on a dolphin's back' (2.1.150). But with the wood scenes played in pervasive gloom (the only lighting appeared often to be the single massive lightbulb dangling on its cord in mid-stage), the action accompanied almost constantly by strange music with a strong gamelan component, this has to be the darkest, bleakest view of the play ever taken.

If Brook's production used Kott to underline a certain degree of terror in the experiences of the night, Lepage's removed any vestige of pleasure in favour of fear and panic. Bottom's 'most rare vision' (4.1.202) was one of the purest animality, a sustained, terrified awareness of his transformation (like Pinocchio on the way to becoming a donkey), marked by the sheer difficulty of enunciating, his tongue transformed with his head. His hands turned to hooves, Bottom had to carry Robin on his back, Laurier's feet serving as expressive ass's ears. Titania's erotic interest in him was

14. *A Midsummer Night's Dream* 2.1, Royal National Theatre, 1992: Oberon
(Jeffery Kissoon) and muddy fairies

particularly bestial, her normal humanity making the ass even
more grotesque and frightening. In 4.1 Bottom's sex with Titania
was like the rutting of wild beasts (nasty, brutish and short). This
is unremittingly coarse as a view of the play: Titania's desire to
'wind thee in my arms' (4.1.39) does not mean 'have sex with you'
(a reading which sits oddly alongside the first part of the line,
'Sleep thou') and noisy humping rather distracted from the image
of the ivy and the elm; 'O how I love thee' (44) became, inevitably,
a deep post-orgasmic sigh.

Titania had had to order off the bed her attendant fairies, blue-
faced and near-naked like Congolese Kota undergoing puberty
rites (an identification I take from the programme). They had
obviously wanted to turn the event into a group orgy. Rarely standing upright, the fairies slid malevolently through the pool like evil
children beyond parental control, their monarchs dark deities
who have clearly 'Come from the farthest step of India' (2.1.69).
This dark world increasingly muddied the very young lovers whose
scenes raced by until, with the dawn in 4.1, the huge black back
walls of the stage lifted to reveal exquisite morning light, accompanied by the cast chanting, and the lovers left the stage through

showers, washing away the experience and reappearing cleansed and freshly dressed for Act 5.

But the damp night-world seemed to have affected the workers, here inhabitants of cardboard city, led by Bottom (Timothy Spall) in platform shoes and flared trousers far too short for him. What comedy there was in their rehearsal and performance was in tension with the dank, degraded world they inhabited. Grimy figures, more miners than tradesmen, they sat hunched up brewing tea in a dirty billy-can, crouched in the frame of the hospital bed that, as in too many experimental productions I have watched, was the play's single major prop.

Throughout, the production offered strong overtones of dream. The opening, with Theseus and Hippolyta perched on one end of the bed as Philostrate poled it in circles, had the lovers slumped in a heap asleep on the bed, half-waking as the action called for them, as if the dream had begun long before the play left Athens. My dreams and my view of *A Midsummer Night's Dream*, though, are certainly not as sustainedly melancholic as this one. But the play had become a drama of directorial imagination and caprice, the text disdained for the most part, though Sally Dexter is too fine an actress not to make something powerful of the 'forgeries of jealousy' speech. Lepage's theatrical imagination is rich and exciting but it was simply not interested in the material of the play it was ostensibly illuminating, as opposed to the one Lepage would like to have been devising. With Lepage's *A Midsummer Night's Dream*, I have seen the future and it is muddy.

CHAPTER 6

1992–1993: London and Stratford

Hamlet (RSC, Barbican Theatre); *Richard III* (Northern Broadsides); *King Lear* (English Stage Company at the Royal Court Theatre); *Macbeth* (Royal National Theatre); *Much Ado About Nothing* (Queen's Theatre); *Julius Caesar* (RSC, The Other Place); *The Merchant of Venice, King Lear, The Tempest, Love's Labour's Lost* (RSC, Royal Shakespeare Theatre)

If there is one cry heard more often than any other whenever the state of the arts in England is being discussed, it is the accusation that the arts are treated far too much of the time as if nothing significant ever happens outside London. Sponsorship, Arts Council grants, National Lottery money and, above all, press coverage are all subject to the grave charge of being London-centred. Of course the claim is put too strongly but there is truth in the argument none the less.

For Shakespeareans in England the similar accusation might be 'Stratford-centrism'. Niky Rathbone's annual listings in *Shakespeare Survey* show the sheer quantity of Shakespeare activity in the professional theatre across the country. Yet few Shakespeareans, even those most devoted to productions, see more than a tiny fragment of them. For 1991, for instance, Rathbone lists 94 professional productions of 31 Shakespeare plays, 14 by the Royal Shakespeare Company.[1] The most-produced plays in 1991 were *Macbeth* (7 productions), *A Midsummer Night's Dream* (8), *Romeo and Juliet* (8), *The Tempest* (7) and *Twelfth Night* (10). For 1992, my count of Rathbone's listings is 101 professional productions of 26 plays, of which 14 were by the RSC.[2] The most-produced plays that year were *As You Like It* (7 productions), *Hamlet* (11), *Macbeth* (14), *A Midsummer Night's Dream* (8) and *Twelfth Night* (7). Such statistics are only of generalised validity: Rathbone does not claim

145

comprehensiveness. Similarly, the variations between the popularity of individual plays from one year to another are statistically insignificant, accidents of the patterns of theatre culture. But it is striking to me how many of the companies performing Shakespeare are ones of which I, as an attentive observer of British theatre, have never heard. That producing Shakespeare is financially demanding, not least in cast-size, does not seem to inhibit companies large and small from continuing to perform the plays.

But, even for the most Stratford-centred of observers, it was also striking how firmly the centre of attention to the Shakespeare theatre industry shifted to London at the close of 1992 and early in 1993: the RSC opened a Shakespeare production in London; an innovative touring production arrived at the Riverside; the Royal Court, the Royal National Theatre and the West End were all responsible for important productions. In a year in which there were fewer new Shakespeare productions in Stratford than had been usual in recent years, only five in total, there was equal balance between Stratford and London in the ten productions I shall be reviewing in this chapter.

LONDON

For the first time since the company's opening productions at the Barbican in 1982, the Royal Shakespeare Company premiered a new Shakespeare production at its London home. The decision to open Adrian Noble's *Hamlet* there marked a clear policy change and its overwhelming box-office success proved its worth to the company's coffers. The idea was also a consequence of the company's difficulties in cajoling star-performers into a two-year commitment; Kenneth Branagh, Noble's Hamlet, was far too busy to stay with the RSC that long. Instead the production ran in London from December 1992 until it moved to open the 1993 Stratford season in the main house with a straight run of performances, playing opposite Sam Mendes's production of *Richard III* which, after its tour, had moved to the Swan Theatre, and it had closed by late spring, never to be seen again. In a short time-span it thus had as many performances as most RSC Shakespeare work spread over the normal two-year cycle.

If the production's advance publicity was, inevitably, dominated by the presence of Branagh, the production itself was as much dominated by Noble's decision to use a fully conflated text of Q2 and F. Basing his decision less on any textual theory than on a delightfully innocent greed to do as much of a *Hamlet* as he possibly could (given that he was unlikely to direct the play for many years to come), Noble created his own conflation and allowed the enormous result full rein. The production ran at least four and a quarter hours, with a five-minute pause before the play scene (3.2) after nearly two hours, and only one full interval after the Fortinbras scene (4.4), forty-five minutes later.

As the vast expanse of the text unfolded, some scenes, played at fuller length than usually allowed, took on new weight and scale. Claudius's duologue with Laertes (4.7.1–134), for instance, was striking in its extent and spaciousness; yet, in spite of the fine performances by John Shrapnel and Richard Bonneville, the scene was shorter on tension and conspiracy than in its normal truncated form. The gulling of Laertes and Claudius's fascination with Lamord did not justify their larger presence in the shaping of the whole play. The uncut text does not necessarily reveal a more dramatic form. The director's responsibility is to prove the theatrical viability of the text, not necessarily through a belief in the sacrosanct nature of the text but through the individual director's choice about the sheer quantity of text to be spoken in a particular production. Noble, choosing to play such a scene at the full extent of the conflated text, had to justify the choice and failed to do so here.

Cutting is shaping but Noble's production was unequivocally shaped by Bob Crowley's design. The colour changed for each of the performance's three segments, from white through red to a grey drained of all life, demanding the audience's attention to colour as a controlling motif. Where Noble's *Henry IV* had explored height (see chapter 4, above), his *Hamlet* explored the stage's depth. In front of the downstage edge, as it were in the orchestra pit, was a rank and unweeded garden, with flowers and herbs rather obviously in place for Ophelia's mad horticulture; the crosses in among the plants keyed the presence of death and provided for the grave-digging later. Not content with Shakespeare's opening, Noble added an entry for the ghost who emerged, hand first, through the soil of the graveyard like a corpse in a poor horror film, before stalking the whole depth of the stage and, as the broad cyclorama at the back lifted, exiting at the furthest upstage point, establishing for the production its full extent of depth.

The space at the rear beyond the cyclorama, a space marked as a world beyond, was the entry-route for the players and for Fortinbras and his army, in both cases apparently at the Elsinore railway station, where Hamlet appeared to be leaving Denmark for England by the boat-train. It was also the direction in which the funeral procession headed at the end where, as the cyclorama lifted again, the ghost could be seen with outstretched arms welcoming his most loving son. Such evident structuring enforced a pattern of formal articulation on the rhythms of scenic structure that might have shaped the performances. Designer-architecture is not necessarily in conflict with the form of the dramatic text but here it imposed shape on to something that, consequently, appeared shapeless, a dramatic form apparently in need of such shaping.

Crowley's extravagances often made life difficult for the actors: the glaringly scarlet closet created on the abandoned stage of the players' performance had no correlation with Jane Lapotaire's nervy and vulnerable Gertrude who was supposed to be living in it – only the photograph of Claudius on the dressing-table suggested her touch. But the bedroom had to be surrounded by the accoutrements of the court stage so that Claudius could turn a spotlight on Hamlet when interrogating him later, echoing Hamlet's turning the same theatre light on him during his disruption of the play. For the last section of the play, the stage was covered in grey parachute silk, under which, as Ophelia pulled it away, were found large heaps of decaying wreaths and a piano, all offering a mass of obstacles for the actors to negotiate.

The piano exemplified the production's frequent obviousness of design. There is little point in putting a piano on stage unless someone is going to play it (see above on ponds for people to fall into, p. 133). It had earlier been seen in Ophelia's room in 1.3, still a nursery with her doll's-house lodged on top of her wardrobe. Joanne Pearce's Ophelia, first seen in bed wearing nightdress and bedsocks, washed perfunctorily at the wash-stand (a child's cat's-lick and a promise) before cuddling her brother on the bed, and started playing the piano when Laertes left. Polonius (David Bradley), a strictly authoritarian father as well as efficient bureaucrat, loomed large beside her as she played, leading her off by the hand like a small child, as he pocketed the silver-framed photo-

15. *Hamlet* 4.5, RSC, Barbican Theatre, 1992: Laertes (Richard Bonneville),
Ophelia (Joanne Pearce), Claudius (John Shrapnel) and Gertrude
(Jane Lapotaire)

graph of Hamlet that had stood on her bedside table, a prefigura-
tion of Gertrude's bedside photo of Claudius.

Pearce's Ophelia's closeness to her father was already strongly
marked, as was his concern for her, strikingly differentiated from
his attitude to Laertes whose parting embrace he spurned while
giving him a ring (which, in due course, Laertes would later give
his distracted sister). In 2.1, set in Polonius's office, with a sky-
scraper tower of filing cabinets, Bradley in frock-coat combined
magnificently the natural spy, the far-thinking politician and the
now anxious father, putting a coat around the shocked Ophelia
who had thrown a shawl over her nightdress. After the 'nunnery'
scene, when Hamlet came close to raping her when she tried to
kiss him, throwing her to the ground and finally spitting on her,
Pearce's distraction was terrifyingly inevitable. When she now tried
to play the piano to calm herself, Polonius firmly closed the piano-
lid to stop her.

Her madness in 4.5, played both as extreme in its neurosis and detailed in its naturalism, was deeply distressing. Clutching the suitcase in which she had earlier kept Hamlet's 'remembrances' (3.1.95) on top of her wardrobe, she combined loss of lover and loss of father, with Polonius effectively superimposed on her existence by her wearing his clothes, blood-stained shirt and all, a powerful invention. But when she headed for the piano to accompany her mad songs and to play a fragmented version of the piece she had played in 1.3, the large prop seemed a glib reference to her father whose presence was more effectively present in costume than prop.

It is this curious cross between intermittently satisfying depth and frequently frustrating superficiality that characterised Branagh's Hamlet. First seen with his back to the audience, wearing a black coat with a prominent black armband, Hamlet had very carefully separated himself from the court, placed on the opposite side of the very wide stage, a group dominated by Claudius in a comfortable white suit with a glass in one hand and a fat cigar in the other, easy and confident. Claudius's summoning of Hamlet into the action (1.2.64)[3] brought a light up on him as he turned first away from the court before facing them, hands clasped tightly behind him like Prince Charles, stiff and unmoving as Gertrude tried to embrace him. The rigidity of grief, though, did not sit comfortably on Branagh whose easy warmth as an actor and natural preference for comedy, as in his Coriolanus (see chapter 5, above), was continually being reined in behind a mood of introspection. Branagh's earlier stage Hamlet (for his Renaissance Stage Company in 1988) was accused of being too dashing and impetuous.[4] Now there was a clear superimposition of thoughtfulness, focused, above all, on the profundity of his love for his father. At his best in acerbically mocking Polonius, Branagh's Hamlet seemed so intensely on the verge of swashbuckling action that it was increasingly difficult to see what was preventing him from stabbing Claudius at once and dashing off stage with Ophelia tucked under one arm. The melancholy was too self-evidently performed (by Branagh rather than Hamlet), a disguise laid over his normal style. Only in his delivery of 'How all occasions' (4.4) did the stillness grow out of the character and the soliloquy as the expression of thought convince. Only in the savagery of his treatment of Osric did the aggression towards people become more than mannered. By comparison, the brutality to Ophelia and to Gertrude, whom he came close to feigning to rape in the closet scene just as the ghost entered, was designed more as theatrical effect than credible facet of character. Branagh also, I must report, acted much of the performance on autopilot, lazy in his responses, confident in the anticipation of the standing ovation he duly received; it is some time since I have seen an actor quite so contemptuous of the audience.

Branagh and Noble, who had worked so successfully together in *Henry V* years before, now made an uneasy partnership, with the director trying both to showcase the star-actor and to deliver a fresh production. The result was heavyweight in the worst sense, its invention unfocused. In a production that seemed for the most part to perceive the play as family drama (for Noble was predictably uninterested in its internal or international politics), the spectacle of set and star became an obstacle submerging the play's language. Perhaps a cut text is better; at the least, Noble proved the blurred effect of conflation.

While Noble's *Hamlet* indulged in its length, no one could accuse Barrie Rutter's production of *Richard III* of taking its time. Spoken at high speed, the text whistled by, concentrating attention on the thrill of the unfolding narrative, the vitality of the characters' relationships and the verve of the actors. Only rarely so fast as to be breathless, the lines had an easiness and immediacy, almost a contemporaneity, in the way they seemed to fit the actors' tongues so naturally.

Rutter's company, Northern Broadsides, had toured the production triumphantly across the north of England before a season at the Riverside Studios in London, taking over the mantle of popular Shakespeare after the collapse of Michael Bogdanov's English Shakespeare Company which had lost its Arts Council funding. The particular advantage of Northern Broadsides lay in an attitude to voice: the actors, mostly from Yorkshire, were allowed, usually for the first time in their professional careers, to use their natural voices in a classical play. The company was mocked by some critics for doing Shakespeare in Yorkshire accents, most noticeably by John Peter in a swingeing attack on 'a piece of karaoke theatre in which Shakespeare provides the orchestra, and the actors have fun providing the voices'.[5] But the actors were not choosing accents; instead they allowed their voices to relax from conventions of Received Pronunciation and official Shakespeare diction so that the text was not mediated by an imposed accent, the convention of classical theatre that all speech has the accent of London. If the result was that 'Naught to do with Mrs Shore?' (1.1.99) sounded more like 'Nowt to do wi' Mistress Shawah?' or 'Something we will determine' (3.1.190) was adapted into 'Summat we will do', it seemed a small price to pay for the infectious energy of the production.

Audiences in the north of England, for whom the production had been conceived, were not required to see Shakespeare as an expression of a Home Counties middle-class culture which patronised them. Far from being condescending, as John Peter claimed, Northern Broadsides reclaimed Shakespeare in a piece of cultural annexation that reappropriated high culture and its geographical polarity. Inevitably, it was only when seen in the capital, displaced from its own context, that Rutter's *Richard III* was widely reviewed in the national press.

Even more than in Sam Mendes's RSC touring production (see chapter 5, above), Rutter's production was defiantly played as cheap theatre, with a shoulder-pad borrowed from Bradford Northern Rugby League Club for Richard's hump, and an old fur coat as the queen's robe passed from Elizabeth to Anne and then offered by Richard to Elizabeth again for her daughter. The rival armies of Act 5 slowly donned boiler suits and clogs, making the costume change visible during the build-up to Bosworth where the generals were wheeled around mounted on porters' trollies and the armies stamped thunderous rhythms in their clogs. Richard died at the hands of the ghosts whose sticks and clogs enacted a folk-ritual of exorcism of the devil. His corpse was placed inside the wire enclosure that had been a permanent presence on audience right and on whose perimeter fence articles symbolising Richard's victims had accumulated in the course of the performance. The drumming of the clogs slowed and quietened and eventually stopped as Richmond spoke of 'this fair land's peace' (5.8.39). The soldiers, copying Richmond, took off their clogs and dungarees, dumping the paraphernalia of war on the body of the cause of bloodshed, closing the enclosure fence on him and leaving on the opposite side of the stage towards a strong light streaming through open doors. I have never before found the sense of purification of the demonic so absolute, the calm of the

16. *Richard III* 4.4, Northern Broadsides, 1992: King Richard (Barrie Rutter) asks Queen Elizabeth (Ishia Bennison) to help him woo her daughter

new order so effective. It was fine theatre, powerfully clear in its communication of what Bosworth had accomplished.

The battle sequence was, by some way, the largest of the production's effects. More often, the energy of narrative came through with the rapidity of naturalism. The disputes of the rival factions took on overtones of a family squabble in a gritty northern realist drama of the 1950s, with Ishia Bennison's splendid Queen Elizabeth someone who the others clearly thought had got above herself in her gold dress and mink coat. In 4.4. Polly Hemingway's Margaret, a bag-lady who has wandered into the court, could kick Elizabeth to the ground, pull the hair of the Duchess of York, and leave the stage with clenched fist raised triumphantly aloft like a street-fighter who has beaten up rivals. But none of these moments diminished the text; the implications of the struggles of dynastic factions or the threat of Margaret's prophetic curses were no less powerful for the recognisability of the characters. Rutter's Richard was no less dangerous for appearing an engaging comedian with a prancing walk (wearing one shoe and one clog) and one hand permanently thrust in his trouser pocket. The audience could not help but admire Richard's brass-neck, that northern word for arrogant nerve, even as his actions disgusted. The worried conversations of the citizens (2.3) came over all the more concerned since the fate of the nation was in hands insufficiently different from their own. The class gaps closed with the voices: there was no accentual linguistic divide between aristocrats and citizens.

Rutter's production proclaimed its regionalism but it also trumpeted its unabashed pleasure in the play. Where some productions seem almost to be apologising for doing Shakespeare at all, Northern Broadsides showed why he was the English Renaissance's most popular dramatist and why he should continue to be the centre of vitality in our theatre culture. If that is 'condescending' it is a condescension more companies should copy.

Part of the problem that Northern Broadsides addresses is the placing of Shakespeare in English culture. Central to the work of the RSC or a classical company like the Royal National Theatre, Shakespeare is a figure on the periphery of the vision of the English Stage Company at the Royal Court. The last time the company had turned to Shakespeare had been in 1980 (*Hamlet* directed by Richard Eyre, starring Jonathan Pryce); now, as his valedictory production to mark the end of his long reign as the theatre's artistic director, Max Stafford-Clark directed *King Lear* on the Court's tiny stage.

Eyre's *Hamlet* is best remembered as the production where the ghost's lines were spoken by Hamlet himself; Stafford-Clark's *King Lear* will probably be remembered as the production where Fool (Andy Serkis) made his first entry in drag. It might also be remembered for the way its opening conversation between Kent (Philip Jackson) and Gloucester (Hugh Ross) was set in a urinal, or for Oswald urinating over Kent (not in the stocks but buried up to his neck), or for Fool, obstinately refusing to vanish after 3.6, graffiti-spraying on the back wall 'What a piece of', leaving open the question whether the quotation is to end 'rubbish' or 'work is man'. But such mockery of tradition, while they may be part of the Royal Court's own traditional pose of liberal radicalism, suggests a production more glib than was the case.

More thoughtful, though equally predictable, was the production's attempt to provide a context of contemporaneity by staging the last scenes as echoes of Bosnia. Across the battlefield wandered refugees with their possessions loaded into a supermarket trolley[6] or clutching a ghetto-blaster or a bicycle, taking cover as they fled from the explosions that blasted chunks out of the brickwork of the set. At the end, as Kent prayed by the corpses of Lear and Cordelia, two grave-diggers rapidly shovelled up mounds of earth, two soldiers in sunglasses and holding automatic weapons unrolled barbed wire, and two women lit candles. But such images of civil war and torment, for all their power as theatrical imitations of all-too-familiar newsreel, were intrusions into the production's play-world, over-emphatic additions to make a point more superficially than the resonances created elsewhere.

Earlier, Stafford-Clark's view of the play's politics had emerged from the production's creation of a dominantly male, public-school homosocial world. Entering in riding-coat and breeches, Tom Wilkinson's Lear, nowhere near 'fourscore', was an energetic colonel with beetling eyebrows, walrus moustache and a monocle, an efficient ruler busy signing the papers Gloucester handed him, smug in his authority and enjoying his elder daughters' glee at their shares of the kingdom. It seemed natural, in this militarist context, for Kent's exile to be marked by Lear's cutting off his uniform ribbons. At Goneril's house, Lear, in red hunting-coat, goosed the serving-maid who was setting the dinner-table and loved the officers'-mess games as Oswald was kicked in the groin and his mouth stuffed with butter by Lear's two knights. Fool, a camp queen in full Edwardian evening-dress, kissed Kent full on the mouth and mocked Lear by bending him over, pretending to spank him with a whip and to bugger him to the cheers of the others. Goneril's fury was not only fully justified by these 'not-to-be-endurèd riots' (1.4.186) but by the exclusive masculinity of Lear's attitude to gender. This Lear, who knew, even as he ignored Cordelia's exit in 1.1, that he had made a terrible mistake, would have found it a questioning of his sense of his own masculinity to change his mind. His self-assurance in contradicting Kent in the stocks ('No, I say', 2.2.196) revealed the absolute confidence of a man who simply cannot bear to be wrong. Only the gay Fool, whose working-class accent broke through the sounds of camp whenever he was moved, could be perceived by Lear as caring for him. In 1.5 Fool powdered his nose and then, movingly, showed Lear his own reflection in the mirror in the lid of his powder-compact.

Goneril and Regan had adopted differing ways of dealing with their father, Goneril (Lia Williams) adopting riding breeches as if to be Lear's son, and Regan (Saskia Reeves) playing at being daddy's little girl, an act she repeated with her husband. But neither strategy would work, for women could not possibly penetrate this Lear's shell. Madness was a retreat into a still more private world. Edgar's 'Look where he stands and glares' (Q13.19) was an accurate description of Lear's post-traumatic shock. Death, too, became another form of privacy as Lear's death-rattle in his throat and drumming heels, an extraordinarily long drawn out agony, shocked and horrified the audience on and off stage, even as Kent lovingly cradled the dying man. It was inevitable that a man of such physical strength should be stretched inordinately long on the 'rack of this tough world' (5.3.290).

Beside the clarity of Lear's progress, the production's gimmicks were only distractions. It was difficult to concentrate on Lear's death as the corpse of the hanged Fool swung to and fro at the back of the stage, providing a cheap referent for Lear's line. In the tiny space of the Royal Court, the immediacy of Edgar's individual pain spoke more eloquently of Bosnia than the activity of the company's supernumeraries. The threat beyond was better captured by the distant rumble of the tube-trains always to be heard under the theatre than by offstage gunfire. The company's radicalism lay in its emphasis on the play's despairing humanity in a state in which central authority had collapsed, not in the gestures of heterodoxy in stage effect.

Richard Eyre's 1980 *Hamlet* at the Royal Court was strikingly fresh; his *Richard III* at the Royal National Theatre (see chapter 2, above) strong and provocative. But his *Macbeth* at the National was simply awful. Alan Howard's way with Shakespearean verse used to be quite mannered; by comparison with his Macbeth his past excesses were moderate. The lines were screamed and chanted, twisted and fragmented, stretched and gabbled into a nonsense that harked back to satiric descriptions of the worst nineteenth-century barnstorming styles. Anastasia Hille, as Lady Macbeth, could hardly be blamed for keeping her distance from this Macbeth, a man perfectly capable of making his wife go with him at the end of 3.2 by the simple expedient of picking her up and carrying her off over his shoulder. By the end Macbeth seemed to have turned into Dracula, biting Young Siward in the neck, before fighting a duel with Macduff in which the actors were all too plainly counting their moves. It was a sad experience.

A Shakespeare production opening in the West End, rather than transferring there, is an even rarer event than one opening at the Barbican or the Royal Court. Courageously, Thelma Holt backed a production of *Much Ado About Nothing* by the promising young director Matthew Warchus. The pre-publicity for Kenneth Branagh's film may have helped and may even have conditioned the choice of play. Certainly the production deserved to succeed. I would, however, be hard put to it to indicate in what ways Warchus's production differed from an RSC one. Some under-casting of the smaller roles went with a certain obviousness of playing but worse has often been seen in Stratford. Janet McTeer (Beatrice) and Mark Rylance (Benedick) have both played major roles for the RSC. Perhaps Warchus's production took especial care to underline the plot, with Borachio at the end of 2.2 left alone on stage as he silently imagined, with the help of projected photographs, his encounter with Margaret; but such clarification of narrative is positively desirable, even if this was not necessarily the best way to do it.

By comparison with the banal populism of Branagh's film version, Warchus's work was thoughtful and often perceptive. Far from being overly centred on the stars, this *Much Ado* was full of fine detailing of other roles: Margaret sitting in mourning outside Hero's monument in 5.2, trying to be witty but crushed by her part in the events; Don Pedro (Jack Ellis) in the last scene deeply shamed by Don John's capture and his humiliating share in the plot against Hero; Kevin Doyle's Don John, immured indoors in a dark interior with a massive window through which he could watch Claudio embracing Hero in 2.2, a trapped and caged man, bitterly angry at being defeated by his brother.

There was good comic business as well: Dogberry (Gerard Kelly) interrogating his prisoners in a lawyer's gown like some would-be Irish Marshall Hall; Benedick in the opening scene, bested by Beatrice in the dialogue, suddenly sinking down clutching his heavily bandaged head (hence her accusation of 'a jade's trick', 1.1.138), before flinging the bandage aside to reveal no trace of a wound, when left alone with Claudio at 1.1.154. Beside such invention, the playing of the dance in 2.1 in Wild-West costume and cod John Wayne accents was a banal mistake.

Neil Warmington's design was dominated by cupids, three of whom, armed with bows, hovered over the gulling of Beatrice and Benedick. But these benign cupids were offset by an image of a painted cupid with the eyes torn off, an emblem of love blinded that was only healed when the missing strip of painting was found watching Hero's 'tomb' inside the monument, a canopied space previously used as the wedding-chapel in 3.5. The set for the gulling had a net of roses descending from a cupid's hand, a net of love for Benedick's concealment. The cupids' bows allowed for targets on stage, behind which Beatrice hid, becoming, quite literally, a moving target for the surprisingly brutal attack on her 'carping' by Hero.

McTeer's Beatrice, tall and, from the start, at ease with herself, bare-legged and wearing sensible brogues, strode the stage in complete control, giving Hero a glass of Dutch courage before the wooing or coming to call Benedick to dinner (2.3.233) munching a banana. The gulling unsettled her magnificently. After her soliloquy at the end of 3.1, spoken slowly and mournfully to the accompaniment of a melancholy viol, the scene ran straight on, as Benedick entered newly shaved of his drooping moustache, trying to sing 'Sigh no more' in a cracked voice. The two sat awkwardly on benches, not knowing how to start the conversation, how to begin to express what they felt, until, at the entry of Don Pedro, Claudio and Leonato, Beatrice ran off and Benedick stuffed the paper with the words of the song in his mouth. His complaints of the toothache (3.2.20 and 64) were justified by the large lump in his mouth caused by the paper. By the end, her willing acceptance of his kiss ('Peace, I will stop your mouth', 5.4.97) echoed and transformed her earlier advice to Hero ('Speak, cousin. Or, if you cannot, stop his mouth with a kiss', 2.1.291–2), advice which, when Hero followed it, caused Beatrice a loud groan.

McTeer's Beatrice was perfectly balanced by Rylance's Benedick. Rylance looked particularly short alongside McTeer who could swing him around in the dance in 2.1 whenever Benedick tried to escape. Always fresh in his conception of a role, Rylance equipped Benedick with a Belfast brogue, enabling him to combine both the gift of the gab and an offhand delivery, almost, but never quite, throwing lines away by muttering them half to himself. Almost coarse early on, the 'bugle' he does not want to hang 'in an invisible baldric' (1.1.226) unequivocally phallic, Benedick was left a complete wreck by his treatment at the hands of the conspirators. 'Love me! Why, it must be requited' (2.3.212–13) became 'Love me! Why? It must be requited' and the audience, looking at this bedraggled crushed figure could find no answer to the question other than laughter. Increasingly gentle as the performance developed, this Benedick was engagingly awkward in his wooing in 4.1, and his concern in 5.2, putting his arm caringly round Beatrice as he asked 'And how do you?' (5.2.82), was sincerely moving. Throughout, Rylance increasingly showed the private, vulnerable man behind the public show. Often understated, always provocative, this was a fine Benedick. In generating and accommodating central performances as fine as these, Matthew Warchus showed that the Queen's Theatre in Shaftesbury Avenue is a convenient staging-post on the route to Stratford, where he was to be found the following year.

STRATFORD

Though the Stratford season may have been foreshortened by the runs of *Hamlet* and *Richard III*, it was certainly not short on anything else. It was, quite simply, one of the greatest Stratford seasons I have seen, production after production of a quality of imagination and achievement of the highest order, both in the company's Shakespeare work in the Royal Shakespeare Theatre and The Other Place and, even more emphatically, in the non-Shakespearean work in the Swan and The Other Place.[7] Not all were great productions but cumulatively they were a magnificent vindication of the approaches that, falteringly in the previous two seasons, Adrian Noble had established.

David Thacker, for instance, whose work in the previous season had been so disappointing, was firmly back to form. I must admit to having approached his production of *Julius Caesar* in The Other Place with depressing expectations. There were two particular grounds for impending gloom: the first was the sad history of the play in recent Stratford productions (see chapter 4, above, on Stephen Pimlott's); the second a general dislike of promenade productions.

The settled perspectives of the audience to the action in a conventional seated theatre deserve to be disrupted sometimes but I always find in promenade shows that, sooner or later, I end up in the wrong place to see a particular scene. In this, *Julius Caesar* was no exception. I cannot be sure that I made the right sense of the quarrel scene since I was staring at Brutus's back rather than seeing his face, and my concentration on the battle wavered while I nursed the bruises caused by a soldier planting a size eleven army boot squarely on my foot as he charged off stage through the smoke. On the press night, when I saw it, there was the added distraction of watching the critics. The sight of Michael Billington of the *Guardian* taking notes was almost as intriguing as whatever Casca was doing standing next to him.

None the less promenade is one possible answer to the perennial problem of the crowd, always a disaster in the Royal Shakespeare Theatre as Pimlott had found in 1991 and Hall would find in 1995. Thacker staged the Forum scene brilliantly, with the promenading audience and a few actors mingled among them staring up at Brutus or Antony on their towers as the light gently accentuated the crowd's rapt faces; helped by the hard-working concentration of the crowd-actors, the audience was bound together into a group, if not a mob. In fact only half of the audience was promenading, for those seated in the gallery of the theatre could observe both action and 'onstage' audience. Strikingly, in the scenes of privacy, promenaders made an almost voyeuristic intrusion into Brutus's attempt to weigh his commitment to the conspiracy alone (2.1.10–34) or the attempts by Brutus and Portia to define the nature of their marriage (2.1.232–308).

Almost convinced by the promenade style, I had more serious hesitations about the production's contemporaneity. Playing Caesar as a cross between Yeltsin and Ceaucescu, Calpurnia as Raisa Gorbachev, and allowing the battle scenes overtones of civil war in Bosnia, have peculiar consequences, here as in the Royal Court's *King Lear*, for, if *Julius Caesar* celebrates, as we were celebrating, the overthrow of dictatorships like those of Eastern Europe, it is also a play far more uneasy about the manipulability of the mass of the people than I would like to be about the fall of Ceaucescu or the events of Tiananmen Square. That republican conspiracy can lead to further empires disdains the people's yearning for freedom. It was another case where the analogy would not hold. Still, the sight of David Sumner's Caesar playing to the TV cameras with the assurance of Yeltsin or Clinton on walkabout, beaming but surrounded by bodyguards, was too good to miss.

The weaknesses of the analogy matched a lack of concern with the production's politics. The production's obeisances to the issues of contemporary political history were little more than dutiful. Like the RSC's ambivalent (effectively reactionary) attitude, under Noble's guardianship, towards making visible its political or cultural readings of Shakespeare, Thacker offered generalised connections whose implications the production consistently evaded. This is of a piece with a post-Thatcherite position which renders oppositional theatre almost impossible within the massive institutions of centrally funded and business-sponsored theatre.

The political analogy also controlled the production's visual language. Fran Thompson's set – a red-carpeted circle with blue surround with four massive platforms at the corners of The Other Place – carried in its colours and in its banners with their central stars strong overtones of Soviet style. But it also left resonances of an arena or a circus ring within which the drama was played out. The drama of Thacker's production was not one of the politics of ideology but of the human and hence corrupted nature of commitment, a commitment generated by individual psychology rather than political analysis. In the cautious indirections of Brutus's language ('What you would work me to I have some aim', 1.2.164), could be heard here the dangers of being overheard, the risks in speaking too plainly. But while Jeffery Kissoon's Brutus articulated his actions in terms of a political theory, Rob Edwards' Cassius was driven by a personal loathing for Caesar of frightening intensity.

This Cassius foregrounded his sneering contempt for the gap between the public image of Caesar (marked by his face staring from the walls in a mass of posters) and the private limitations (echoed by Caesar's superstitions about dreams and his hiding behind his wife's fears as a mask for his own). In his wild behaviour in the storm (1.3), he was able to focus this personal hatred, ripping one of the posters as he talked to Casca. In the quarrel with Brutus, Cassius allowed us to see his real concern, a simply desperate need to be loved by Brutus: 'Have not you love enough to bear

with me / When that rash humour which my mother gave me /
Makes me forgetful?' (4.2.175–7) – and Edwards' rasping,
mocking enunciation of 'mother' suggested the unloved child in
need of the love and reassurance that an adult man alone could
give him. Not in any way homosexual, Edwards' Cassius could only
find meaning in the homosocial world, the male camaraderie of
conspiracy.

Julius Caesar became a play centrally about this male bonding in
a fiercely patriarchal society, to the extent that Brutus's willingness
to listen to Portia in 2.1 appeared almost abnormal, at least in this
world where women could be so easily marginalised, such as when
Calpurnia rushed out of the room choking back tears when Caesar
had decided to 'go forth' or when, in a rather glib image, a woman
pushed a dead soldier in a pram across the battlefield of Philippi.
When Portia (Francesca Ryan) explored what her marriage to
Brutus meant to both of them, she spoke of a modern partnership
of which the play has no other exemplar, and even the news of her
death became only grist to the public image of Brutus before his
officers in 4.2. Cassius, hugging Brutus as the conspirators left the
orchard at 3 a.m., became some sort of rival to this marriage.

Caesar, oscillating between his suit and full army uniform,
heavily bemedalled, for ceremonial occasions, met his death in the
full panoply of public event, standing at a lectern with a microphone to address the senate, turning 'Are we all ready?' (3.1.31)
into a tutting aside at the conspirators' nervous whisperings whose
words he could not hear. But Caesar's very visible self-confidence
in public, echoing that extraordinary moment when Ceaucescu
realised the crowd were booing not cheering, modulated into the
private self-confidence of Barry Lynch's Antony.

There is always something dangerous about Barry Lynch's smile,
as in his Proteus in *The Two Gentlemen of Verona* in 1991. After
making his private speech to Caesar's corpse ('O pardon me, thou
bleeding piece of earth', 3.1.257ff.) into a violent verse paragraph
of rage, Lynch played the whole forum scene in a low key, appearing almost unable to control the energies he had unleashed.
Wearing Caesar's bloodied and ripped jacket, hanging loosely on
him like a giant's robe upon this dwarfish thief, he seemed
wrapped up in himself. Only when Octavius's officer arrived as
Antony was hanging on one of the set's ladders (3.2.254) did the
play of that smile over his face show his real relish of what he had

achieved, intensified later as he rocked his chair back, so easy with himself as the triumvirs pricked the names and a woman shredded dangerous documents. Lynch's charm suggested a remarkable Iago to come.

The battle scenes were a logical culmination of the production's concerns; the casual slaughters, the 'deaths put on by cunning and forced cause' (*Hamlet*, 5.2.337) were dominated by the moment when one of the guards killing prisoners removed his Balaclava and turned out to be Caesar's ghost who smiled mockingly at Brutus. Philippi was, we know, a blood-bath, its casualty list enormous for a battle of the period. It was also civil war. Here the indistinguishability of the two sides in their battle fatigues added immeasurably to the moral as well as visual murkiness of the fighting; there were not even the racial divisions that differentiate the sides in Bosnia. The deaths of Brutus and Cassius seemed almost incidental, certainly unheroic, and the last speeches of Antony and Octavius provided no summing-up. There could be no full close here, only the exhaustion of self-destruction.

Thacker's production of *The Merchant of Venice* was also outstanding proof that he had exorcised the demon of the main house, proof that the Royal Shakespeare Theatre need not be an insoluble problem for directors. Played in modern dress in a context of the yuppie explosion of business-dealing in the modern City of London, *The Merchant*'s attitude towards exploitative capitalism risked nonsense. As with *Caesar*, Thacker refused to follow through the logic of the analogy, for Shylock's exorbitant interest charges and ability to make money would surely have been widely applauded in the social setting Thacker had chosen while Antonio's willingness to lend out money interest-free would seem the height of folly. Money as the sole principle of value assimilates Shylock into the centre of its moral system. Yet Thacker found, through the analogy of setting, a means to reveal much else about the social organisation of the play, its exploration of both belonging and being an alien within a tightly controlled community. In this the analogy worked far more effectively than the ESC's *Merchant* in 1991.

I have always preferred to believe that *The Merchant of Venice* is not anti-semitic but that directors have usually lacked the perceptive ability to show how it is not. Thacker's production was the most coherent and convincing demonstration that the play need not be. Bryan Cheyette's review in the *TLS* argued that the production showed that 'If even an assimilated and cultured Jew can become a bloodthirsty skullcapped and gaberdined racial killer, then how can we possibly trust any of them?' But Cheyette seemed to have missed Thacker's careful use of Tubal to place and define the audience's attitude to Shylock.[8] Thacker increased Tubal's presence in the play. He was on stage in 1.3 when Bassanio and Antonio come to borrow the money from Shylock. David Calder's Shylock really did not have the 3,000 ducats available (1.3.51–4) and Tubal's whispered offer solved the problem: 'Tubal, a wealthy Hebrew of my tribe, / Will furnish me' (55–6). Skullcapped from the start, offering advice about Shylock's biblical analogy to Jacob like a resident rabbinical scholar, Nick Simons' Tubal increasingly marked his distance from Shylock's maniacal pursuit of Antonio. When Shylock announced 'I will have the heart of him if he forfeit' (3.1.117–18), he put his hand firmly on an open book, a prayer-book I presume, on his desk and Tubal registered horror at this abuse of religion. In Shylock's confrontation with Salerio and Solanio (the two halves of 3.1 were reversed), Tubal made clear his total rejection of Shylock's course of action, a response underlined by placing the interval here as Shylock and Tubal exited in different directions. It was an unspoken plea from Tubal that drew from Shylock the acerbic 'Tell not me of mercy' (3.3.1) as Antonio was going to jail. At the trial scene, while Antonio was backed by his friends, Shylock was conspicuously alone, the seats behind him empty.

Calder's approach to Shylock was clear and logical. He began as a man desperate for assimilation (no skullcap for him), his voice cultured and anglicised except when he mocked the stereotype jew his visitors expected to find ('Fair sir, you spat on me on Wednesday last', 1.3.124). His statement 'I would be friends with you, and have your love' (1.3.136) was totally sincere and he really could not understand their gentile contempt. At this stage Shylock's desire for integration made his jewishness ambivalent; Antonio's comment 'gentle Jew' (1.3.176) drew from Shylock compliant laughter, followed by a grimace at the audience asking for complicity in his mockery of these odd things gentiles found funny. Such a view of the character had, of course, to underplay Shylock's aside of hatred (1.3.39–50) as much as possible and the speech left a jarring resonance across the scene.

But, seen at home in 2.5, listening to Schubert on his CD player and hugging a photograph of Leah, this cultured man did not deserve his treatment. It made of Jessica's betrayal both something incomprehensible and something far more culpable, a commitment to the triviality of the yuppie culture, all champagne and mobile phones, of the production's view of Venice as modern stock exchange. Everything that followed in Calder's performance was a direct response to the traumatic shock of the loss of Jessica, as he searched desperately through the crowd of animal-masked carnival revellers, shouting her name in a sequence added to the end of 2.6.

The revenge on Antonio was simply the consequence of Antonio's availability as victim. Wishing Jessica 'hearsed at my foot and the ducats in her coffin' (3.1.83–4), Shylock tore open his shirt to reveal the Star of David underneath (as Antonio's open shirt in the trial scene revealed a crucifix). By the trial scene, Shylock had turned himself into the image of a religious jew, with skullcap and gaberdine and with the Star of David now worn outside his collarless shirt. His use of the symbols of religion was now demonstrably an abuse of religion and race, becoming a jew only because it focused his traumatised existence. It was Shylock himself who now appeared the anti-semite.

Calder was matched by Clifford Rose's Antonio, tight-lipped and precise, a man whose hidden sexual habits were probably very nasty indeed. Shaking uncontrollably with terror in the trial scene, needing guards to hold him down, as Shylock marked out the pound's-worth on his chest with a marker-pen, he ended up, legs buckling, draped over Bassanio, which was where, I presume, he wanted to be. He had tried embracing Shylock and been rejected (3.3.4); he had tried shaking hands with the Duke and been rather pointedly ignored. Only Bassanio could console him now. Owen Teale's cheerily good-natured Bassanio missed the caddishness of the man, first cousin to Claudio in *Much Ado About Nothing*, though there was something endearingly clumsy about his suggestion to 'Wrest once the law to your authority' (4.1.212), rating horror from everyone else at its corruption of law, and something ingratiating about his appearance at Belmont, unruly hair now slicked down like the Prince of Morocco's.

Thacker's vision of Venice was of a generalised racism: when a black yuppie spoke feelingly to Solanio and Salerio, in the bar

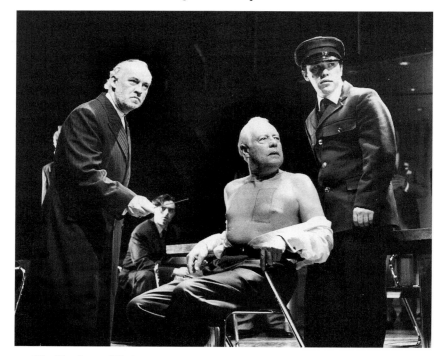

17. *The Merchant of Venice* 4.1, RSC, 1993: 'Tarry a little': Shylock (David Calder) and Antonio (Clifford Rose)

where they had gone with a couple of secretaries, of Antonio – 'A kinder gentleman treads not the earth' (2.8.35) was transferred to him – he was very pointedly ignored. It was a pity then that Thacker had not allowed the racism in Belmont, for Portia was neatly sanitised by the cutting of her vicious final comment on Ray Fearon's sympathetic portrayal of Morocco, 'Let all of his complexion choose me so' (2.7.79), a line which deliberately echoes Morocco's first line in the play, 'Mislike me not for my complexion' (2.1.1).

Penny Downie, caught in a sterile Belmont backed with a translucent screen, blossomed unexpectedly when Bassanio chose correctly. Suddenly there were flowers and a brilliant costume, replacing her earlier black dress. But the arrival of Salerio with the news of Antonio's arrest had suddenly allowed sight of the Venetian high-tech world through the now transparent screen. The process was reversed when for Act 5 tree projections filled the back wall of the stage and Venice seemed invaded by the spirit of Belmont, a takeover bid entirely in keeping with the monetarist world of the production. But Thacker's attentions were hardly directed at the Belmont scenes and that side of the play seemed dull by comparison with the events in Venice.

One of the great strengths of the season was the casting in depth. Mark Lockyer's Graziano, wearing a mesmerisingly awful tie, grew brilliantly from shallowness in the first scenes to a near-hysteria of impotent rage at the trial when he was left spitting at Shylock. Christopher Luscombe proved that Lancelot Gobbo, long thought the least funny of Shakespeare's clowns, can be deliriously funny, extracting the humour from the lines, not from comic business.

Only once did the production falter, when, at the end of the trial scene, Shylock, crawling to his feet with his back to the audience, trying to control himself in the gathering darkness, suddenly rounded on the audience and glowered threateningly. I realised it was offered as a parallel to the prim and smug authority of Antonio spotlit at the very end of the play but the look was too enigmatic.

There were many enigmas in Adrian Noble's production of *King Lear*, facets of Anthony Ward's design and passages of the play that never came fully into focus. But, after the disappointments of his *Hamlet*, it was satisfying to find Noble so unquestionably back to form. Using a conflated text, cut by about 400 lines, the production was as vast and cosmic as the play demands, creating a vision of the play as powerful and as moving as one could wish for.

Productions of *King Lear*, however good, are foredoomed unless the Lear himself is good enough. Robert Stephens possessed the role with an authority as absolute as Lear's own rule. When a teenager, I remember complaining, with all the arrogance of youth, of the fluffs and doubles in Schnabel's recordings of Beethoven piano sonatas. 'Ah but', a far wiser mentor told me, 'never mind about the few wrong notes. Just listen to all the right ones.' It was appropriate advice for Stephens' Lear. There were many lines fluffed and rewritten – on some nights many more than on others. Sometimes the new lines were nonsensical; sometimes the metre went haywire as a result. Certainly there were nights when, for Shakespeare scholars, the fluffs loomed large and troubling. But then Shakespeare scholars are by their very nature a pedantic breed. And one would have had to be, like the onstage audience Lear addresses at the end of the play, 'men of stones' not to be wrenchingly moved by Stephens' Lear. If with John Wood's Lear, in Hytner's production in 1990 (see chapter 2, above), one could not help but observe the technique that was producing the effects, admiring the actor's skills that created the emotional charge of the performance, with Stephens it seemed wrong to hold oneself removed, observing how he did it. If this Lear did not make one weep, no performance ever would. Capable of terrifying violence, as when he threatened Goneril with his riding-whip in 1.3, and capable of equally terrifying love, as when Cordelia was stood on a chair like a prized pupil for her answer in the first scene, Stephens' Lear became increasingly trapped in a world of his own making. Kent (David Calder) could not help, nor, even, could contact with Fool, played by Ian Hughes much less eccentrically than most other recent Fools – no need for drag here – and much more tender and moving as a result. Fool touchingly made his final exit in 3.6 in the wrong direction, away from Kent and Lear, in a state of suicidal despair, carrying a knife which Lear had dropped.

No one could really touch this Lear, wrapped up in the private terror of the descent to madness. Even the scene with the blind Gloucester was frighteningly lonely, with Edgar, immobile through most of the scene, able to do no more than touch his father's shoulder consolingly as Gloucester wept uncontrollably. The steps down for Stephens' Lear from the authority at the start were controlled and plainly marked. The trauma of the loss of control was as much physical as mental as the anguish appeared almost like a succession of heart attacks – as in a sense they are. This transformation of the mental into the physical was crushing, leaving the audience as helpless as observers as the other characters on stage. Above all, it was a descent of which Lear himself was painfully aware: Stephens made of 'O Fool, I shall go mad' (2.2.459) nothing more or less than a statement of fact, all the more chilling for his consciousness of the inevitability of the process. The collapse was a self-inflicted wound.

To call Lear's agony self-inflicted is to give a hostage to fortune. But Noble's treatment of the evil elsewhere in the play removed it far from Lear himself. The grand guignol of Simon Dormandy's psychopathic Cornwall, searching Edmund's wound with intrigued fascination in 2.1, or the mannered playing of Goneril and Regan, making them more than ever like Cinderella's ugly sisters, did not deny the horror of their actions but put them into a different play-world, one which could not really affect the solipsistic universe of Lear. Only as they stared after Lear towards the impending storm, trying to convince themselves that they had had no choice and had done the right thing (2.2.461–5), was there a hint of a child's affection.

Something similar happened in the Gloucester action. David Bradley, like Stephens, started quietly, almost underpowered as he coasted through his scene with Edmund (1.2). Only at his blinding did this Gloucester unleash his power. Bradley awfully demonstrated the sheer physical pain of the blinding, where usually the discovery of Edmund's evil and of the wronging of Edgar is allowed to take precedence over the enveloping agony of the act. Bradley, by contrast, caught in the coldest possible white spotlight, let the horror of torture have its fullest unbearable extent, so that the care for Edgar ('Kind gods, forgive me that, and prosper him!', 3.7.90) existed in spite of and through that overwhelming experience of the extremity of physical suffering. Taking the interval after the blinding (as Hytner had done and Peter Brook before him), Noble left Bradley's Gloucester staring sightlessly at an immense moon suspended over the stage as the biggest of all the big effects of Anthony Ward's design came into its own: the huge globe cracked and sand poured from it as, as Lear predicted, 'all germens spill at once' (3.2.8). The impact of this extravagant device was perfectly in keeping with the play's cosmic vision.

Great productions of plays like *King Lear* understand the rhythm of the text. Where Noble had imposed shape on to *Hamlet*, he allowed *King Lear* to unfold, building slowly towards the emotional extremes of pain and grief that would be needed in the last stages of the action. The result was a necessary but disappointing underplaying of the opening. Lear's stylish regency court, a world of apparent rationality which would disintegrate to the limits of unreason, turned tensely at the King's approach, but the production did not reveal a cause for that nervous anxiety. Stephens' Lear certainly believed himself to have been 'So kind a father' (1.5.33). He was, as Michael Billington commented, 'a man spoilt by a lifetime of adulation' (*Guardian*), beaming at everyone, until, just before his exit (1.1.265), he paused, marking both the power and regret at what he had done, signalling a man who had never had to undo anything and was incapable of starting to do so now. Later, too, he settled to 'pray' (3.4.27), framing the word to hint at its unaccustomed significance. There was too much geniality in 1.1 with its polite court laughter and even applause at Cordelia's 'Nothing', little sense that the future of the nation was at stake.

Noble's production was played out over a map of England which papered the stage floor and on which Fool, gagged and with odd stockings like some bizarre footman, painted the red lines of the division of the kingdom, as the court – and Cornwall in particular – craned to see how the shares would be established. Gradually the paper map ripped and shredded from the moment of Edgar's entry as Poor Tom in 3.6 until it was finally removed in the civil war of the last battle. But the production did not seek to explore the politics of the play's view of nation. Only the careful nature of the apportionment of the three shares, with Cordelia's third a wedge that prevented the lands given to Goneril and Regan from touching at any point along their borders, suggested a politics of rule here. Instead the line from individual through family led without interruption to the pitiless universe beneath which these characters crawled.

Many characters had to make this journey until the survivors could line up facing the sand-heap and the globe as the production's final image. John Normington's Albany moved from earlier ineffectuality to a man belatedly trying to make sense of the war he is engaged in ('For this business, / It touches us as France invades our land', Q22.26–7). Simon Russell Beale's Edgar moved from naive bookish scholar, reading in the midst of the court hubbub at the start, to the muddied figure whose body contorted to the poses of the *Icones* of Andreas Vesalius and who sang his fragments of tune with an unworldly beauty. This Edgar was so traumatised by the blinding of his father that he repeatedly sought to revenge it, blinding Oswald with his staff as he killed him and trying to gouge Edmund's eyes with his thumbs at the end of their savage duel, making clear what drove his vision of connectedness: 'The dark and vicious place where thee he got / Cost him his eyes' (5.3.163–4).

But even such performances paled beside Stephens. I must mark four crowning moments. In the scene with Gloucester (4.5), he alone could find the connection between the fragmented shards of his language, revealing the supreme logic of madness, unafraid of the audience's laughter, our temporary comfort while we shared Edgar's simple link of sight and emotion: 'it is, / And my heart breaks at it' (4.5.137–8), though the lines themselves were, surprisingly, cut. Indeed, Stephens encouraged laughs throughout, for instance as he unthinkingly directed 'Follow me not' (2.2.234) at Kent still stuck in the stocks. In the reunion with Cordelia, this shattered king rising from his hospital bed, wearing woolly socks and braces, embraced Cordelia with such force that all the violence of his love came flooding back. At the end, his grief was mixed with equally fierce anger, turning Cordelia's body over roughly, even, in some performances, kicking her corpse, until, at 'Look there, look there', he pulled Cordelia's corpse by the hand, crawling across the stage, and focused his eyes on a vacancy at the edge of the stage that he had filled but which the audience could only find unbearably empty.[9]

Noble's production demonstrated his consistent mastery of the main-house stage. Sam Mendes, who had succeeded with *Troilus and Cressida* in the Swan and *Richard III* in The Other Place, found the transition of scale difficult to make. His production of *The Tempest* was a confident main-house debut but I unreasonably expected something outstanding whereas it was only very good.

The problem lay most particularly in Alec McCowen's Prospero. It was certainly a small-scale performance, underplaying the grandeur of the part and turning him into a grumpy Victorian father, neither magus nor duke. Always a fine comedian, McCowen was happiest with the light touches, blowing the dust off his ducal crown as he took it out of its red velvet crown-box to begin his narrative ('Twelve year since', 1.2.53) or eyeing the affronted Ferdinand whom he has been warning of unchastity with a richly knowing 'Well' (4.1.56). Paul Taylor was not unreasonable in suggesting that this 'donnish, avuncular, mildly eccentric figure' was 'a conjuror who'd go down well at a children's party but not a man who would have to struggle desperately to conquer vengeful desires' (*Independent*). It was easy to see that this man was a fine tutor for his daughter, comfortably self-mocking as he called himself her 'schoolmaster' (1.2.173). But McCowen was not helped by Mendes's predilection for putting him up a ladder at the back of the stage, a point from which I would defy any actor, even Robert Stephens, to dominate that stage. In the Swan, McCowen, whose best work has always been in smaller theatres, would have been magnificent; on the main stage the performance lacked the authority this theatre, as much as the part, demands.

McCowen was also not helped by the production's concentration on Ariel. Noble's 1982 production of *King Lear* is better remembered for its Fool (Sher) than its Lear (Gambon). Mendes's *Tempest* ran a comparable risk, especially given Simon Russell Beale's brilliance as Ariel. The production opened with Ariel emerging from a wicker theatrical skip on stage and swinging a suspended lamp to set the storm in motion, defining from the beginning the theatricality of the production and its domination by Ariel as stage-hand. It is, though, a mistake to have Ariel visibly controlling the storm (with Prospero, too, visible through a scrim), for there are few effects in Shakespeare quite as thrilling as the realisation that the hyper-realism of the opening scene is really only a trick of the play's magician. Mendes made so much come out of or go into the theatrical basket of tricks or a folding screen painted with a cloudscape that he sometimes refused to allow the play its own theatrical effects. The dividing line between theatre and existence that makes of Prospero's connection between the great globe itself and his pageant something hovering between metaphor and reality was too immediately and permanently blurred.

But what Mendes had recognised is Ariel's curious fluidity in the play, the only character not bound to particular groups of other characters, unlike even Prospero himself. This superior servant stage-managed all the play's spectacles, down to the spirits' planting of flowers on the stage floor for the first lords' scene (2.1). It was appropriate that the spirits of this island were not 'of monstrous shape' as Gonzalo suggests (3.3.31) but rather servants displaced from the first-class restaurant of a passing ocean-liner. Ariel as the harpy, in blood-stained mess-jacket and talons from which red streamers spewed, looked like a waiter who had eaten one of the diners.

I cannot better Paul Taylor's description of Ariel's usual appearance: '[Beale's] far from sylph-like form crammed into a blue silk Mao suit, he pads about barefoot making 90-degree turns and looking like a *Stepford Wives* equivalent of Wishee Washee.' This robotic effect drastically delimited Beale's range of expression, turning Ariel's separation from the human world into a fact, rather than an unbridgeable gulf. There could here be no sense of loss or yearning in Ariel's lack of affections, 'Mine would, sir, were I human' (5.1.20), only the efficient tones of service in that deferential 'sir'. As, in a curious echo of Peter Greenaway's film *Prospero's Books*, he transformed Prospero's pattern-book of pop-up toy theatre instantly into a full-size Pollock's for the masque and peopled it with spirit automata, Ariel was the play's shape-changer. As perfect servant of course he did not betray any emotion, even when reminded of his past pains. Prospero's affectionate treatment of him, stroking his cheek or calling him nicknames, met with no response.

There was a genuine earnestness in Ariel's enquiry of Prospero 'Do you love me, master?' (4.1.48), but Prospero waited too long to say 'Dearly, my delicate Ariel' in the gap that Ariel had left and Ariel's 'No' sounded with the response, making it less a question than a regretful statement, the slowness of reply proving the absence of genuine love, whatever Prospero might appear to be saying to the contrary. Freed at the end, Ariel met the benign gaze of Prospero by spitting full in his erstwhile master's face, a superb invention, pinpointing the patronising nature of our assumption that the perfect servant enjoys serving and that Prospero's treatment of him is not in its own way as brutal and humiliating a servitude as Sycorax's. His final exit, through a previously invisible door in the stage's back wall, from the stage's blue room into a world of dazzlingly white light, was poignant and enigmatic: what after all is there behind the back wall of the stage?

Ariel's service was parodied by Stefano (whose costume echoed the island spirits), played by Mark Lockyer as a cross between Bluto in *Popeye* and Barry Humphries' Australian cultural attaché, Sir Les Patterson. Stephano inevitably turned Caliban into a version of himself; his servant was as like himself as a servant as he could manage, just as David Bradley's Trinculo, a jittery northern ventriloquist with Little Tich boots, was accompanied by his own mirror likeness in his dummy. If the dummy inhibited Bradley, locking his hands in supporting the prop, it also gave Ariel's ventriloquism ('Thou liest', 3.2.45) a physical focus as the dummy moved uncontrollably in Trinculo's hands. Characteristically the clowns' exit to 'Freedom, high-day! High-day, freedom!' (2.2.185) was back into the wicker skip under Ariel's control, not into freedom at all but the entrapment of the actor in the role.

The Stefano and Trinculo scenes were helped immeasurably by David Troughton's Caliban, bald and with long hooked fingernails only on his left hand (all the better to dig pignuts with), able to

18. *The Tempest* 2.2, RSC, 1993: 'Freedom, high-day! High-day, freedom!':
Trinculo (David Bradley), Stefano (Mark Lockyer) and Caliban
(David Troughton) in the costume skip as Ariel (Simon Russell Beale)
enters to pull it away

move from the huge rage of hatred to child-like cowering as Sarah Woodward's gutsy Miranda flew at him at 'Abhorrèd slave' (1.2.354). His announcement 'This island's mine' (1.2.334), spoken while hiding in the basket, sounded like a child's grumble from behind the bedroom door. This Caliban – or was it only a spirit version of him? – turned up as one of the reapers in the masque, breaking out of his role to roar threateningly at Prospero and thereby cueing the abrupt ending of the masque. It was no surprise that this Caliban should so touchingly describe the island's noises. What was unfairly harsh was Mendes's cutting of the text at the end so that, rather than being able to hope for pardon in return for a bit of housework ('As you look / To have my pardon, trim it handsomely', 5.1.296–7), he was locked into the theatrical skip, still roaring in pain. Throughout, the disconcerting coldness surrounding Ariel redirected audience sympathies towards Caliban.

With lords' scenes that never quite caught fire, Mendes's *Tempest*, for all its ingenuity and strong lines of interpretation, was still hampered by the very size of the stage. Anthony Ward's set, enveloping the actors in a single massive space, part cell, part shore, often left characters unhelpfully lost in space. Only in the fine celebration of theatricality in the masque did the change of scale from the Swan appear fully accomplished. Throughout there was always much to admire but admiration seems too objective a response, as cold as this Ariel.

The strengths of the season did not continue to the final Shakespeare production. Ian Judge's vision of *Love's Labour's Lost* began promisingly by choosing to set the play in an Edwardian Oxbridge. The loss of a court setting, as in Hands' production in 1991, was here more than offset by the immediately recognisable world of 'academe' in which young men, in single-sex colleges, had to balance their commitment 'to live and study here three years' (1.1.35) against such temptations as 'to see a woman in that term' (37). Nathaniel became a college chaplain, Holofernes a 'Professor of Latin' (according to the programme), Mote (Christopher Luscombe) a well-scrubbed student chorister and Costard a local delivery boy – though it was not clear where Daniel Massey's dull Don Armado fitted into this community. The dons discussed the hunt in 4.2 while watching a town-vs-gown cricket match, Costard making his entrance (4.2.81) as a batsman just bowled. In 5.1, they arrived somewhat the worse for wear after dining at High Table, Holofernes (John Normington) clutching his napkin like a miniature Pavarotti and rising to peaks of drunken fury at the barbarities of Don Armado's assaults on orthography.

With the stage floor littered with piles of books, like those in Prospero's cell in Mendes's *Tempest*, and, when the walls of the college drew away, a prospect of Oxford's dreaming spires revealed in the distance, the pastoral ambiguities of the play could be precisely focused in groves of academe. The arrival of the Princess and her entourage was not only a matter of gender but also of style, their superb costumes by Deirdre Clancy looking like a series of Edwardian fashion plates and contrasting sharply with the students' blazers. In response, the men metamorphosed into white ties and tails, though they were also to be seen in dressing-gowns and pyjamas in 4.3 as they wandered the college courts at night with their love poems.

All this was promising and supported by a fine quartet of men:

Jeremy Northam's breathlessly enthusiastic Biron, Owen Teale's nervous King of Navarre, on the verge of fainting at the prospect of mockery (5.2.390), Guy Henry's very long Longueville and Robert Portal's Dumaine (whose *risqué* jokes embarrassed the others at 4.3.278–9). It was helped too by Paul Greenwood's Boyet, thankfully free of the camp that usually dominates the role.

But such ample resources of comedy must in *Love's Labour's Lost* be balanced by an understanding of love and this the production signally failed to provide. Every expression of love was heavily underscored by Nigel Hess's overscored music swelling beneath; the young men's poems became songs and Don Armado's farewell to valour (1.2.172–6) an excess of musical ardour. The saccharine sentimentalism of musical pastiche smothered any possibility of accurate depiction of emotion under its clichés. Judge's versions of love were all of a piece with such faked romantic feeling. Jenny Quayle's Princess, for instance, fluttering her eyelashes and gazing with big round eyes, offered an engaging parody of naivety but her self-mockery was left stranded when her invitation to the King at the end, 'Come challenge me' (5.2.798), was made with an unexpectedly sensuous promise of sexual desire. Even the pain of the Worthies mattered far less than it should, especially against the operatic excesses of the heroes' performances, though the blocking of the scene was effective, young men clubbing together on one side of the stage while the women stiffly showed their annoyance on the other.

Judge's transpositions at the end epitomised the problems. Don Armado's line 'The words of Mercury are harsh after the songs of Apollo' (5.2.914–15) followed Mercadé's last line (714). The ladies too left the darkening stage, the King's offer to 'bring you on your way' (860) spoken to the Princess's departing back. In a melancholic gloom and to the sound of distant gunfire, Biron's ironic comment on the time-limits of plays now corroborated the change of mood and told the audience exactly when the experience of the play had taken place: it was the long summer of 1914 and the young men would never live out their year and a day in the trenches, a more absolute solution than the text's open-endedness.

The audience began applauding an apparent end. Only after the first bows did Armado offer the song. The opposition of Spring and Winter was lost, as the two sides were identical, Nathaniel in a cuckoo costume set against Holofernes' owl complete with mortar-board. A final company chorus to ram home the fun of a good family show was followed by Don Armado pointing the way to the exits: 'You that way, we this way'. Such treatment denied the play's discriminating perception of the knife-edge of loss, replacing it with theatrical banalities. This production seemed to be aiming rather too obviously for a West End transfer (which it never achieved), a different conjunction of Stratford and London from the RSC's usual bifurcated existence.

CHAPTER 7

1993–1994: the problems of history

Hamlet (Birmingham Old Rep Theatre); *As You Like It* (English Touring Theatre); *King Lear* (Talawa Theatre Company); *The Merry Wives, A Midsummer Night's Dream* (Northern Broadsides); *A Midsummer Night's Dream, Twelfth Night, Henry V* (RSC, Royal Shakespeare Theatre); *Henry VI: The Battle for the Throne* (RSC, The Other Place); *Coriolanus* (RSC, Swan Theatre); *Measure for Measure* (Cheek by Jowl); *Measure for Measure* (RSC, Royal Shakespeare Theatre); *Macbeth* (RSC, Barbican Theatre); *Pericles* (Royal National Theatre)

Shakespeare productions intersect with many histories. When the Duke tells Angelo 'There is a kind of character in thy life / That to th'observer doth thy history / Fully unfold' (*Measure for Measure*, 1.1.27–9), he is probably as wrong about Angelo as commentators tend to be about any theatre production. Thomas Postlewait's brilliant analysis of the difficulties of writing theatre history, using as his example the first London production of Ibsen's *A Doll's House*,[1] is as applicable to the problems of writing about a production one has seen as to the problems of recovering information about a production one has not. Only parts of the history can be unfolded.

Productions intersect with the stage-history of the play, with the history of the theatre company and with the individual histories of all those associated with the development of the project (actors, director, designers). They engage with specific historical moments: the moment of the play's first production, the moment of their own production and the moments of history to which a production may allude. Their historical connections may interconnect with their geography, their place in the theatrical map as well as the places in which play and production are set: *Measure for Measure*'s Vienna means different things at different times and a production in Stratford-upon-Avon means something different from a production in Stevenage. These problems have been apparent throughout this study but I want to foreground them to analyse the productions in this chapter.

HISTORY AND TRADITIONS

Richard Dreyfuss's production of *Hamlet* for the Birmingham Old Rep Theatre offered the spectators two intersecting perceptions of history. The attempt to locate the play at a precise historical moment had the surprising consequence of locating the production at an equally precise historical moment. Dreyfuss's vision of the play's world as a barbaric society straight out of sagas, as if nothing much had happened to the fable in its transition from Saxo Grammaticus to Shakespeare, was fired by his commendable belief in the virtues of story-telling and by his mistaken belief that tenth-century Denmark was a culture that, as he was fond of saying in interview, was 'pre-fork and pre-Christian', the former as true as the latter false. The resultant design by Alice Purcell was full of wassailing, drinking horns and serving wenches, rough-woven tunics and Anglo-Saxon necklaces. The resultant performance style seemed to be strenuously eschewing anything that might remotely suggest poetry, imagination or complication.

A cynical response might see this as an attempt to turn *Hamlet* into some version of Hollywood epic, Dreyfuss inappropriately importing his own experience as a film star. But the effect was rather more strongly to reveal the connections between film and nineteenth-century theatre. George Bernard Shaw, reviewing a production of *Hamlet* in 1897, began wryly:

The Forbes Robertson Hamlet at the Lyceum is, very unexpectedly at that address, really not at all unlike Shakespear's [*sic*] play of the same name. I am quite certain I saw Reynaldo in it for a moment; and possibly I may have seen Voltimand and Cornelius; but just as the time for their scene arrived, my eye fell on the word 'Fortinbras' in the program, which so amazed me that I hardly know what I saw for the next ten minutes.[2]

At the Old Rep there was no sign of Valtemand or Cornelius. The Reynaldo scene was present but the character renamed Osric, at the expense of the metre. Fortinbras was missing in Act 4 and the play ended, as it nearly always did in nineteenth-century productions, immediately after 'flights of angels sing thee to thy rest' (5.2.313) as the stage darkened leaving a spotlight picking out Hamlet cradled in Horatio's arms. Film is a medium that cannot tolerate much spoken language. The play rattled by. Yet, as the music swelled up under the speeches (e.g. at 'within a month' in Hamlet's first soliloquy or at 'What a piece of work is a man!' in 2.2), it suggested both the prevalence of film-music, literally to underscore emotion, and the source of such pervasive accompaniment in the incidental music of nineteenth-century theatre.

No nineteenth-century actor would have tolerated the ineptitude of Dreyfuss's staging, for instance in the placing of Hamlet's near-rape of Ophelia in the nunnery scene on top of a gallery which left Claudius and Polonius, standing under the gallery, twisting their necks to try to see what was happening. Dreyfuss wanted an audience of fourteen-year-olds while denying them any way of perceiving that Hamlet is not Rambo. The production was a historical curiosity which registered the huge gulf between film and theatre.

Dreyfuss's reputation ensured that the production was much hyped. Work like Stephen Unwin's *As You Like It* for the English Touring Theatre is often barely noticed. Unwin's commitment to touring classical theatre is impressive and deserves respect for bringing professional Shakespeare productions to Barnstaple and Darlington, Crewe and Worthing. But this production disappointed.

Unwin's programme-note promised much, for it would indeed be 'revealing to look at Shakespeare's comedy of unrequited love from a sociological, even agricultural perspective'. As Unwin recognised, the play does touch 'on many of the great changes in the Elizabethan countryside'. But the possibilities of such an approach never reached production. By comparison with Cheek by Jowl's brilliant production of the play (see chapter 4, above), revived and on tour at the same time, the English Touring Theatre's production seemed tame and conventional. Even Kelly Hunter, an actor of exhilarating risk, turned in a Rosalind of dull predictability. The production spoke eloquently of a tradition of easy, unthreatening Shakespeare in which the achievement of the play's ending had far too few obstacles to overcome.

A production may show a theatre company making a statement about itself, seeking to rewrite its place in theatre history. That was the case with the Talawa Theatre Company's production of *King Lear*. Talawa is a black theatre company, the only British black company to be 'building-based', that is a company with its own theatre, the Cochrane Theatre in London.[3] *King Lear*, directed by their artistic director, Yvonne Brewster, starred Ben Thomas as Lear. All the publicity took as its keynote the statement that Thomas was the first black actor to play Lear in a professional production in England for 135 years, since a performance by Ira Aldridge.[4]

There is of course no reason why a black actor should not play Lear, no reason why black actors should be restricted in playing Shakespeare to Othello, the Prince of Morocco in *The Merchant of Venice* and Aaron the Moor in *Titus Andronicus*. Companies like the RSC now regularly include black actors and are developing the practice of what is known in America as 'non-traditional casting' and in England, more punningly, as 'colour-blind casting'. We have grown used to seeing siblings of different colour so that Cheek by Jowl's *Measure for Measure* (see below, pp. 206–9) had a black Claudio and a white Isabella, a step beyond Nicholas Hytner's production for the RSC when both Isabella and her brother were black. I have stopped worrying about the parents in such cases; I observe the performances without trying to view colour as realist. The actor's skin colour becomes unimportant. The development of such equal-opportunity casting has been gradual and largely successful. Alongside the ethnicity of Ben Thomas, the publicity for Talawa's *King Lear* also emphasised the broad multi-racialism of the company: 'never before has a *King Lear* been performed by such a culturally varied cast in Britain', including white, black and Asian actors.

But the production offered nothing to suggest itself as the creation of a company as distinctive as Talawa. In other words, the production achieved one part of its clear aim: to be taken as a production of *Lear* to be judged like any other, a presentable example of the work of a company whose strength has been in the performance of new work and who now declared its interest in a major classical text, like Max Stafford-Clark's *King Lear* at the Royal Court (see chapter 6, above). But precisely in the measure that the company achieved that aim they obscured any reason to foreground the ethnic identity of the leading actor or the multi-racial company. The company's own publicity emphasis was effectively denied by the conventional classicism of the physical movement of the cast and the Received Pronunciation of most of the voices (except David Webber's Kent when disguised as Caius and the occasional piece of rap from Mona Hammond's Fool). While the aim of the production was a deliberate intervention in the history of black actors in Britain, the success of the production was that it denied its own publicity. Mark Ford (*TLS*, 1 April 1994) complained that, apart from the electronic music that the composer Matthew Rooke described as 'the pulse of Africa', 'there is little else directly African in this production', but Ford missed the point. The cultural ambivalence of black theatre in Britain, required to be simultaneously visible and invisible in its ethnicity, is especially exposed within the context of classic theatre. Talawa's *King Lear* represented precisely this ambivalence of cultural perception, both foregrounding difference in its music and Lear's colour, and demanding assent to its cultural assimilation in its electronic treatment of that 'pulse of Africa' and in Ben Thomas's conventional performance.

There are times when a company's response to ethnicity is more clear-cut. The Alabama Shakespeare Festival, based in Montgomery, Alabama, has long been aware that African-Americans are under-represented in its audiences. In 1992 the company received $1 million from the Lila Wallace Fund to spend over five years specifically to increase the proportion of African-Americans visiting the theatre as well as developing its repertory of plays reflecting black and Southern experience. It was no surprise then that in 1994 the company mounted a production of *Othello* as a way of encouraging African-Americans to attend the backbone of the company's repertory as well as its productions of new plays. Producing *Othello* and casting a black actor as Caliban in its production of *The Tempest* were direct consequences of the company's funding and its commitment to transforming its audience from the white, middle-class and elderly audience that is the traditional theatre-going public of the region. Here function is clear. In Talawa's case the cultural politics of colour in the theatre had blurred.

AN ALTERNATIVE HISTORY

It might appear that I intend only to carp about the forms of engagement with history that productions offer. But, following the success of their *Richard III* (see chapter 6, above), Northern

Broadsides continued to suggest a different and far more successful engagement with the historical structures of Shakespeare production than the English Touring Theatre and Talawa managed to
present. As their publicity proudly proclaims, the *OED* defines a
broadside as a 'powerful verbal attack' and their demonstration of
the vigour of Shakespeare's language shows the definition has
been taken to heart. Where Talawa's actors were confined by a
concept of orthodox Shakespearean acting, Northern Broadsides'
casts work with a relish that communicates to the audience with
great immediacy. Their heterodoxy of voice is part of the
company's heterodoxy of style, shown not only by the 'poor
theatre' of minimal sets and simple costuming but also by refusing
to cover the text with the production. As an alternative to the mainstream, the company successfully maintained its impact and its
quality.

Northern Broadsides toured two productions: *The Merry Wives*
(*sic*) in the autumn of 1993 and *A Midsummer Night's Dream* in the
autumn of 1994. As with their abbreviation of the title, there was
no mention of Windsor anywhere in *The Merry Wives*. The 'wise
woman of Brentford' had moved north to 'Bradford' and the cast
had accompanied her. The play lost its connection with the court
and castle, its sense of a noble world present in the same town and
of London being only twenty miles away. It did not lose anything
of the sense of a town community, a bourgeois world in which the
characters lived. Dressed in contemporary costumes, the characters were placed with great exactness in their society: Conrad
Nelson's Host, with shirt-collar up and buttons undone to reveal
his gold chains, clearly ran karaoke nights at the Garter and saw
himself as a pop star *manqué*; Ishia Bennison's Mistress Quickly, in
apron and with a duster always at the ready, earned her living as a
cleaner and had ambitions to retire as a Blackpool landlady;
Edward Peel's Ford, when metamorphosed into Brook, donned
sandals, sleeveless sweater and flat cap, becoming the archetypal
put-upon husband of the seaside postcard. Even the 'foreigners'
were precise manifestations: Lawrence Evans's Caius patriotic in
his red, white and blue clothes with long shorts and knee-length
socks with tricolour garter tabs, his catch-phrase 'By Gar' turning
by the end of the play into a good northern 'Bugger' (pronounced
'Booger'); David Crellin's Pistol a smooth customer in Italian shiny
trousers and white socks. Most powerfully of all, Barrie Rutter's

Falstaff, a tough figure in blazer and grey trousers, sported a variety of awful ties, ending up with an MCC tie to which he obviously had no right whatsoever.

Falstaff's aim here was purely financial. With boundless self-confidence he assumed the wives would fall for him. While he was happy to take the 'entertainment' (1.3.39) Mistress Ford offered, his motive was her 'rule of her husband's purse' (47–8) and his eyes grew as big as saucers at the sight of Ford's 'bag of money' (2.2.167), a silver suitcase full of neatly arranged bundles of notes, out of any gangster film. If later, disappointed at the failure of his amorous adventures, he became an overblown child, able to be pulled around by the women as a great baby, and grinning sheepishly from ear to ear whenever either wife tickled his belly, the venom returned at the end when he seized on the failure of Mistress Page's plot for the marriage of her daughter, relishing seeing the biter bit as he directed 'I am glad . . . that your arrow hath glanced' (5.5.226–7) very sharply at her. Falstaff's love of money took on distinctly regional overtones, a man brought up in the belief that 'where there's muck there's brass'. This was no Londoner out of his depth but a northern schemer with a firm conviction that there is such a thing as a free lunch.

But Rutter also played the comedy, using his padded size to fine effect, especially as he nearly crippled Mistress Ford by leaning on her knee to help get over a bench, or when he attempted to get into a buck-basket that seemed impossibly small to contain such a bulk, until finally, unable to climb in, having to fall backwards into it, with Mistress Page then jumping on top of him to squash him down. In these scenes he was aided and abetted by Elizabeth Estensen's Mistress Ford and especially Polly Hemingway's Mistress Page, in a purple suit with a tight skirt that always suggested a woman ready to burst out of her clothes. In the letter scene (2.1), this Mistress Page was amused but also genuinely intrigued by Falstaff's offer, only sure she would reject it when Mistress Ford's copy appeared. As sure of herself as Falstaff of his own abilities, Mistress Page's delight in the trickery was infectious. She was quickly reconciled to her final defeat, a supreme pragmatist enjoying her life.

Throughout, the production played the narrative with clarity, even managing to show what was happening in the revenge of Caius and Sir Hugh on the Host where the text is unhelpful and incomplete. Even the catechism of young William Page (4.1) worked, especially when I saw the production in Bangalore, India, performed to a local audience who had had a proper classical education and understood the Latin jokes. As the legacy of colonialism ensures that Latin continues to be taught in all English-language schools attended by middle-class Indians, the scene could be properly laughed at for Mistress Quickly's mistakings. Even – or, perhaps, especially – in a production where Herne's Oak was a ladder and Falstaff's horns were bicycle handlebars mounted on a colander, the production's energies were all being generated by the company's pleasure in the text.

The same held true for Northern Broadsides' *A Midsummer Night's Dream*. Rutter, as Theseus and Oberon, demonstrated a flexible and delicate response to the verse, allowing the rhythms of the lines to underscore meaning throughout with proper attentiveness to the variation in the metrics of blank verse. This *Dream* was especially full of doubles and mirrorings: not only the doublings in the casting which are now a commonplace in productions (Theseus/Oberon, Hippolyta/Titania, Egeus/Quince, Robin/Philostrate), but also the less common doubling of workers and fairies, a piece of theatrical thrift that was recommended for small-cast productions of the play as early as 1661.[5] But Rutter's production also explored mirrorings of moves so that Hermia's running leap high in the air into Lysander's arms in 1.1 as they contemplated flight metamorphosed into the same move at the height of the confusions in the wood when he rejected her with 'Get you gone' (3.2.329) or when the blocking for the workers' horror at Bottom's transformation into an ass was repeated and echoed in their joy at his return in 4.2.

It was also a world of music where Titania's lullaby became a big choral number with all the cast joining in. But music and song were often the accompaniments to striking dance. Northern Broadsides' *Richard III* had used traditions of clog-dancing; in *A Midsummer Night's Dream* the sources were more eclectic, including a dance of amity for Oberon and Titania to the sound of gypsy music, suggesting the links between fairies and another race of travellers. Choreographed by T. C. Howard, who also played an athletic dancing fairy, the performers danced and sang energetically and enchantingly. The dominant style was drawn from morris-dance with fairy king and queen wearing long coats covered in ribbons and the other fairies costumed in versions of male morris costumes, as if the production had deliberately misunderstood Titania's reference to 'The nine men's morris . . . filled up with mud' (2.1.98). Morris-dancing suggests a style of dance that is complex and formalised, an echo of the patterns and permutations which the characters go through in the course of the play. But it also, much more significantly for the production, recalls dancing as a genuine rural tradition, a major part of the history of popular music in England. This was not a nod to some weak version of Merrie England; instead the dance tradition offered a dignified resonance of a working-class form that commanded respect as well as nostalgia. It also allowed Andrew Cryer's Robin to carry echoes of the jester/fool of morris into his cocky wide-boy.

From the first moments on, Rutter's *Dream* showed deep affection for the play's depiction of a proletarian world more in touch with truth than anything in the society of the play's aristocrats. The performance's prologue showed the Athenian workers hard at work but their tinkering and tailoring, weaving and carpentry turned into a combined and harmonious rhythmic tapping. Throughout, the workers were funny but never ridiculed. Their first scene (1.2) began, as in Peter Brook's famous 1970 production, with the sound of a factory siren, so that the casting took place in a tea-break. In their overalls and their enthusiasm, these workers enjoyed the prospect of their amateur dramatics and we shared their pleasure, without ever patronising them. Each of them found new riches in the play's comedy: Flute rehearsing Thisbe with tea-towel round head and table-cloth round waist, Snug plainly terrified at the prospect of the long speech of explanation Bottom was composing for the Lion.

They were led by John Branwell as Bottom, a confident man of down-to-earth good sense, plainly the star of the local workingmen's club where he spent most evenings. Abandoned by his friends, wearing an ass's head magically created by Robin's turning inside out the cushion on which the sleeping Titania had rested her head, Bottom sang 'The ousel cock' (3.1.118–26) to the tune of 'On Ilkley Moor'. Titania was far from amused at being woken – 'What angel' (3.1.122) was snarled in annoyance, for Oberon's drug does not work on her hearing but her sight. Exiting with the fairies at the end of the scene, seated on the hospital trolley that was Titania's bower, Bottom looked totally bemused but also a man perfectly willing to try anything once and able to get used to the life of luxury with attendant servants that seemed to be on offer.

Precisely because these earnest workers had never been mocked by the production, their own play could modulate rapidly from comedy to something unexpectedly moving, as, for instance, when Thisbe's summoning of the 'sisters three' (5.1.331) drew the three women on stage (Hippolyta, Hermia and Helena) tenderly towards him/her, finding their own sympathetic echoes in Thisbe's plight. Yet there was space for a fine wild bergamask.

But Rutter's minimalist approach to production was well accomplished by Jessica Worrall's set in which the transition to the wood was achieved by unrolling a long ribbon of green carpet, and the return to Athens was defined by the workers, entering for 4.2, rolling the carpet back up again. In both productions, Northern Broadsides demonstrated the sheer power and delight in simplicity, the pleasures of theatricality, the exhilaration of theatrical metamorphosis. The result was that the actors' skills and the characters' work dovetailed together to produce a belief in the dignity of work that was never sentimentalised. Unlike Unwin's *As You Like It*, where the processes of rural life had seemed so alien to the actors, Rutter's *A Midsummer Night's Dream* found labour always worthy of respect, whether actor or weaver, John Branwell or Bottom.

STRATFORD HISTORIES

While Rutter's *A Midsummer Night's Dream* carried a few distant echoes of Brook's, the moment of the play's recent theatre history against which all productions now seem to be measured, Brook's *Dream* is bound to be present with particular intensity for the RSC. All productions in Stratford since Brook's have negotiated with it by defining their distance from it, defiantly taking very different approaches from the abstraction of Sally Jacobs' set, for instance. Adrian Noble's 1994 production chose instead with great boldness to confront Brook head on, allowing for the echoes but defining its own view of the play.

From the first sight of the set, I could not get Brook's production out of my mind. Part of the cause lay in Anthony Ward's design. It was not so much the red room, strong central doorway

and swing for the first scene – though they did seem like a dream-
echo, a coloured transformation of Sally Jacobs' white box and
trapezes for Brook. The echo was much stronger in the costuming,
particularly of the lovers, where the strong colours and the indistinguishability of Lysander and Demetrius, differentiated only by
a blue or green shirt over their white trousers, was extraordinarily
like the earlier production.

But the resonance of Brook's *Dream* was much more significantly
apparent in other ways. First was the energy and athleticism of the
lovers. As they careered over a bare stage, banging in and out of the
line of doors at the back of the stage that appeared for the wood
scenes, or the two doors that could rise out of the stage floor unat-
tached to any walls, their frenetic speed turned them into the
puppets of farce, driven by the unidirectionality of the desire they
happened to be feeling at any particular moment. It was both
absolutely right and extremely funny, particularly the men shuffling around at high speed on their knees or leaving for their duel
so literally 'cheek by jowl' that it looked as if they were about to
tango. The lovers are largely puppets of their emotions, forced to
live out their feelings. What Noble perceived was the women's pain
within this process; Hayden Gwynne's Helena had begun as the
woman doggedly determined to win Demetrius by being submissive; a woman who announces 'I am your spaniel' (2.1.203) positively wants to be told to 'Stay' (2.2.93). But in the middle of the
chaos of the chases of Act 3 she could not help the tears coming.

The lovers became mechanical creatures in a farce which, like
all good farces, depended on doorways. But dreams have doors too
and the worlds of the play here met. Theseus and Oberon,
Hippolyta and Titania and even Philostrate and Robin were
doubled yet again, though I yearn for a production that will
explore the difference between the roles rather than their connections by using six actors rather than three. But it need not follow
from the doubling that the events of the night are therefore a
dream dreamed by Theseus and Hippolyta. Theseus comments on
Pyramus's death, played here by Bottom so movingly that
Hippolyta cried at the sight, 'he might yet recover and prove an
ass'(5.1.305–6) and the last word triggers all the associations, all
the echoes that riddle the play. But Alex Jennings' Theseus
offered the word as a very deliberate nudge to Hippolyta, as if to
say 'this is the man who was the ass in your dream' and Stella Gonet's

Hippolyta later offered Bottom her hand at a moment of mutual recognition, suggesting that for them, like the lovers, the convergence of dream, 'their minds transfigured so together' (5.1.24), is a happy memory. Theseus had to put himself rather rapidly between them, for fear that the balance of their marriage might prove fragile. Connecting the world of the forest and the world of the court in this way diminishes the real power of the play: the play's glorious awareness of the parallel, usually unseen world of the fairies.

Like Rutter's, Noble's *Dream* had that most unfashionable of achievements, a real relish of the play's verse. Memories of verse-speaking tend to be golden. I remember well how Alan Howard (Brook's Oberon/Theseus) made the play's poetry sing. Alex Jennings was even finer. From the first line of the play, he allowed the language all its musicality. He was equalled by Stella Gonet, initially content, eyes closed in sensuous anticipation of her approaching wedding-night but, like Ishia Bennison for Northern Broadsides, made furious by the treatment of Hermia, storming off stage at 1.1.122 to leave Theseus following her rather awkwardly. Jennings' command in his approach to the language matched the command of his presence, but as Theseus and Oberon his authority was troubled.

Jennings' Oberon was isolated; all the fairies belonged to Titania. Only Barry Lynch's sexy little Robin seemed to accompany Oberon, a wicked imp who pulled down his trousers to be scolded by his master, revealing a bottom covered with shaggy hair. This Oberon began with a malicious glee, laughing outright at the news that the changeling boy's mother died in childbirth. But he was also capable of stroking Helena's hair caringly, and later the malice was tinged by melancholy. The sight of Titania and Bottom filled him not with triumph but with pain. It was not the pain of the cuckold, though there was no question in this production but that Titania and Bottom had sex: the sight of Bottom's bottom bouncing rhythmically up and down on top of Titania, as the inverted, cushion-filled giant pink umbrella that represented the bower rose at the interval, told as much; so too did Bottom's sexual exhaustion on his reappearance in 4.1, while the fairies giggled and smirked at every possible double meaning (like 'weapons' and 'nuts', 4.1.11 and 35). Oberon's pain was instead a lonely exclusion from their happiness, an isolation of a man whose revenges had exacted a harsh price even as he gloried in his power.

Bottom's happiness was complete, shown by the broad grin with which he contemplated the pink brolly as he left the wood. Desmond Barrit's performance was controlled and brilliant clowning. Though the text suggests that Robin gives him only an ass's head, Barrit's ass's ears seemed to have exploded through his motor-cycle crash-helmet while his false teeth made him into an asinine Ken Dodd. Robin has not endowed him with an ass's penis and the mournful gaze down the front of his trousers at 'Methought I had' (4.1.206) was a vulgarity. But the immense confidence with which he took control of his first scene modulated finely into the gormless vulnerability of the transformed Bottom later, nervously singing to himself in a 'monstrous little voice' at Titania's appearance. Moving and funny – a rare combination – this Bottom returned from the wood with much of his bumptiousness gone.

Noble, like Rutter, had doubled workers and fairies but Noble's worker-fairies were costumed with parodic echoes of their other selves: the Snug fairy with a lion's mane, Flute wearing a version of the little brolly he had worn in his hat in 1.2 and so on. But as their fairy alter egos, the workers moved with a new lightness and airiness appropriate to their new status as spirits of another sort. If this suggested that the worker-fairies are projections of Bottom's dream-imagination, it made no sense for them to be present in 2.1, before Bottom has entered the world of this dream, an unnecessary confusion of the dream-structures Noble was developing.

Noble is not naturally a director of comedy; his comic invention for *A Midsummer Night's Dream* was too often made up of very old pieces of comic business. But overall his control and imagination were assured, matched throughout by the playing of his cast and the wondrously inventive imagination of Ward's design, especially his forest of dangling light bulbs or the dangling cocoons in which the lovers slept, awaiting the sound of the hunting horns to bring them out of their chrysalises into a new world.

Noble's *A Midsummer Night's Dream* proved extraordinarily successful, touring to great acclaim in England and the United States and providing the basis for Noble's film. Yet it is difficult to find its success as a particular consequence of its own merits, other than its easy and undemanding style. Other productions have been as rapturously received, yet do not tour the world. The significance of the production lay primarily in the RSC's need for such a success and the opportunity of a US tour provided the fillip necessary.

It seemed to be raining a lot in Noble's Athens. Though the weather cleared up by the interval, the workers arrived for their first scene to the sound of pouring rain, and Robin and the first fairy descended into the wood of pulsing light bulbs sheltering under green umbrellas. The effect was to make this Greek wood take on overtones of England, that dankness which Angela Carter so brilliantly ascribes to the play.[6]

This suggestion of a geographical transposition was much more strikingly dominant in Ian Judge's production of *Twelfth Night*. This was Ian Judge's third Shakespeare production for the RSC, following *The Comedy of Errors* and *Love's Labour's Lost*, and I did not like any of them. Paul Taylor, writing in the *Independent*, described this *Twelfth Night* as 'tourist-friendly' but its attractions were clearly wider than that: all audiences took great delight in it and I felt like Malvolio in standing out against it. Talking to his cast, Ian Judge announced, according to the programme, 'When I look through the hedges of New Place or sit in the gardens of Hall's Croft, I understand Illyria', echoing J. B. Priestley's comments in *Seeing Stratford* (1927), also quoted in the programme. While the play's costumes were conventionally Elizabethan, Stratford was brought in by the presence on the horizon of a row of half-timbered houses, to which a church was added before the entry of Olivia and the priest in 4.3. The locale and the costumes made of the play's events an episode in the history of the town where the audience was watching the production, Illyria made a part of local history, rather than the romantic otherness more usually identified in *Twelfth Night*'s location.

The storm had certainly brought a fair number of tourists to Shakespeare's Illyria, if not quite as many as to Stratford in the summer. But the dark and troubling world of Shakespeare's play is not as reassuring either as the view through the New Place hedges or as Ian Judge's production made of the play. Russell Jackson, in a fine review in the *TLS* (3 June 1994), summed it up perfectly: 'the darkness of the play is made wistful, the cruelty muted, and the gender confusions are amusing and wittily set out – but not so as to cause undue apprehension'. This *Twelfth Night* was trying very hard to be charming and as a result it seemed to me unpleasantly ingratiating, ironing out most of the dangers and troubles of the play. It is not being subservient to a concept of text to argue that the pleasures of this play should be hard-won, worrying, uncertain.

When Malvolio arrives to complain about the late-night drinking-party, 'My masters, are you mad? Or what are you? Have you no wit, manners, nor honesty, but to gabble like tinkers at this time of night?' (2.3.83–5), we should have some sort of sense that Malvolio is right, that there is here 'no respect of place, persons, nor time' (88). Olivia's is a house of mourning, a fact Judge defined through a dumb-show before 1.3, as Olivia grieved at her brother's tomb in the rain, though it was too comically dominated by the disjunction between the enormous figure of Desmond Barrit's Malvolio and his tiny umbrella which could barely keep him, let alone Olivia, dry. Sir Toby's carnival is both attractive and ill-mannered, selfish in its rejection of Olivia's grief. The ambivalences of rank present in Malvolio's calling this crew 'my masters' must carry a charge. But the party in this production was so tame, its threats so muted, even its singing so tidily harmonised with the interventions of the theatre's musicians, that all attention at this moment focused on Malvolio's excesses.

With Desmond Barrit as Malvolio excess was the order of the day. For some reason, Malvolio was Welsh; if the suggestion was that his puritanism is like Welsh chapel morality, it did not square with the way he crossed himself at every mention of Jove (e.g. 2.5.171). I shall long remember his desperate attempt to manoeuvre his mouth into a smile, the muscles making the lips twitch uncontrollably until his hands pushed them into a semblance of a grimace, but I am afraid I shall also remember how Barrit changed Malvolio's error in his reverie so that 'play with my—' (2.5.58) was no longer the character's automatic reaction of toying with his steward's chain, which Count Malvolio would no longer wear, but instead became a hand toying with his genitals. At this point Barrit picked on a member of the audience, cast a disapproving glance at her and pointed with his parasol towards the exit. But the dirty mind was Barrit's, not ours, the line coarsened for a cheap laugh. Malvolio is not Frankie Howerd and the humour of *Twelfth Night* has nothing to do with the rather different culture of the English seaside postcard.

The sheer nastiness of the tormenting of Malvolio was properly in place in the scene in the dark house. But the terrible sight of a man trying to gather the last remnants of his dignity at his final exit was cheaply lightened again when, throwing down his ruff and boots, he arranged the last few long strands of hair over his bald pate before leaving. The gags, funny though they were, were working against our attempts to respond sympathetically to a man so deeply unsympathetic.

The whole production was always too reassuring, even at the end as the line of rejects (Sir Toby, Sir Andrew, Antonio) trudged through a thunderstorm ('With hey, ho, the wind and the rain') down the Stratford street before Feste was unceremoniously thrown out of the front door. This ending was much more restrained than Judge's previous explorations of the end of Shakespearean comedy but the image made too comfortably explicit the disturbing way that at the ending of this comedy so many characters have vanished.

In the same way, Viola's anguish at her brother's loss was smoothed over by the sight, immediately after her rescue in 1.2, of Antonio carrying Sebastian safe to shore. But for the most part the love-tangles were more effectively in place than the rest of the play. Emma Fielding's Viola moved from a full-throated romanticism in the storm scene, played against billowing sea-cloths straight out of any nineteenth-century production, to a boyhood that was deliciously troubling in its ambivalence. She was both a convincingly boyish Cesario and an extremely attractive one, the sexual charge lying not in androgyny but in her male beauty. No wonder that Cesario's grief made Orsino kiss him at the end of 2.4, one of a series of perplexing kisses that confused the couples. Sebastian's easy kiss of Antonio as they parted was met by an openly homoerotic response from Antonio. Hayden Gwynne's Olivia was disturbed by Cesario's lips, half-suspecting the real gender of her object of desire. This Olivia, so confident and sure of herself early on, in her grey and gloomy house, was thrown completely off balance by her desire, a woman who has never before felt anything remotely like this.

Clive Wood's Orsino was a complex performance, not diminished by the production's over-frequent recourse to sentimental music swelling up at each scene's end. At first Wood's Orsino, swooning on cushions in his dressing-gown and pyjama bottoms, languorously self-indulgent in the romanticism of the music, seemed of a piece with the genial sentimentalism of the production but the abrupt transition of 'Enough, no more' (1.1.7) placed the excess. This Orsino, whose puffed-up chauvinist sense of the largeness of masculine emotion ('There is no woman's sides / Can bide the beating of so strong a passion / As love doth give my heart', 2.4.92–4) matched his confidently displayed hairy chest, was reduced by his perplexity to threatening violence, brandishing a dagger at Olivia before turning it on Cesario where it was met by a wide-eyed masochistic hunger for any expression of his love, a driven appetite that pushed Viola's body down into an animalistic crouch. There was here a frightening emotion that was unusual in a production whose care and tact was exemplified by Malvolio's carefully practised dance-steps in the letter scene. But such disruptive emotional power was out of keeping with the way that Viola's new costume for the second half turned out to be identical to Sebastian's new costume when the latter has, as far as I can tell, had no chance to go back and change.

Where Judge diminished *Twelfth Night*, in part by turning it into a piece of local history, Matthew Warchus turned *Henry V* into a complex piece of national history. Warchus's thoughtful production gained substantially from Charles Edwards' extraordinary lighting design, by far the most intriguing exploration of the main-house stage's potential for many years, setting spaces and shadows, creating closed arenas with lowered spots and using much side-lighting to produce startling changes in the perspectives on the actors.

Warchus investigated the play as a series of overlays of history. Its opening and closing image, with Henry's red regal gown with a gold collar placed on a dummy, roped off like an exhibit in the Imperial War Museum, established a sense of royal myth. But the robe was surrounded by tall red poppies, the strongest modern symbol of the cost of war. Tony Britton's Chorus was an old soldier, in military camel-coloured overcoat and campaign ribbons; the poppy in his buttonhole and his rich theatrical voice summoned up past wars. With the house lights still up he strode to an electrical box on stage, turned the handle and put out the house lights, taking the audience from his contemporary perspective on the history of war into the play's sense of its own history. The action inverted the effect of Jacobi's Chorus in Branagh's film who turns a switch to illuminate the film studio. But Britton's Chorus was also a reminder of what will happen to the myth of Agincourt, so that in the middle of the battle, at Henry's lowest ebb, he could come forward and help the King to his feet, reassuring him of the outcome that the Chorus, the military historian of the future, already knew.

Chorus's perspective, a survivor's connection to past wars, was set against the frequent appearances of a crowd of English non-combatants, principally women and children, dressed in 1940s costumes, both visitors to the 'museum' and a reminder of the civil cost of war. This was a less successful ploy, as was the return of the poppies, planted on the field of Agincourt: they became too obvious a symbol of loss, a clichéd image of Flanders. The fertility of Warchus's imagination needed restraining at such a moment. The sleight-of-hand at Agincourt that draped the corpses of the murdered boys over the corpses of the French prisoners offered another too easy equivalence. But the decision to follow Gary Taylor's suggestion[7] of having the prisoners killed on stage brilliantly produced a reaction of protest and horror from Clive Wood's Pistol, a coward forced to kill and loathing it, nearly vomiting after the killing, an unwilling participant in the actuality of the war off which he has been freeloading.

Occasionally hit and miss in its effects, Warchus's *Henry V* was also not helped by the unevenness of the cast. At times the players were lost under the exhilarating scale of scenic effect that Neil Warmington had designed. Some seized their chances. Monica Dolan as the Princess found the comedy of the wooing scene: when Henry mentioned 'armour' (5.2.138) she touched her arm, remembering one of the words she had learned in her English lesson. But she also registered blank incomprehension as Henry went on and on in English, blithely unaware, as he started to enjoy his own rhetoric, that it was all passing her by. But there was also her suspicion that Henry's ability to understand French was greater than he was letting on and hence that she dare not speak to Alice at all. It made of the scene something dangerous, even as she copied his gesture, holding out a hand for him to shake, learning the body language of the conqueror. And the scene modulated uncomfortably as the English nobles, returning to the stage, giggled at the very male sexual innuendos the King's conversation with Burgundy (often cut) conjured up (5.2.279–316). It was characteristic of the production that this advantage was followed by the regrettable transfer of the Dauphin's lines to Bourbon, following the Quarto text, which meant that there was no point in

19. *Henry V* 4.4, RSC, 1994: Pistol (Clive Wood), Monsieur le Fer
(Sean O'Callaghan) and Boy (Daniel Evans)

keeping Henry's final triumph over the Dauphin: the French King's disinheriting his son and nominating Henry as his heir (330–9).

There were many such moments of uncertain gain and loss. I have never heard the listing of the dead at Agincourt spoken with such a sense of mourning, when even Davy Gam Esquire was well known to the survivors and his death a reason for mourning. But the long roll of the French dead, a mounting litany of the obliteration of the French nobility, should have been balanced by the French King's listing of some of the same people earlier in the play (3.5.40–6), a speech Warchus cut. The connection was not in place, the local effect powerful but insufficiently resonant.

But the local effects were exhilarating, especially the use of the upstage area to suggest tableau visions of a heroic version of the narrative, images from a *Boys' Own* history book. The finest was an Agincourt icon of the defeated English yielding under the hooves of the French cavalry, the vision of what the French anticipate from the impending battle, the last image before the interval. Earlier, as the invasion fleet embarked, Henry was incorporated into a heroic tableau of the spirit of adventure, a photo-pose waiting for the court painter to capture it for posterity, and then, as the pose was held through the narrative of Falstaff's death, Henry turned out of the static image, glancing back at his old companions. Henry would never forget (as when, for instance, he explained the reason for Bardolph's execution for theft to the Boy, 3.6.108–14) but his memory was beautifully counterpointed by the way that, in 4.7, Fluellen cannot remember Falstaff's name. The tension here between the heroic and the personal was strongly underlined.

Other effects were similarly well judged: having a female Governor of Harfleur feminised the city and provided a direct response to the horrendous threat of rape and murder that Henry had offered, his language and her body directly connected. Other large effects manifested ambivalence: as the dawn rose at Agincourt, with a fiercely rising spotlight of the sun capturing Orléans's 'The sun doth gild our armour' (4.2.1), the stage floor tipped to a steep rake, revealing that the rake carried the dates '1387–1422', the limits of Henry's life, so that the battle was fought across his tomb.

It was also fought under a collection of pieces of armour hanging down on chains (no longer the set of swords that had dangled down for the aristocrats to choose from at the announcement of the expedition at the end of 1.2), an eerie reminder of Williams' warning about the King's reckoning, 'when all those legs and arms and heads chopped off in a battle shall join together at the latter day' (4.1.134–6). There was, at moments like this, a remarkable combination of performance and commentary, sufficient to offset mistakes like the grotesque costumes at the French court.

We have had enough for now of theatrical, rhetorical Henries, shouting the big speeches to the upper balcony. Iain Glen's Henry, needing to encourage his troops before the battle, did so quietly, allowing the lines to make small local points, refusing to let a rising tide and rising volume overwhelm meaning. At the end of the speech he could isolate words in a line, letting the audience hear the point of 'with us' in the conclusion: 'whiles any speaks / That fought with us upon Saint Crispin's day' (4.3.66–7).

The Renaissance calendar was far more aware of saints' days than we are but Henry's definition of the battle's day as the 'Feast of Crispian' had never seemed so right before. Glen's Henry was a deeply religious man. Others may talk of the reformation of the wild Prince Harry but this King Henry was born-again in a rather modern sense. Canterbury's assessment in the first scene, 'Never was such a sudden scholar made; / Never came reformation in a flood / With such a heady currance scouring faults' (1.1.33–5), was entirely accurate. Henry turned to his books to remind the others of the threat from the Scots; he knelt to the Archbishop and kept with him throughout the rest of the play the crucifix his spiritual father had given him. Every time he mentioned God he spoke in genuine humility. The scenes the night before the battle did not here show Henry 'Walking from watch to watch, from tent to tent' (4.0.30) but instead a man who desperately wanted to find a quiet place to pray and kept being interrupted. As Henry says 'I and my bosom must debate awhile' (4.1.32) and the line was not the usual pretext to allow a little surreptitious wandering around in disguise. The scenes built towards the prayer itself and, later, the deeply felt tones of the culmination of this sequence, the last line before the battle, 'And how thou pleasest, God, dispose the day' (4.3.133).

The *Non nobis* that Henry calls for after the victory became a large-scale chorus, giving the request an importance entirely in character for this king who would hand over the cause of victory to God. Serious-minded, sincerely religious, this Henry, often seen shouldering a huge pack like his troops, took his share of the work of war. He was part of a band of brothers and was respected for it. Glen is a handsome actor but his performance had nothing to do with his good looks. Instead there was acute intelligence at work here, thinking through the lines and the role as he charted Henry's life.

Warchus explored the overlays of history, the historicising of Henry and the Agincourt campaign into a peculiarly national myth. Katie Mitchell's production of *Henry VI Part 3* for the RSC's tour was a far more rigorous recreation of a sense of history, a single-minded investigation of the possibility of creating a past world of ritual and gesture. The productions shared an interest in the motifs of religion but what had been restricted to the King in Warchus's work now became a general truth, a continual counterpoint to the action.

This was the first time that *Henry VI Part 3* had been performed on its own in Stratford, though it has often been seen, heavily abbreviated, as a part of productions of the first history cycle. 'Part 3' is an unenticing title for a touring production and Mitchell retitled the play *Henry VI: The Battle for the Throne*, summing up her identification of the play's action as an endless series of battles unfinished by the end, with Richard of Gloucester a malevolent presence outlining his future plans. Mitchell trimmed the text, eliminating or combining characters to fit the limitations of a fifteen-strong touring company, but the cutting and pasting was neat and efficient. The result was a bleak exploration of the viciousness of human behaviour, a tense vision of political brutality.

Mitchell was concerned to place the aristocratic ambitions and political manoeuvrings in a play in which, unlike its modern meaning, the personal is political, as power is sought by hungry individualists. The framing of the action was achieved by three devices. The first was typified by the weather. Heavy rain, snowstorms, bright, falling autumnal leaves and clear dawn light – the full gamut of the English climate was heard or seen. The production's meteorology was supported by hints of an animal world, bird-song and sheep bleating, sounds that were both reassuring in their normality and disturbing in their transformations into the sounds of horses in pain during the battles. There was a reminder of a natural world in the bark that covered the stage floor, as in

Mitchell's RSC production of Thomas Heywood's *A Woman Killed with Kindness* in 1991, and in a pine-tree on the side of the stage from which Margaret tore a branch to serve as the mocking crown she put on the Duke of York before killing him in 1.4. It was echoed too in the rough crosses of twigs tied together that accumulated along the sides of the stage as the production unfolded. Most strongly, it was present in the white and red roses, the symbols of a natural world abused for human ends and civil war. It was there most exquisitely, to the accompaniment of bird-song and a babbling brook, in the tuft of feathers Henry plucked from one of the wings that dangled on the belt of a gamekeeper and blew into the air: 'Look as I blow this feather from my face, / And as the air blows it to me again' (3.1.83–4). Suggesting continuity in a world beyond the political, the device belittled the high terms which the characters invoke.

Their actions were also placed by the production's borrowings, from *Richard II* and from *Gorboduc*, of lines defining the horrific impact of war on the state, spoken most often by characters marginal to the action, warning ineffectually of the consequences of others' actions: Exeter, borrowing the Bishop of Carlisle's words from *Richard II*, warned at the end of the first scene that 'Disorder, horror, fear, and mutiny / Shall here inhabit, and this land be called / The field of Golgotha and dead men's skulls' (*Richard II*, 4.1.133–5). It is a language of apocalyptic political prophecy substantially missing from *Henry VI Part 3*. Like the language of pastoral, it was generated for the production by the emblematic scene that was the still centre of the performance, Henry VI's meditations at the battle of Towton and the grief of the two anonymous figures who define in their acute pain the impact of war on family, the son who has killed his father and the father who has killed his son, a scene played with intense awareness of its symbolic power. Characteristically the two soldiers brought in no corpses, finding the identity of their dead in two roses they unwrapped.

The third frame, again a device Mitchell had explored in *A Woman Killed with Kindness*, was an acute sense of the immanence of religious practice in Renaissance culture. The stage was dominated by a picture of St George, the patron saint invoked in the play, an image often left spotlit on a darkening stage. Beside the double metal doors through which the various armies crashed was a medieval wooden statue of a *pietà*, before which characters often

20. *Henry VI: The Battle for the Throne* 1.1, RSC, The Other Place, 1994: Henry VI (Jonathan Firth) swears an oath with Richard, Duke of York (Stephen Simms)

knelt muttering prayers, while yet another step in the faction making and breaking unfolded and ignored them, as, for instance, when a half-naked servant prayed during the scene in the French court (3.3). Above the stage hung an immense bell whose sound resonated endlessly, a church bell pressed into unholy uses, as when it was rung to summon the Duke of York's troops to compel Henry to nominate him his heir in the first scene.

Throughout, the action was punctuated by liturgical chant and procession. Over the corpses of the two slaughtered young men, Rutland and the Prince Edward, a woman keened a 'Miserere' before the dead figures rose to be led out by the hand through the audience. More elaborate choral Kyries marked the murders of the two most significant adults, the Duke of York and King Henry himself, the singing led by a woman holding the bloodied napkin and mocking crown for the former and a feather and rosary for the latter, as the smell of incense filled the theatre.

This framing was not just a reminder of the central importance of religious ceremony in medieval and Renaissance life. It contrasted with the savage use of religious gesture by the warring factions: in the first lines of the production, as Warwick made a vow (1.1.21–4), he knelt to confirm the oath; a parley between the Yorkists and Lancastrians was preceded by all kneeling and crossing themselves; under the rusty, well-used armour, the men wore rosaries, a very visible mockery when in 3.2 the three York brothers, a distinctly unholy trio, ridiculed the prostrate form of the mourning Lady Gray, supplicating with her arms out-stretched. In a play of repeated oath and prayer, in a world in which the forms of religion were a conventional recourse to underline and validate all action, the echoes of a genuine religion in turn underlined the political manipulation of the divine for entirely worldly ends. Only 'the good King Henry the Sixth' seemed removed from it.

The cast were almost all new to the RSC, a welcome infusion of new blood. Tom Smith's Richard of Gloucester, shaven-headed and with his withered arm strapped to his body by belts, always biting his nails, made the most of his amazed self-discovery of his potential for evil, the logical outcome for this frustrated child in an adult's body. Jonathan Firth's Henry VI, a young man who has been king from nine months old, coughing and red-eyed after long imprisonment, showed brilliantly the terrifying irrelevance of contemplative goodness in the play's politics.

A production as slow and unrelieved in its intensity as this is not easy to watch but the action was set out with exemplary clarity, making the programme's careful provision of a family-tree unnecessary. *Henry VI Part 3* may have seemed an eccentric choice for Mitchell's first professional Shakespeare production but the outcome superbly demonstrated the high standards with which the RSC approaches its touring and with which Mitchell approaches all her work.

Where Warchus had spread his view of *Henry V* across its afterlife in history and Mitchell had defined *Henry VI Part 3* as a historic moment, David Thacker's *Coriolanus* took a more familiar route, the choice of a particular historical moment as analogy. Unlike other analogies I have found wanting, the choice here was provocative and coherent, supporting a production of *Coriolanus* more generally successful than any of the ones I have so far considered. Thacker's *Coriolanus*, played in the Swan Theatre, pinpointed the moment of the play as the *ancien régime* teetering on the brink of the French Revolution. Without the direct claim of relevance in Bogdanov's production (see chapter 4, above), the choice was still immensely suggestive: a world of popular uprising against oppression, a revolution that was overtaken by a dictatorship, a world of ideals betrayed, above all a moment of historical possibility, 'a republican Year Zero whose future is a blank sheet' (Irving Wardle, *Independent on Sunday*). Coriolanus became, from this perspective, a potential Napoleon and I thought I saw Toby Stephens' hand occasionally straying towards his belly, hinting at Napoleon's most clichéd gesture. The history of the French Revolution can be seen as a series of attempts to become Rome, from the hairstyles and furniture (both seen on stage in this production) to the imperial dream. *Coriolanus* is set in a Rome that is still only a small republic city-state, not yet an empire, a Rome that is, in effect, not yet Rome, not yet the potent symbol it will become, as France is not the Rome its leaders have so often wished it to be.

There were imprecisions in the analogy. As Thacker made clear at the opening, the potential for revolution in Rome is the result of starvation, not solely of political oppression. The striking opening image of corn cascading into an open trap on the stage, watched by Coriolanus in supremely arrogant pose, set the tone for the opening crowd scene, full of plebeians who really were starving, picking over grains that missed the chute, rocking and staring, twitching and drooling. It was a moment counterbalanced by one after Coriolanus's banishment when the grainstores were open and the plebeians could collect corn by the bowlful. The people's tribunes, especially Linal Haft's Sicinius, were genuinely concerned for their charges. Yet, as the tribunes basked in the adoration of the crowd, it was easy to see why, for all their good intentions, these middle-class leaders, tightly buttoned-up over their well-fed bodies, could so easily become potential Robespierres.

Their actions seemed far preferable to Philip Voss's Menenius, a smug patrician whose whole attitude was typified in a remarkable gesture on his first entrance: as the plebeians held up hands, palms upwards, beseeching him for food or money, he turned their hands and shook them, offering the politician's genial expression of solidarity and friendship but no act to relieve their suffering. Voss's performance was outstanding, work of consistent intelligence and subtlety, a superlative investigation of the language of the role to construct both the politician and Coriolanus's substitute father. Even the tribunes had to respect Menenius's perceptiveness; it was his warning about starting a process that one cannot control – particularly in the First Senator's lines, spoken here by Menenius: 'The other course / Will prove too bloody, and the end of it / Unknown to the beginning' (3.1.329–31) – that made them realise the necessity of giving Coriolanus a second chance. By the end of the play, the hollow emptiness of his response to his rejection by Coriolanus, 'I neither care for th' world nor your general' (5.2.102), was devastating in its despair while fully justifying the guard's awestruck response, 'A noble fellow, I warrant him' (108). 'Noble' was now much more than a definition of social class, a powerful transformation of Menenius's earlier comment on Coriolanus, 'His nature is too noble for the world' (3.1.254), a line which Voss played for its laugh.

There was a problem in the analogy over the backing image of the play, an unfinished sketch of Delacroix's 'Liberty Leading the People', for Delacroix's image was a response to the failed revolution of 1830, not the 1790s. But the potency of the image lay not only in the symbolism of the revolution in arms. Strikingly, Delacroix accords symbolic power to a woman; Delacroix's Liberty became the iconic expression of the control over the political world that Volumnia would have wished to have. For, in this male world, female power is necessarily vicarious: Volumnia cannot go to war except through her son. At the end of the play she becomes the saviour of Rome, 'the life of Rome' (5.5.1), but at the point where she was the centre of political activity in her own right, she could only wear an appalled mask of grief, even while Virgilia and Valeria were enjoying their own part in the procession and the crowd's response.

In *The Importance of Being Earnest*, Lady Bracknell advises Cecily: 'The chin a little higher, dear. Style largely depends on the way the chin is worn. They are worn very high, just at present.'[8] Caroline Blakiston's Volumnia had obviously heeded the advice: her power was seen in the angle of her chin, a woman prone to looking towards the heavens in ecstatic anticipation of her son's triumphant return to Rome. At the Herald's announcement in 2.1, she alone looked out towards the audience, again her head held high. The distance from that to her lying prone at her son's feet, imploring him to give way, charted the immense changes in their relationship. But this was also a woman who loved her son; her one loss of control came after Coriolanus left Rome, a wailing wild animal who was as mad as the rumour Sicinius reports (4.2.11). Her attack on Virgilia's grief, 'Leave this faint puling and lament as I do' (55), was a hysterical scream at a woman whose puling had the dignity that Volumnia had for the first time in her life abandoned.

Volumnia's rival in this production was not Virgilia but Aufidius. Barry Lynch's Aufidius was a subtle representation of the warrior as politician, a man who, from our first encounter with him, was in total control of events in Volscian power politics. It was only right that he was, in the second half of the play, always accompanied by the two spies, Adrian and Nicanor. His love for Coriolanus was epitomised in the caressing of his rival's body in their embrace at his house, as Coriolanus stood with his arms stiffly around Aufidius, unsure how to react. Lynch picked up the tremendous homoerotic charge in Aufidius's language, the man who compares Coriolanus's arrival to his own wedding-night. Yet the achievement of that love, the transformation of military rivalry into co-leadership, is Aufidius's crucial political misjudgement, love clouding his acuity, leaving him vulnerable to Coriolanus's charisma. In the final image of the production, Thacker resisted the last stage direction, 'A dead march sounded. Exeunt bearing the body of Martius'. Instead Aufidius, having been the first to attack Coriolanus and having kicked the dead body and stood on it until a Volscian senator stopped him, now found that 'My rage is gone' (5.6.147), without a trace of the irony the line can bear. Trying to lift the corpse under the armpits, he called 'Assist' (154) but the others scurried off the stage and he toppled back with the dead body on top of him. His final gestures, like a beetle turned on to its back, were both an embrace and an attempt to extricate himself from under the oppressive weight of the corpse, an ambiguous moment of love and submission perfectly in keeping with the production.

Like his mother, Toby Stephens' Coriolanus looked the part. Stephens was far younger than Dance, Pennington or Branagh. This young buck, full of himself, captain of the first XI at school, leader of the Officer Training Corps, had barely scraped a couple of A levels after much private tutoring. Aufidius's taunt of 'boy' was a real threat for someone still unsure of his adulthood, comfortable in his arrogant posing but reluctant to reveal a body that was not only scarred but also showed a physical vulnerability. At

Aufidius's house, dirty, barefooted and barechested, his hair now combed back rather than forwards in the high Roman fashion, Stephens' Coriolanus was unrecognisable – we, like Aufidius, needed him to name himself. Stephens played the garrulity of a man who cannot control his speech and finds himself whipped along by his own unmediated attitude towards language. If the whining tone became tedious it was because Coriolanus himself can be tedious. Not a great performance, it sat comfortably in a production of clarity and imagination. *Coriolanus* is a frighteningly difficult balance to achieve; Thacker very nearly managed it.

HISTORICAL MEASURES

That almost any play can define different relationships to the present is obvious but *Measure for Measure* occupies an especial position in its negotiations with contemporary society. Where Nunn in 1991 had sought to find its place in Freud's Vienna, the two major productions in 1994, by Declan Donellan for Cheek by Jowl and by Stephen Pimlott for the RSC, plotted the play's modernity in contrasting ways: Donellan in making it immediately contemporary, Pimlott in gesturing at the development of British society across history from the nineteenth century to the present. Where for Donellan *Measure* was a definition of the moral relativism of the modern state, Pimlott found in it a recapitulation of the male ethos that defines the history of the establishment. Both productions followed the logic of their position with rigour and power.

Cheek by Jowl played on a minimalist set by Nick Ormerod: a black desk and some stacking chairs with a single strip of red material, suspended upstage and off-centre, offering the merest suggestion of a state banner, echoed at the end by the red carpet unrolled for the Duke's return to the city. Objects on stage could, in this context, take on different valencies: Angelo's desk, beside which he knelt in prayer before taking on his new role at the end of 1.1, could become the altar at which Isabella prayed simply by her placing a cross on it at the start of 1.4. When in 2.4 he came close to raping her on the desk, the place of assault carried with it both its meanings, both an assault in his office and a blasphemous act at her shrine of veneration.

There was in all this little to distract the eye from the actors but,

21. *Measure for Measure* 3.1, Cheek by Jowl, 1994: 'She should this Angelo have married': The Duke (Stephen Boxer) and Isabella (Anastasia Hille) talk across Angelo (Adam Kotz)

in his treatment of the interrelationship of scenes, Donellan made the actors into parts of the set. Frequently the first line of a scene would be pitched loudly across the final image of the previous one before the tableau broke, the furniture was rearranged and the next scene properly begun. The technique gave first lines especial portentousness but also became a part of the simultaneity Donellan was exploring. This simultaneity was also present in the sight of characters left on stage for scenes in which they had no part, silent reminders of the play's problems: hence, for instance, Angelo wrote away at his desk through 1.3 and Claudio was seated on a chair upstage from the end of 1.2 until his encounter with the Duke in 3.1. Their mute presence meant that other characters could talk about them across them. They counterpointed and interwove with the language of the scenes, visual reminders of the issues literally personified.

But the scenes were also imbued with nicely observed realist details: Angelo's officer handed Isabella a cup of tea as she waited to talk with Angelo in 2.2 with the result that she then had the problem of where to put the cup down; Escalus gave Pompey a cigarette which he tucked behind his ear for later; Mariana shrieked with laughter as Isabella explained to her the 'good' she 'comes to do' (4.1.51); Isabella and Mariana checked the scripts the 'friar' had given them while waiting for the Duke's return in 4.6.

　　The strength of Isabella's religious belief made it only right that she should encourage Claudio to kneel beside her and recite Psalm 23 after he had accepted in the single word 'Yes' her instruction to be 'ready . . . for your death tomorrow' (3.1.106). But his anxiety then caused him to interject lines into the psalm while she continued to recite all the more strongly, trying to block out what he was asking of her, until he had to put his hand over her mouth to stop her chanting. Claudio was often to be seen kneeling in silent prayer. His faith was apparently as fervent as his sister's, each ready to respond to anything by trumpeting their faith so that after her first interview with Angelo Isabella prayed ecstatically downstage, counterpointing his soliloquy (2.2.168–92). Against this, comfortable social behaviour became a thin veneer to cover a desperate emptiness beneath for those for whom religion was not an immediate living presence, so that, for instance, Lucio asked the Duke 'I prithee pray for me' (3.1.439) while on his knees, crying and holding on to the Duke's waist, before switching back into his usual streetwise mode with its bravado now hollow.

　　Initially, the Duke, Isabella and Angelo seemed to be starting from the same moral position. But as the action developed, Isabella (Anastasia Hille) clung to her sense of virtue and ethical behaviour with a fervour that was increasingly desperate and therefore shrill in her continued espousal of a code whose integrity was no longer in keeping with the universal corruptibility that Angelo's fall manifested. Cold and hard in her beliefs, Isabella was at the same time passionate and physical, able to place her head on Angelo's breast, stroking him as she encouraged him to 'Go to your bosom' (2.2.140). But with her nun's habit she had adopted an absolute doctrine that removed her from the world's reality, so that her lesson to Angelo, 'man, proud man' (2.2.120), was both teacherly and spoken through tears, tears which would flow ceaselessly through the rest of the play as she tried to staunch them with a hankie and was left shaken and snuffling.

　　Terrifyingly isolated, Isabella found her code irrelevant to the world. She was rejected brutally by Claudio (Danny Sapani) at the end of the play as he embraced Juliet and kept his back firmly turned to his sister; he found it easier to hand Lucio a cross and kneel to pray for him as he was dragged off to marriage than to respond to his sister's plight. Isabella finally tried to sneak away and was herself dragged back and forced, passively resisting, to hold the Duke's hand as the couples stumbled from the stage. Only in Mariana, who sang 'Take, O take those lips away' herself while taking large gulps of vodka, did Isabella find a genial companion. (Pimlott's Mariana, incidentally, had turned not to drink but the paint-brush, working at huge abstracts in her moated grange.)

Angelo (Adam Kotz) and the Duke (Stephen Boxer) began the play as two connected points from which their position allowed them to diverge. Each could have done what the other did. But in their attitude to Isabella they were as one: as Michael Billington commented in the *Guardian*, 'the Duke is Angelo's double in his furtive attraction to an Isabella who represents the sexual temptation of corrective chastity'. In their exercise of rule both men explored the possibilities of power without responsibility so that their similarly logical approach to law and morality resulted only in revealing their own hypocrisy; Angelo's assault on Isabella was no different from the Duke's fixing. When the Duke proposed the bed-trick (3.1.245) Isabella reacted by leaving the stage in shock and walking round the auditorium while he was left on stage trying to convince her. Acquiescent rather than enthusiastic, she returned to the stage, the interval coming at this point.

For the trials of Act 5, Donellan's Duke, a director in control of his assembled cast, set up a microphone into which Isabella and Mariana, isolated in the empty spaces of the stage, had nervously to speak their accusations straight out to the audience, checking their scripts at awkward phrases like 'concupiscible intemperate lust' (98). Pimlott's Isabella and Mariana were similarly isolated but not through the bare spaces around them; Pimlott had taken the extraordinary step of recruiting 'citizens of Vienna' from 'the citizens of Stratford', as the programme put it, so that each woman in turn was a lone female presence on the stage floor while behind them were ranged dozens of middle-aged men, clad in gowns, wigs and mortar-boards, the embodiment of the male system of the law and government, against which their pleas seemed especially vulnerable. Mariana in her red dress was discrepant enough from

22. *Measure for Measure* 5.1, RSC, 1994: Isabella (Stella Gonet) intercedes with the Duke (Michael Feast) for Angelo (Alex Jennings, left)

the black robes of the men but Isabella (Stella Gonet), now for the first time wearing a man's suit – by implication her brother's – and a large crucifix, seemed deliberately transgressive in her cross-dressing, an affront to the principles of religion reminiscent of recent reactions to the ordination of women. As Isabella spoke of sex with Angelo the language itself was offensively public, speaking of the most private of acts, the kind of language that, in this establishment culture, should never be spoken in the presence of a woman, let alone by a woman. But her simple statement 'And I did yield to him' (101) was greeted by the violent ridicule of raucous smutty male laughter so that she yelped an interjected 'No' back at them.

The main part of Ashley Martin-Davies' huge set consisted of a curved back wall with a gallery above and, as this scene unfolded, Juliet, gagged and held back by a warder, brutalised by her experience of prison, wrestled in helpless hysteria with the appalling revelations. Her wordless witness placed the onstage action as, for instance, she pounded with her feet, desperate to stop Isabella pleading for Angelo's life. The shocks of the sequence registered with violent emotional force so that the news of Angelo's 'private message' (457) had Isabella screaming and Mariana pounding on Angelo's weeping body. By the end, the Duke's proposal of marriage was met by Isabella's slapping his face, then kissing him and then, just as the audience was starting to feel uncomfortable with the cliché, rejecting him sharply and standing apart in tears, twitching. The Duke's final speech was spoken nervously as the stage darkened and Isabella cried helplessly. It could not have been a more disconcerting ending.

Though Pimlott's control of the huge sweep of Act 5 was outstanding, it had an excellence that the rest of the production lacked. Too often the play was burdened by the production's materials. On either side of the forestage, for instance, a massive ducal throne confronted an electric chair which seemed its grey mirror-image. But the electric chair was only indicated when spotlit as the interval came, and the throne used only for the Duke to sit in during the Act 5 events. The chairs offered a symbolic discourse that the production substantially refused to follow up.

Pimlott did, however, explore clashes of comedy and violence. At his first appearance, before Escalus in 2.1, Bille Brown's Elbow was the archetypal P. C. Plod, an amiable joke; but as he hauled Pompey on stage in 3.1 there was a strong threat that Pompey was facing a serious beating from which only the presence of the Duke as 'friar' at first saved him. The picklock that defined Pompey's crime (285) was blatantly planted on him by Elbow and, when Pompey in desperation bit Elbow's ear and the blood flowed, the risk of police brutality was stopped now only by Lucio's entrance. The state's violence was seen too in the bloodied and bruised prostitutes who accompanied Mistress Overdone to prison.

Lucio (Barry Lynch at his most streetwise and charming) could threaten at the slightest excuse. As he munched an apple through his dialogue with the Duke in 3.1, he could drag the unwilling 'friar' into a waltz. At the end of the conversation he dropped the apple core in the friar's hood and, when the Duke plucked it out and threw it at him, he turned aggressively – before pulling another apple out of his pocket and smiling with infinite malevolence.

If violence was as much a work of the state as of its subverters, then the Duke's abandonment of power was all the more culpable. Michael Feast's Duke, cultured and ironic from the start, had never had control and found in his new position of outsider the opportunity to speak of his pained knowledge that he has long seen 'corruption boil and bubble / Till it o'errun the stew' (5.1.315–16). Nervously incompetent, he was in striking contrast with Alex Jennings' ramrod-stiff Angelo, his babyface with its smirk in contrast to the brutal authority he enjoyed wielding. Jennings' easy assumption of power meant that he could keep Isabella waiting while he finished his papers in 2.2 before slamming the book shut and striding over to shake hands. When Isabella pointed out one passage in her ever-present bible, Jennings could instantly counter it by finding a contrary passage to show her (2.2.77–84). As his growing awareness of his own desire took over his body, he sat hunched and crushed, his sense of his own worth destroyed and turned to pitiless self-loathing. The climactic scene with Isabella moved from a hypothetical debate, a series of intellectual proposi- tions, until he crashed to his knees at 'Plainly conceive, I love you' (2.4.141), a fall from which he quickly recovered to make 'Answer me tomorrow' (167) into a sneer that raised a laugh from the audi- ence. This Angelo's power seemed dangerously limitless: when he remarked to Alfred Burke's slightly tipsy Escalus that the Duke's 'actions show much like to madness' (4.4.3) he seemed to be plan- ning to get himself off the hook by having the Duke declared insane and taking over the state himself. Crushed by the play's end, he walked off to marriage so fast that Mariana was left to follow some way behind in his wake.

Pimlott largely succeeded in anchoring his view of the play's moral politics in a construction of English society as a historically coherent object, a world whose genial acquiescence in the forms of nineteenth-century social behaviour could be threateningly exposed by the problems of the play.

PROBLEMATIC HISTORIES

Directors have their own histories. Their previous work – their the- atrical biographies – set out a context within which their approach to a particular play may be defined. This is especially true when they return to a play they have previously directed. Max Reinhardt's series of productions of *A Midsummer Night's Dream* was a life-long sequence of encounters with the play, each time finding new emphases and new possibilities. But sometimes the success of one production prejudices the chances of success of a subsequent one.

Adrian Noble's 1986 production of *Macbeth* for the RSC with Jonathan Pryce in the title-role was a remarkably complete triumph, a dense and thoughtful consideration. Returning to the play in 1993, Noble seemed to have nothing left to say. There were echoes of earlier effects, like the playing of the cauldron scene at the banquet table of 3.4, but their repetition seemed now drained of interest, a gesture towards a previously strong moment of theatrical imagination. Elsewhere Noble offered 'hardly more than a sketch' (Irving Wardle, *Independent on Sunday*). Indeed some scenes, played in front of a downstage curtain like Victorian front-cloth scenes (e.g. 1.7 and 2.4), were more concerned to cover elaborate scenic effects being set upstage than to be investigated for their own potential: as the Macbeths embraced at the end of 1.7, now fully resolved in their plans, the curtains parted to reveal the Scottish court at a banquet, strongly lit by candles, at the sight of which the guilty couple started before the effect dissolved as the banqueting table trucked back upstage, as if the entire scene, so rich in possibility, had existed only for this one rather uninteresting surprise.

At the production's centre lay the decision to cast Derek Jacobi as Macbeth. Jacobi is unusually capable of exploring the attractions of goodness but that is hardly a qualification for tackling Macbeth. He started as a decent and honourable soldier, apparently without any ambition, confused by the witches and ready to laugh off their prophecy until the sudden confirmation of his new title disturbed him. A sensitive man, he remained far too full of the milk of human kindness, never finding the single-mindedness of brutality – at least until he carefully hacked at Young Siward's arms and legs before breaking his neck in an act of casual violence. Until that point Macbeth stayed vulnerable in his increasing isolation. Jacobi reined in the lyricism of his voice: only in the world-weariness of the last scenes was there a glimpse of his range, eloquent in his vision of the infinite sadness of lonely old age, beautiful in his slow uncovering of the poetry here.

But it was only at this late stage that the language was allowed to take over. As John Peter commented (*Sunday Times*), 'this most elemental of tragedies needs as little machinery as possible: hydraulics and massive, sliding furniture simply divert attention from the thunder and terror of the words'. This set was over-mechanised but the mechanics did nothing to suggest the supernatural, inhibiting rather than helping the witches. Only in the Porter scene, as the swirling dry ice took on strange shapes and the Porter was 'momentarily immobilized by some ugly intimation of hell' (Paul Taylor, *Independent*), did the production acquire the supernatural dread and the fearsome presence of evil so greatly lacking elsewhere.

If Noble seemed hamstrung by the exhaustion of his own invention, Phyllida Lloyd was hamstrung by the inexhaustibility of her imagination in her production of *Pericles* for the Royal National Theatre. In a play with little stage-history, the director's decisions can be untrammelled by the pressures of expectation.

In the event, the production lost sight of the play. There were two sets of irreconcilable oppositions that meant that the play was bound to disappear in the process. The first was between Lloyd's interest in narrative and her investigation of the play as dream, a world of infinite possibility. As Peter Reynolds sets out in his interesting account of the rehearsal process, Lloyd 'insisted on the need for everyone to keep in mind the need to "tell the story clearly"'.[9] But this laudable aim, the play as 'a literal journey', was in tension with her view of the play as 'Pericles' dream; a fantastic journey in time and space, one which breaks all the rules of logical progression' (Reynolds, p. 6). Mark Thompson's set was dominated by a massive vertical disc with a huge central doorway, encrusted to suggest a moonscape and mirrored in the giant circle of the Olivier's revolve; the powerful image offered both the world of dream and of madness, 'another form of wandering in the mind' (Reynolds, p. 6). But the performance denied the connections of narrative, the repetitions and mirrorings that give shape to the play, so that the production retained only the fragmentation of a dream and left the dream unanalysed.

The second opposition was between actors and set. Where Thacker's 1989 RSC production in the Swan left the play relatively unencumbered, Lloyd was seduced by the potentialities of the Olivier stage for scenic spectacle. As Reynolds describes, the production processes of the National, like those of the RSC, mean that the set design has to be fixed long before rehearsals begin. Thompson's set, elaborate in conception and technically demanding in execution, created immense difficulties for the National's technical crew, with lifts repeatedly sticking and revolves demonstrating a predisposition not to revolve. After the first week of performances, some of the technical effects were simply abandoned and the programme carried an extra slip announcing that performances would not 'encompass all elements of the original design' but the changes, 'taken for safety reasons', had resulted in a 'slightly modified version . . . re-worked by the Director' – as frank an admission of failure as one could expect to see.

From their first encounter with the set model, 'some of the cast felt disempowered', a feeling intensified as the rehearsal process moved the focus 'from acting to staging' (Reynolds, p. 4). The reunion between Pericles and Marina was initially staged with the whole disc of the revolve raised to create a sunken space, with the result that this most intimate of scenes began with Pericles, curled up below the lip of the revolve, completely invisible to the audience and with Marina able to be seen only from the waist up. The reunited pair stayed either invisible or dwarfed by the machinery throughout the scene. The restaged version, played on a flat stage floor, allowed Douglas Hodge's Pericles and Susan Lynch's forceful Irish Marina a space in which they could at last act freely; if not outstanding, the second version was at least a marked improvement.

Lloyd and Thompson's free-associating dream denied the play's geography. No longer a precise voyage round the Mediterranean, Pericles journeyed to places of myth: a Welsh Simonides lived near the North Pole where the dance of the knights was accompanied by Pericles and Thaisa playing icicles like a xylophone; Tarsus was somewhere in Inca culture with a statue of Pericles treated as an object of cult veneration, while Mytilene, dominated by Kathryn Hunter as a pox-ridden, rasping Bawd modelled on Barbara Windsor, was nowhere in particular. Like Viola, I kept wondering 'What country, friends, is this?' (*Twelfth Night*, 1.2.1).

There was much cross-gender casting to weird effect: Selina Cadell's Helicanus was the worst kind of girls'-school-play Polonius, Tom Yang a Dioniza of screeching camp, and even the virtuosic Kathryn Hunter (playing a very odd triple of Antiochus, Cerimon and Bawd) was reduced to appearing up a ladder as Antiochus, with a long beard, sunglasses and apparently ten-foot tall, waving stick-like extensions to her arms, a position in which no performer can be expected to do much. It was only too predictable that at Ephesus, as Pericles announced to Diana the story of his life, everyone else on stage was wearing a head-dress like a lampshade or jellyfish that covered their faces so completely that the only way one could identify Thaisa was by her bare arms (she was the only black performer in the scene) and there was no possibility of seeing her face respond to the news.

Such a disastrous production creates its own niche in the history of Shakespearean performance but it is a history that I would rather not have had to chart. The staging of some plays suggests that directors are only too willing to ignore the lessons of history while leaving behind them a trace that their successors will perhaps not heed either. No one could respond to the experience of such catastrophes with any belief in the inevitability of progress. Theatre historians cannot be Whiggish.

CHAPTER 8

1994–1995: two by two

A PAIR OF *HAMLET*S

The year's two productions of *Hamlet* came with such hype that they provoked the postponement of a third, Sam Mendes's planned production with Simon Russell Beale. Both expunged the disappointing memories of Noble's 1992 production. Each was sharply defined by its choice of theatre. To mark the renaming of the Globe in Shaftesbury Avenue as the Gielgud Theatre in honour of Gielgud's ninetieth birthday, Peter Hall directed *Hamlet* in the West End with his own company, starring Stephen Dillane, Horatio to Mel Gibson's Hamlet in Zeffirelli's film. It was a tribute to Gielgud as the greatest Hamlet of his generation but also a way of defining a distance from the poetic Prince Gielgud had made so emphatically his own between the wars. Jonathan Kent's production for the Almeida company starring Ralph Fiennes, which must have been originally planned for the small scale of the Almeida, needed, in the aftermath of Fiennes' huge success in *Schindler's List*, to find a larger space. This *Hamlet* moved east, using the Hackney Empire, an enormous, once splendid theatre designed by Frank Matcham, now more commonly used for music-hall.

Dillane's performance negotiated brilliantly with the ghost of Gielgud. While his Hamlet foregrounded its modernity, it did so only after emphasising Dillane's ability to offer a lyrical Hamlet in the Gielgud mould. Indeed, initially, in the first court scene (1.2), Dillane surprised by his attention to old-fashioned virtues of eloquent verse-speaking, as if Hall's long-standing obsession with the beat of the verse and the force of line-endings had created a new Gielgud. But the trauma of the encounter with the ghost of his father generated in this Hamlet a bitter jokiness and a harsh modernity that, immediately and irrevocably, made him disjunct from the rest of the characters. Dillane, unlike many recent Hamlets, was consistently funny but the humour had an edge that was defined by the reactions of those at whom it was directed: the accuracy of Dillane's mimicry of Sinden's rich and fruity pronouncements and *sotto voce* mutterings as Polonius did not, as usual, pass Polonius by; instead the audience was made insistently and disturbingly aware of the anger the mimicry caused its object.

Sinden's Polonius was certainly not a figure to anger lightly. Dressed, like the other courtiers, in red frock-coat and breeches, black stockings and black top-hat, Polonius looked laughably like some rare variety of beetle, but behind the brilliance of the comedy which one might have expected Sinden to achieve were clear markers of something very different: his comment to Ophelia 'I do know / When the blood burns' (1.3.115–16) was a sudden and very personal memory cutting through the facade of the efficient, harsh old man. But Sinden's Polonius was also still an astute and powerful politician, gazing as intently as Horatio and Hamlet at Claudius's reactions to the murder of Gonzago, as if he knew what had happened or now realised the truth about the death of old Hamlet, or making his recommendation to Claudius, 'confine him where / Your wisdom best shall think' (3.1.189–90), into an explicit suggestion of imprisonment in a dungeon.

The processes of this court were defined by its paperwork, as Laertes offered his petition to return to France and Hamlet his written request to return to Wittenberg, the former accepted by Claudius, the latter firmly rejected before Claudius passed the paper to Gertrude who tore it in two as Hamlet helplessly acquiesced. Though Michael Pennington's Claudius was often drunk, always reaching for a glass of whisky or red wine, his aggressively male presence was insistently dangerous, as politically astute and pragmatic as his chief counsellor. He was also sexually charismatic, inducing in Gwen Taylor's Gertrude a painfully inappropriate girl-ishness in the intensity of her desire for him, as she grinned far too much throughout the court scenes, and making her rejection of Claudius after the closet scene a transforming moment for her. As Claudius tried to close in on her, Gertrude firmly kept her distance, as if the 'rank sweat of an enseamèd bed' (3.4.82), which Hamlet had forced her to smell face-down in the sheets, had been transferred to the once overwhelming object of her passion. After the interval, Gertrude had changed costume to a dignified and matronly black, now, as it were, being her age, rejecting her sexuality at precisely the moment when Ophelia would most fully express hers.

Gina Bellman's Ophelia carefully laid out Polonius's clothes on the ground to suggest his corpse and then obscenely rode on them, like a parody of sex. It was with great difficulty that, later in the scene, Laertes held Ophelia away to avoid the full, open-mouthed kiss she was trying to give him. Hall was centrally concerned with the characters' finding of their own sexuality: his talk to the company at the start of rehearsals (printed in the programme) argued that 'shifting sexuality, uncertain sexuality, is at the heart of the play' and that 'for the Renaissance . . . there wasn't heterosexuality or homosexuality, there was just sexuality'. The ease with which Dillane's Hamlet could discard Ophelia suggested that Hamlet found sexuality unimportant by comparison with the isolation in which he found himself. The isolation was marked in his question to Rosencrantz and Guildenstern, 'what make you at Elsinore?' (2.2.271), asked in the full knowledge of the inevitability of yet one more betrayal to add to the world's stock.

Reviews of the production drew attention to the moment at which Hamlet stripped naked on the stage but there was nothing remotely sexual about it. In 4.2, as a direct consequence of lugging out Polonius's corpse, Hamlet was covered in blood. Calmly and neatly, he took off his clothes and stuffed them in a laundry-bag until, as he was led off to Claudius, his naked body became a comic robot in his mocking walk. For the confrontation with Claudius Hamlet was now dressed in a nightgown, his nakedness clothed but in such a way as to ridicule Claudius, especially as he tried to hop off to England like a pantomime fairy waiting for the flying wire to work. The act of stripping was comic but also a rational response to the bloodstains, rendered absurd and humorous by its transposition to an inappropriate place and moment, a climactic moment in Dillane's presentation of the character as a figure who, in the aftermath of the encounter with the Ghost, now found himself consistently in the wrong place at the wrong time. Hamlet's response to this displacement was to use all his powers of thought, but without ever finding in thought a solution or a resolution. The isolation produced in him actions that were entirely logical for him but, equally completely, bound to appear madly illogical to everyone else, as the rest of the cast stayed in the social world Hamlet had been forced to abandon.

The different facets of Dillane's performance came together magnificently on Hamlet's return to Denmark. His encounter with Alan Dobie's wry and precisely real Gravedigger was a game of two equal wits, enjoyed by both of them, both outsiders at Claudius's court. The wit was not here an act of hurtful patronising, as it had been and would be again when he forced Laertes at dagger-point face-down into Ophelia's grave so that he could sweep the mound of earth on all three of them. His entry into the funeral scene (5.1.250–4) allowed the re-emergence of the full-throated lyrical and heroic style, the Gielgud voice, unheard for hours in this long production, but in its new context, so completely changed from its earlier resonances, this too came over as only another mockery, a vicious reaction to Laertes' grief.

By this stage, Hamlet was in remarkable control, almost able, it seemed, to prevent the play's continuation. His response to the proposed duel, 'How if I answer no?' (5.2.131), completely floored Osric who took a long pause as he tried to find an answer. In the final scene, Hamlet thrust Claudius through the leg to render him immobile before killing him with a lunge vertically down through his back, an act of extreme brutality, leaving Claudius slumped like a drunk in the gutter as the wine poured down from a very large goblet. Only death now left Hamlet surprised.

Throughout, the production modestly stated its brilliant insights. In the closet scene, for instance, Hamlet set up two large court portraits as if to give his mother a lesson in art history, before he slashed at Claudius's portrait, turning the picture into a thing 'of shreds and patches' (3.4.93). Most satisfying was a double so obvious I wonder why it is not more often explored: Michael

Pennington played both Claudius and his brother. The latter's torments were explored in an eloquent lyrical voice, the huge verse
paragraphs effortlessly placed. The degeneration from old Hamlet
to Claudius, the move from the heroic to the cruel and bloat king,
was all the sharper as it played across the actor's own appearance.[1]

As Claudius stormed out of the play scene, Dillane's Hamlet
grabbed a prop crown and seated himself in Claudius's place,
neatly suggesting an ambition that Hamlet could perform but
never feel. He was still holding the crown as he saw Claudius at
prayer and put it down, stopping only to consider the murder on
his way out. The crown was an unemphatic touch. At the parallel
moment at the Hackney Empire, Ralph Fiennes' Hamlet played
with various pieces from the players' costume skip, trying on an
orange robe and a mask, experimenting with heroic postures and
strange walks. Hamlet the performer is a familiar trope but here,
with the prayer scene played in front of a drop like a front-cloth
scene in a nineteenth century melodrama, the costume became
Hamlet's way of freeing himself by experimenting with the role of
an active avenger. But when, in the closet scene, Hamlet's orange
robe was echoed by Gertrude's dressing-gown, the effect lost
meaning, the logic of the disguise no longer followed through.

Jonathan Kent's production was full of such inconsequentiali-
ties. But what marked it above all was its sheer pace. An emphasis
on speed was a strong feature of a number of productions in
1994–5. Here it made lines and scenes rattle by as if the determi-
nant on the production were a three-hour time-limit. As Matt Wolf
suggested (*Herald Tribune*), Kent's was an 'impetuous yet unin-
flected staging' in which Fiennes' was a Hamlet 'for whom events
cannot happen fast enough'. There could be no pause here for
reflection. The soliloquies were gone through at a speed which left
the audience marvelling at Fiennes' technique but never engaging
with Hamlet's processes of thought: for John Peter in the *Sunday
Times*, 'To be or not to be' 'sounds, not like thought moulding
itself into speech, a subtle intelligence grappling with a problem,
but like an obsession that has already been rehearsed more than
once' and, while he was prepared to read this as the character's
'spiritual equivalent of probing and probing an open wound', I
found it only a demonstration of an actor's skills, a superficial
effect that damagingly disengaged actor from character.

Where Dillane's Hamlet had been emphatically modern,

Fiennes' was a throwback to a romantic tradition of aristocratic Hamlets. As he shouted 'My fate cries out' (1.4.58) he struck a yearning diagonal pose as if waiting for a nineteenth-century engraver to capture the moment. It was of a piece with the set and costumes of Claudius's court as a nineteenth-century world of frock-coats, where both the play scene and the duel were after-dinner entertainments for an audience in evening-dress clutching brandies. It also provided a firm context for Terence Rigby's First Player, a consummately professional actor-manager, tossing his trilby to another actor as he began the Pyrrhus speech, but holding on to his cigar which, after he had finished speaking with sobbing emotion, he calmly puffed on again.

Peter J. Davison's design for Hackney created a series of fully walled rooms, a country house that could suddenly, for example for Hamlet's first soliloquy (1.2.129ff.), take on the eerie empti-ness of a deserted mansion, powerfully mimicking Hamlet's isola-tion. But Claudius's world, an establishment smugly pleased with itself, provided a firm context for the most startling and intriguing performance in the production: Francesca Annis's Gertrude. Beginning as a fashion-plate, with her stylish elegance and china-doll make-up, Gertrude proved to have created for herself a brittle facade. The closet scene was the turning point: opening in a warm glow of autumnal light, the scene transformed as the dying Polonius pulled down a long curtain to allow a cold, dawn light to fill the stage and remove all traces of romantic lighting.

Hamlet's sexual violence had been clear in the nunnery scene where he had poked at Ophelia's crotch with his hand and finally pulled up her skirt to rape her, very quickly, from behind. Through the play scene Ophelia (Tara FitzGerald) had been a traumatised rape victim, perched on the edge of her chair as she suffered the physical pain consequent on Hamlet's actions. Now, in the closet scene, Gertrude would receive similar treatment and with similar consequences. If Gertrude was not actually raped, Fiennes' Hamlet certainly imitated rape. On Claudius's touch she shrieked and pulled away in revulsion, weeping but also traumatised, pulling the covers around her in a parody of decorum as Rosencrantz and Guildenstern entered. Through the second half of the play, Gertrude's control collapsed and she quivered on the edge of madness. By the final scene she sat with her head twitch-ing, her make-up a terrible mask, her suffering ignored by all

about her. I have never seen the consequences of Hamlet's treatment of Gertrude so graphically and horrifyingly exposed,
counterpointed by the aggressive sexuality of the mad Ophelia,
who sang of 'St Valentine' while eyeing Claudius's crotch. By
comparison with the women's suffering, Hamlet's madness
seemed only an actor's performance and his treatment of them
unmistakably brutal, callous and self-regarding.

A COUPLE OF *ROMEO AND JULIET*S

The year's two productions of *Romeo and Juliet* both typified the
problems of artistic directors and their companies. Neil Bartlett,
the artistic director of the Lyric, Hammersmith, is best known for
his experimental work with his company Gloria and for fine productions of French classical drama; his *Romeo and Juliet* was his first
Shakespeare production in England. For Adrian Noble, on the
other hand, *Romeo and Juliet* was a play that had come round yet
again in the RSC cycle, after Leveaux's 1991 production.

The twin promptings for Bartlett's production both deserved
respect: a desire to create a style of Shakespeare stripped to its
essentials and a wish to work with Emily Woof, a young performer
who had established a reputation in solo performance theatre.
Bartlett wanted a production that emphasised narrative pace,
removed the accretions of the play's stage-history and left a bare
acting-space. The opening music mixed echoes of musical transformations – Prokofiev, Tchaikovsky, Leonard Bernstein – as if to
summon them up and then firmly discard them. What would stay
behind would be the empty space.

As explained in his programme-note, Bartlett's intentions
derived from a respect for the text: 'it is only in the movies or at
the ballet or the opera that Shakespeare acquires landscapes,
scenery, the baggage of "period"'. Instead he aimed to 'honour the
pace of its storytelling, because it is in the pace that sex turns out,
frighteningly, to have the same urgency, the same rhythm and the
same speed as destruction'. The 'stripped' staging that he
described would then be as much interpretative as a means of
revealing the narrative beneath. The production's slogan, also
taken from Bartlett's programme-note, was 'twelve actors, five
knives, one rope ladder and an empty stage'. The source of this
derived from Bartlett's hard look at the 'Bad' Quarto's staging

requirements and even its punctuation. Responding to what he saw as Q1's actor-oriented editing of the longer Shakespeare text, Bartlett created a text that 'uses the lines of the "Good Quarto" arranged into the shape of the "Bad Quarto" . . . removing, shifting or transforming into physical business any words whose late sixteenth century beauty cannot rescue them from their late sixteenth century incomprehensibility'. The result, sleek and efficient, was a hard-driven performance whose losses were rarely glaring.

The design's transformation of the play into a modern street world was disappointing. Bartlett may have argued that Italy was Shakespeare's 'shorthand evocation of sex, violence, glamour and religion' but by dressing the young men in sharp suits and ties he made them into stereotypes of Italian style, offering a glib convention of macho behaviour. If this was a sop to the Lyric's young audience, it was an unnecessary recourse to stock images of Italian street life. But there was also an odd series of reappearances for Mercutio late in the play as Balthasar, Apothecary, Friar John and finally as a ghost who disarms Paris, enabling Romeo to kill him, a directorial intervention at odds with the narrative simplicity and directness elsewhere aimed at.[2]

The production slogan avoided mentioning the centrality the design accorded Juliet's bed, on or in which Juliet was usually to be seen as the rest of the action unfolded around her. This was less a statement about the significance of Juliet as a reference point for the play's action than a desire to leave Emily Woof on stage. Woof's Juliet, young, waif-like but full of strength and energy, belonged firmly in the production's concept of style, checking her hair in mirrors, clutching a copy of *marie claire* from which she seemed to have learned all she knew about the emotional problems of adolescence. This Juliet was less a gauche adolescent than a young woman whose world made perfect sense until her passion for Romeo destroyed it. As Michael Billington commented in the *Guardian*, 'such a spirited girl, you feel, would follow Romeo to Mantua rather than surrender to his banishment'. But Woof found it difficult to work with the other actors, as if her experience of solo theatre had disabled her from responding to other performers. Stuart Bunce's disappointing Romeo may have offered her little but the concentration on Juliet did nothing to help him. Bartlett and Woof may have concurred in their recognition of the play as 'large-scale, passionately physical work focussed around adolescent dreams of sexuality' but it was a recognition that concentrated only on Juliet's dreams, making Romeo an insignificant element in her world.

However, they certainly succeeded in exploring the centrality of sexual desire to Juliet's dreams. It was clear, for instance, just how important it would be to this Juliet that she was 'sold' but 'Not yet enjoyed' (3.2.27–8) when, in the balcony scene, she had asked Romeo 'What satisfaction canst thou have tonight?' (2.1.168), inserting a teasing pause before 'tonight'. The desire reappeared when, after Tybalt's death, she told her mother 'I never shall be satisfied / With Romeo till I behold him', leaving a long pause before 'dead' (3.5.93–4), a reading derived from Q1's punctuation.

If the production was undeniably limited, it intelligently maintained its energy. At Stratford, by contrast, Adrian Noble's production flagged from beginning to end. Noble too had cut the text hard but the performance still ran for three hours. Noble had also created a stylistic problem. On the morning after the Capulet ball, as the waiter was setting up the tables at the cafe (the focus for piazza life in this Verona), Mark Lockyer's Mercutio staggered on upstage, nursing a painful hangover, entering down one of the long vistas of Kendra Ullyart's set. The waiter dropped his metal tray with a clang and Lockyer winced, clutching the ice-pack ever more firmly to his head. The audience laughed, remembering the feeling. But why did the waiter drop the tray? It could have been an accident: busy with his chores, he had let the tray slip from his grasp; he could have been annoyed and thumped it down on the table in irritation. But the waiter dropped the tray only so that Mercutio could wince and Lockyer gain an easy laugh. The action was solely conditioned by its immediate effect. The realist detail, the action that provoked the possibility of the gag, was inadequately grounded. The realist method as well as the period setting (nineteenth-century Italian Risorgimento) suggested a novelistic resource for its detailing. Noble's stylistic choice meant that the stage business had to emerge out of the dense social life of Verona, where, for instance, Capulet talked with Paris in 1.2 on his way home with a cake-box, which he carefully handed to Peter, precisely so that there would be a grand cake at the party to be cut and distributed among the guests.

The implications of the social world conjured up on stage were not followed through. Far too often it was as if the lines had not been heard, their meaning not considered. When, for instance, Lady Capulet tries to turn her daughter's thoughts towards marriage, she comments 'By my count / I was your mother much upon these years / That you are now a maid' (1.3.73–5). Though Lucy Whybrow's 'Alice in Wonderland' Juliet was certainly not thirteen, she looked very young indeed. But Darlene Johnson's Lady Capulet had not seen her twenties for a while. There is no reason why Lady Capulet should be, say, twenty-eight, as the line suggests, but the gap between the performer's age and the clear statement in her lines ought to have produced a little reaction, something that registered the point. Here it skated by unremarked.

Ullyart's mobile set pitted black buildings against a white sky, all marbled and hence cold and implacable. As oppressive as the tomb it would become by the end of the play, its alleys all narrowed disturbingly so that the space crowded and confined the characters who bustled inside it. It was a demanding space for the actors, a space of visibility, as when Romeo, at his first entrance, had to pretend not to notice his parents before being able to come forward, down the alley, to talk to Benvolio. It was a very public arena in which to explore the people of the play but the production never did so.

The only actor to emerge with credit was Julian Glover as Friar Laurence. Most at home at his laboratory bench, mixing up Juliet's potion with the enthusiasm of an amateur chemist, he built up a portrait of a well-meaning man whose actions were controlled by his cowardice. But it was only too characteristic that, at his first appearance, he was seen stopping off at the cafe for his morning espresso, apparently intending to 'up-fill this osier cage of ours / With baleful weeds and precious-juicèd flowers' (2.2.7–8) from the vase of freesias on the cafe table.

Noble's recent approach to Shakespeare had been to step back from the actors, giving them a context within which to play without seeking to predetermine the results through a sharply angled directorial line. It is a risky method that here produced only a bland world where I yearned for an incisive intervention from the director to generate the power and intelligence that the actors were having such difficulty finding for themselves. The clashes and jars of the play only too rarely made a flourish; it was there, briefly and belatedly, when a troupe of singing bridesmaids burst in on the sight of the 'dead' Juliet, but by then the production had gone as cold as its set.

A BRACE OF TEMPESTS

Both the year's productions of *The Tempest* were designed for touring: David Thacker's, for the RSC's small-scale tour, and Silviu Purcarete's, for the Nottingham Playhouse in a co-production with the Hebbel Theater in Berlin and the Amsterdam company Offshore.

Small-scale touring productions have their own necessary limitations which the best turn to strengths. It was good to see, in Thacker's production, a *Tempest* without much in the way of set except a few trunks and boxes. It was good, too, to see the Swan stage stripped back to the bare back wall, an open platform for the action to unfold on. But precious little then unfolded. Undercast, underpowered, underimagined, this *Tempest* was little more than perfunctory.

The production had opened in London and had changed markedly by the time I saw it in Stratford. At first, as Paul Taylor put it in the *Independent*, Paul Jesson played 'an isolated Prospero who remains on stage throughout, brooding over his magic book' or, as Robert Hewison phrased it in the *Sunday Times*, 'Jesson spends a lot of time sitting at a wonky little table with a huge book on it, looking more like a worried manager than a magician'. By Stratford Jesson's continual presence had been eliminated so that this was the first *Tempest* I had seen in which not a single one of the books which Prospero prized above his dukedom was to be seen on stage.

But the change was much more emphatic than that: it had become a *Tempest* less dominated by Prospero than any other I can recall. It was partly the consequence of the generally low-key style of Jesson's performance; Prospero was a genial father, a benign aristocratic castaway but with no glimmering of energy or imagination. As with McCowen in 1993, there was nothing to hint at the magus, the duke, the plotter, the embittered victim. Jesson's Prospero was a thoroughly nice chap, most sharply defined as he comforted and cradled the exhausted Ferdinand who was still moving logs at the start of Act 4. It was too easy to forget, as one

23. *The Tempest* 3.1, RSC, Swan Theatre, 1995: 'I'll bear your logs the while':
Miranda (Sarah-Jane Holm) offers to help Ferdinand (David Fahm) carry a log
(Bonnie Engstrom as Ariel)

looked sympathetically at this caring gesture, that it was Prospero's
enslavement that had exhausted Ferdinand in the first place.

But the diminution of Prospero was mostly the consequence of
the spirit-centredness of the production, for the nearly bare stage
was always cluttered by the on-stage presence of Ariel (played by

Bonnie Engstrom with wide staring eyes) and her three attendant apprentice spirits. It was neat enough to have them play the logs for Ferdinand to carry or the clothes that Trinculo and Stefano were distracted by, but they also responded to much else in the action, so that Caliban's freedom-song induced in them mental torment as they held their hands in agony to their heads like sufferers with acute migraines. If, as with Mendes's production in 1993, Ariel has to appear in the storm, then Thacker's solution was a good one with Ariel as the ship's master creating a storm in the minds of passengers and crew before he literally 'flamed amazement' (1.2.199) with little shafts of fire flicked over the stage.

Engstrom's Ariel was clearly envious of Miranda, always ready to dart angry, jealous looks at her (especially during the masque), and she turned 'Where the bee sucks' (5.1.88ff.) into a sad anticipation of parting from her beloved Prospero, before spending much of the last scene downstage, sitting with her head up, contemplating the sky with longing and loneliness intermixed, balancing Antonio who sat at the other downstage corner, head down. Once released, Ariel took a yearning step towards Prospero as he turned upstage and walked away from her. If a female Ariel seemed like a throwback to an old theatre tradition long out of fashion, Engstrom at least made something significant of it, using her gender to create an additional layer to the master–servant relationship.

Ariel's rival, Dominic Letts' Caliban, emerged from an on-stage trunk, a shipwrecked castaway himself, in rags and tatters rather like old Ben Gunn in *Treasure Island*. Rarely upright, his triumphant moment came as the spirits performing the masque danced with their audience and, with Caliban increasingly controlling the action, Prospero found that the dance was moving out of his control, as most of the other characters, especially the lords, joined in, making the dance less and less a vision of order and harmony and more a wild, subversive carnival. This was a thoughtful moment, taking the masque further through its archetypal sequence than is usually the case or than the text demands, making its disruption Prospero's angry and necessary reclaiming of power over his device. But large swathes of the play unfolded with nothing to intrigue. Uncluttered though it was, the production rarely engaged with the play's demands. When a play as difficult as *The Tempest* appears a little banal, then something has gone seriously wrong.

Silviu Purcarete, a Romanian director, has established a reputation for himself as one of the most exciting of European directors. His production of *Titus Andronicus*, first seen in 1992, was still touring Europe in 1995, visiting the Avignon Festival.[3] The international collaboration for his production of *The Tempest* at Nottingham exemplified a newly inter-cultural strand of current Shakespeare production, the phenomenon of the international show freely transmitted from culture to culture, an item in a structure of global cultural exchange.[4] This *Tempest* followed immediately on his production of the same play in Portugal.

The Nottingham *Tempest* was, however, the first time Purcarete had directed Shakespeare in English. Though he spoke eloquently in the programme-note of his discovery of the English text, of 'the magic of the words' and the 'very special' quality of 'breathing in the English language', Purcarete's vision of the play was dominated by music and visual effect, never by the uncovering of moments of the language. Spoken for the most part extremely slowly and with actors obviously instructed never to be quick on their cues, the scenes of *The Tempest* unfolded with an aural monotony in which actors became pawns in a director's imaginative vision, a form of directorial dictatorship that is sharply opposite to the English tradition of actors' prominence even within strongly conceptual director's theatre. For all the attention the performance paid to the possibilities of language, this production might as well have been in a foreign language, as, for the director, it was.

As the audience entered, they found a set, designed by José Manuel Mela, of an empty revolve across which light played to suggest the sea, and above which stretched steel cords suggesting a musical stave. Upstage stood Prospero (Michael Fitzgerald), bewigged and robed as an eighteenth-century figure, turning every so often as the audience settled. The island was defined as a space of dream and of music. This Prospero, a figure of the Enlightenment, was unambiguously Mozart, the genius of the place. The island's spirits were a masked string quintet who wandered on and off playing, initially as accompaniment to Miranda's singing of Barbarina's cavatina at the opening of Act 4 of *The Marriage of Figaro*, a text that evoked childhood love and the sense of loss. The aria would be heard throughout the performance until, at the very end, as Prospero spoke the epilogue almost to himself as the revolve took him away from the audience, Caliban sat playing the melody on a violin, initially as hideous scratchings but metamorphosing magically and movingly into beauty.

Throughout, music was the locus for beauty and horror, a quality Purcarete found peculiarly acutely mixed in Mozart (used in his *Titus* to accompany the Thyestean feast 'because the moment had to have splendour and horror'). Ferdinand's log was a massive metal skeleton of a double-bass which he kept carrying into 4.1. Unlike Thacker's imaginative exploration, Purcarete ducked the demands of the masque, playing it behind a curtain while Prospero as prompter mouthed his script from the wings, until he pulled the curtain back to reveal the spirits holding up an enormous skeleton, the same one that Caliban had carried on in 2.2 and tenderly arranged on the ground. The skeleton suggested a monstrous Sycorax, a reminder of what lay outside Prospero's eighteenth-century rational and musical universe.

Within this dream-world, Prospero's confrontation was not with his enemies but with the fact of death. *The Tempest* is, for Purcarete, 'about time before death. Death as something final, closed . . . Prospero is the artist. Like all artists he has to face a paradox: the extreme strength of art and simultaneously its weakness, useless-ness.' Prospero dominated his world, until the ending consigned him back to the limited world of bodily fragility and the immi-nence of death. Unlike Thacker's Prospero, there was here no threat to that dominance posed by Ariel, for Purcarete took the typically extreme route of denying Ariel an on-stage presence at all, leaving him merely a voice, heard but unseen.

The production was a cruel paradox: a richly visual world created by a beautiful and striking imagination but dully executed with the actors so subordinate to the director's vision that they became celebrants of the director's power. Purcarete's production was a perfect mixture of the best and worst sides of the stereotype of the European director's Shakespeare, antagonistic to language and the actor but revelling in the visual beauty of the theatre.

TWO HIGH-SPEED ROMANS

I referred earlier in this chapter to the speed-addiction of Jonathan Kent's *Hamlet*. It was the merest dawdle beside Peter Hall's *Julius Caesar* in Stratford. Hall's *Caesar* was about speed, not pace, the exact inverse of his *Hamlet*. As I noted above (see chapter 1), it will be remembered for its timing: two and a quarter hours without an interval. As Irving Wardle wryly commented in the *Independent on Sunday*, 'For once, nobody can say that the play falls off in the second half.' As the play whizzed by, I found myself applauding the vocal virtuosity that enabled the actors to keep going at that speed but such virtuosity soon palls. As, in the middle of the quiet, eerie storm Hall created, Julian Glover's tense and interestingly honourable Cassius belted through his conversation with Michael Gardiner's camp Casca, the language became meaningless at this speed: sound without fury signifying very little indeed. No wonder then that when he first began to work on John Nettles' Brutus, Glover's Cassius generated precious little response, Brutus facing away from him, out towards the audience, musing introspectively rather than finding matter for his thoughts in Cassius's words. It would have been intriguing if the effect had been isolating for the characters, unable to connect with each other from their separate worlds, but instead the effect was isolating for the actors, a feature that did not help the play at all.

John Gunter's set for *Caesar* was a tired recycling of old ideas. I have seen too many productions by now where the stage is dominated by a statue of Caesar. This particular looming head seemed to have been carved out of a giant bar of white chocolate and when the blood ran down it as it hovered over the battlefield of Philippi it looked as though Caesar had a runny nose that needed wiping with a giant tissue. The alarming appearance of segments of animal statues, like the horse that reared through the upstairs window of Caesar's house, hinted at the conventional bestiary of Roman iconology but without doing more than dwarf the characters beneath them. That the characters are dwarfed by the oppressive burden of the history of Rome is a truth about the play but one that a production needs to work with, not merely state. The definition of Rome as alien as well as modern-seeming in its politics is not best served by what Paul Taylor, in the *Independent*, dubbed 'the introduction here of symbols, or rather Symbols'.

Trying to listen to a production moving at this pace was tiring on the ears. The almost unremitting reds and blacks of the costumes and the gloomy set darkly lit were tiring on the eyes. The sense of sprinting a marathon was not helpful. The actors became increasingly off-hand and unconcerned as the play unreeled.

Hugh Quarshie, usually a fascinating actor, made the merest sketch of Antony. Nettles' Brutus was a predictable and conventional portrait of the difficulties of liberalism. Only Christopher Benjamin contributed something new, a Caesar who was frightened and fatalistic, desperately using the pomposity of the language to try to convince himself that 'always I am Caesar' (1.2.213) might become somehow true through emphatic statement and repetition. But the tyrannical anger with which he confronted Metellus Cimber was lost beside the stagey effects of the death, the sudden spurt of blood as Casca stabbed him from behind, and the sound of a thunderclap which would be heard again for the deaths of Brutus and Cassius later, like some Chekhovian breaking string.

Hall notoriously failed, in his 1984 production of *Coriolanus* at the Royal National Theatre, in his attempt to use paying members of the audience as the crowd, clutching their raincoats and shopping. After the success of Stephen Pimlott's use of the citizens of Stratford to play the male establishment of Vienna in his production of *Measure for Measure* in 1994, it must have seemed a good idea to use the citizens of Stratford again for the people of Rome. But crowds are fickle things: on stage and off, they need careful training. It was disastrous to have them, as Hall did, rhubarbing away, mouthing comments to each other at the start and then to allow a few professional actors, career plebeians as it were, to dominate them. Hall's citizenry filled the edges of the stage but they never looked remotely interesting. They were not theatrical, merely awkward. Where Nemirovich-Danchenko famously gave each citizen a personal history in his production for the Moscow Art Theatre, Hall left them as a bland mass, occupying space. They were also oddly unaffected by what happened around them, able to turn their backs on the corpse of Caesar covered in a blood-soaked sheet which Antony had so carefully brought in and placed downstage behind them.

Pandarus ends his interminable tale to Cressida about the hair on Troilus's chin: 'and all the rest so laughed, that it passed'. 'So let it now', replies Cressida, 'for it has been a great while going by' (*Troilus and Cressida*, 1.2.162–5). No one could complain that Hall's *Caesar* was a great while going by, but it was a pity that all one was left with was a feeling 'that it passed'.

Where Hall's *Caesar* was all speed and no pace, Barrie Rutter's production of *Antony and Cleopatra* for Northern Broadsides was a fine balance of the two. Never losing its impetus, this *Antony* had all the qualities of freshness and energy I had come to associate with the company's work. This was Northern Broadsides' fourth Shakespeare production and their appearance on the English Shakespeare scene has come to seem one of the most important interventions during the period covered by this book.

Mike Poulton, in his programme-note, wrote of Shakespeare's Antony and Cleopatra as 'vigorously and noisily alive, up and running, kicking and screaming' and the same epithets can easily be applied to the production. Theatrical energy can be an imposed freneticism that has little to do with the play's language and dramaturgy. Here the energy was being generated by the play moment by moment, line by line. All the characters – not only the title-figures – were vigorously alive; it was not only in the spectacular drumming for the battle scenes nor only in competition with the wide-open spaces and overly resonant acoustic of the Cambridge Corn Exchange (where I saw the production) that this *Antony and Cleopatra* was noisily up and running. It achieved what Bartlett's *Romeo and Juliet* or Thacker's *Tempest* could not: a stripped-down Shakespeare that never had to apologise for any supposed limitations of cast-size or scenic extravagance.

Deliberately eschewing any hint of the play as a spectacle of set-design, Rutter created the opposition of Rome and Egypt in the simplest terms, primarily as an opposition of costume: comfortably flowing trousers and sandals for men and women in Egypt against formal suits and lace-up shoes in Rome. Where Octavius (Andrew Cryer) strutted, Ishia Bennison's Cleopatra ran. Yet, if one allowed one's theatrical imagination to be fired, the fragmentary metonymy fully implied the alternative worlds behind.

The performance opened with a startling contrast. A bare-chested comic spoke as Philo, acting as Master of Ceremonies, as a trolley was wheeled out with a parodied Antony and Cleopatra on it, both male, both sharp mockeries of the lovers, speaking their opening dialogue in 1.1. Watched by a single onstage spectator, Caesar, the action aggressively offered the image that Cleopatra later envisages: we saw the 'quick comedians' and 'Some squeaking Cleopatra boy . . . [her] greatness / I'th' posture of a whore' (5.2.212, 216–17). Then, without a break, the 'real' Antony and Cleopatra bounded on to the stage and, in a single line, the parody was shown up for its lying fictionality, fully vanquished by the originals' power and resonance.

If the parodic could be so swiftly overcome, the production consistently explored the very different threat posed by the characters' own predisposition to undercut their heroic, mythic image. Bennison's Cleopatra was rarely regal, a northern 'lass' whose wryly sharp style could show up Antony's posturing, mockingly applauding his rhetoric in parting in 1.3. It was a risky manoeuvre, having, as Jeffrey Wainwright suggested in the *Independent*, 'no regard for queenliness in the high English fashion' but threatening all the time to make Cleopatra a figure whose coquettish wit was trivial. Yet by her deliberately restrained use of the regal style, Bennison made its occasional appearances all the more powerful and moving so that, as she offered Scarus 'An armour all of gold' (4.9.27), one saw instantly why Scarus was more overwhelmed by her voice and pose than by the generosity of the reward.

The effect was most dangerous in Antony's death scene where her insistent kisses and voluble speech drew from him a repetition of 'I am dying, Egypt, dying' (4.16.43) with the comic exasperation of a man whose girlfriend just will not shut up. But, at his death, her switch of register for 'The crown o'th' earth doth melt' (65–70) redeemed all and Bennison followed the devastating image of emptiness with a wild, animal howl of grief, again the contrast all the more startling because completely unexpected.

Unafraid, the production allowed the audience to make apparently superficial analogies: Octavia (Deborah McAndrew), in her neat blue suit, as an employee of the Halifax Building Society perhaps, or the dirty orange work-jackets of Antony's army suggesting dustmen from the local town council. But the resonances were never able to diminish the action as the characters' language and the staging's power soared above the realist implications. At Actium, Antony, wearing a Herculean lion-skin, and Cleopatra, in a horned head-dress of Isis, took their places at the oil-drums and plastic canisters on which their army drummed, confronting the neat blue of Rome. When Cleopatra put down her drumsticks and walked off and Antony threw down his to run after her, the betrayal was powerfully visualised. The subsequent defections of Antony's men were equally strong as Camidius walked across the stage to join the Roman drummers, an orange-costumed figure now amongst the blue.

In a cast of fifteen doubling and trebling up efficiently, Dave Hill's magnificent Enobarbus stood out, the rich tones of his voice easily matching the eloquence of his description of Cleopatra's barge, and his death a deeply moving consequence of his clear-sighted comprehension of his betrayal. But no performance took undue prominence. At the end, robed in white and with a wreath of flowers on her head, Cleopatra sat on a bench, lit by candles, as, in one of the production's characteristically restrained lighting effects, the stage darkened and the action achieved its image of stasis. *Antony and Cleopatra* is a frighteningly difficult play to stage well: by the simplest means and the utmost trusting of the text, Northern Broadsides achieved far more than most.

The energy the company has always found from its exploration of the Shakespearean text signalled a tradition that was more than just a geographical heterodoxy, a denial of the dominance of southern, London-based Shakespeare. Its brand of popular theatre seemed instead to touch on deep traditions of British performance, of a theatre for all the people, not merely a cultural and social elite. It may be a sentimentalised ideal but the results have been sustainedly thrilling.

TWO STRATFORD EXPERIMENTS

Experimental productions are not common sights on the main stage in Stratford for the restrictions of conventional expectation inhibit radical experiment. Both Gale Edwards' *The Taming of the Shrew* and Stephen Pimlott's *Richard III* were marked by their radical approach to the plays' endings, endings which demanded to be read back across the rest of the production.

Productions of *The Taming of the Shrew* can often be defined by their treatment of Kate's final speech but Edwards' production was also particularly defiant in its approach to the play's opening. The RSC seems to have an objection on principle to playing the Induction using anything remotely approximating to Shakespeare's words. Edwards, the first female director of a production of *Shrew* that I have seen, took a radical look at the Sly scenes. Unlike the class-basis of Alexander's 1992 RSC production of *The Taming of the Shrew*, her *Shrew* was more completely Sly's dream than any other.

The production began, not with a drunken Sly arguing with

'Marian Hacket, the fat alewife of Wincot' (Induction, 2.20), but with an aggressively drunken Sly arguing with one of those intriguingly unseen figures in Shakespeare, Mrs Sly. The Lord and the huntsmen, the whole plot of the Induction, became part of the dream itself with the Lord as a dream-master, summoning up the figures of the dream-world, as with a grand gesture he caused a little proscenium arch to rise up out of the stage floor through which came the troupe of players, including Mrs Sly, who would play out Sly's dream of wish-fulfilment as Kate, the dream of male power that Sly plainly wanted. Edwards had imaginatively found a worthwhile way of setting up the misogyny and female oppression that is for us such a troubling feature of the play.

For the rest of the first half of the performance the production seemed to have forgotten its starting-point completely. On Russell Craig's mobile set, the town of Padua became a farce-world of brash and garish devices. This part of the production was typified by Mark Lockyer as Tranio, overacting shamelessly and scene-stealing maliciously. This Tranio, given the power to be his own master, was transformed from Harlequin in diamond-patterned trousers into the rock star Prince. With its parade of grotesques and caricatures, the production seemed to be offering the broadest, brashest treatment ever, typified by the arrival at the wedding of a bright-red baby Fiat containing a groom in feathers and with one boxing glove, and a servant in a pink tutu. The only actor who seemed to be comfortable in this chaos was Michael Siberry as Sly metamorphosed into Petruccio. His Petruccio, much given to speechifying (Grumio had heard it all before), may have been shaken by the sight of Hortensio and the broken lute but went into round one of his encounter with Kate with boundless confidence, buoyed up by his game-plan worked out in soliloquy.

Beside Siberry's Petruccio, Josie Lawrence's Kate looked and sounded as though she were in a different play or rather as if Mrs Sly were an unwilling participant in Sly's dream. Her voice deep and portentous as if she were in training for tragedy, Lawrence played Kate as a woman playing out a role someone else had defined, a male fantasy of the kind of woman who deserves dominating. The two were clearly smitten from the first time they looked in each other's eyes and the farce seemed to be unfolding genially and happily. By the interval, it seemed as though the frame had been used to simplify the play mercilessly.

But all changed in the second half. Now, with an increasingly diabolic Lord in control, Kate's torments began to become darker and far more painful. A starving, degraded woman in the madness of Petruccio's house, Kate was a pitiable sight, not remotely comic at all. As she sat slumped on a chair, even Petruccio, leaving the stage after his soliloquy of power ('Thus have I politicly begun my reign' 4.1.174–97), was about to caress her tenderly, and she stayed as mute victim behind the following scene for Bianca, the gap between the sisters' experiences now painfully wide. In the scene with the tailor she ended up on the floor in the centre of the stage, cradling a piece of the dismembered gown, a tearful, lonely image of suffering while Petruccio and Grumio argued about the order to the tailor on one side of the stage. Petruccio, victorious, could now afford to be generous to this battered and defeated bride and his tenderness increased her tears.

Smiling, loving, eating and happy in the next few scenes, Kate had found a joy in marriage though it was difficult to see why she should have done. This was, in effect, the climax of Petruccio's plot and Sly's dream. Docile and affectionate, Kate happily embraced Petruccio on the side of the stage while they watched the plot of Lucentio's two fathers unfold. It was in the last scene that the production took its last and most savage twist. As Kate squared up to the Widow, she was clearly unnerved by Petruccio's readiness to bet on her, 'A hundred marks my Kate does put her down' (5.2.37), distressed by his easy retreat to the male world of wagers – as she would be later by her father's flourish of his cheque-book to give her husband 'twenty thousand crowns, / Another dowry to another daughter' (118–19). She was now closely aligned with Tranio, who had entered stripped of his finery, a servant in an apron carrying black rubbish bags, humiliated and back in his real place, as Kate was now discovering the limits of hers.

Before he began his wooing of Kate, Petruccio had collected up the money offered by Hortensio, Gremio and the false Lucentio, scooping it into his hat. Now the wager money on the wives was gathered into his hand. Kate's mute pleas not to have to trample on her hat were overborne and she delivered the speech he demanded of her as a remarkable mixture of emotions: the orthodox language of female submission seemed to be spoken through her, rather than by her, forced to acknowledge that this is how the world is. Her words angered her but she was also close to a break-

24. *The Taming of the Shrew* 5.2, RSC, 1995: 'My hand is ready, may it do him ease': Petruccio (Michael Siberry) and Katherine (Josie Lawrence)

down, her hands pulling at her hair. She ended on the floor, with her hand offered to 'do him ease', an action that was both more threatening and more despairing than any of her earlier violence, and Siberry's Petruccio backed away, dropping the money. The programme helpfully explained that 'Petruccio slowly realises what he has been attempting to do to Katherina in the name of love. By the end of the speech his dream has become a nightmare.' When a Stratford programme announces that '175 lines have been cut', it is rarely cause for alarm. But it is a strong statement to cut 'Why, there's a wench! Come on, and kiss me, Kate' (5.2.185). Now, with hands to head, Petruccio could hardly bear to look at his bride. The scene dissolved, the dream mechanism was unwound and Sly woke to find his wife standing over him as he, on his knees, embraced her, anxiously and, at least for the moment, repentantly.

I have needed to describe this movement at length because it is as radical a reinterpretation of the last moments of this troubling play as any I can recall, even if it has connections with Michael Bogdanov's 1978 RSC production with Jonathan Pryce. But I have also had to reconstruct it because it was only in retrospect that I felt any confidence in having followed the meaning that was unfolding. I came to respect the thoughtfulness of Edwards' production, the way it allowed the garish simplicity of the first half to be re-read in the light of the second, the way it used the dream-structure to make the action move beyond Sly/Petruccio's control, until he became aware of the devastating cost of female subjection, to himself as much as to the women he wished to control. The production was intellectually demanding, even if it could only be so through producing a commentary on the play, reading over it rather than through it.[5] This was the fifth time the RSC had produced *Shrew* in thirteen years and the production justified yet another look at the play. But my high opinion of its intellectual rigour only came *after* the event, overcoming my doubts.

This tension between the experience of watching a production and the post-performance thinking-through of its argument can make a production improve in the memory, the immediate response buried in the pleasurable hard work of analysis. As with Purcarete's *Tempest* and Edwards' *Shrew,* so Stephen Pimlott's *Richard III* has taken on a warmer glow as it has positioned itself in my theatre memory. Again, the logic of the interpretation has come to dominate over the problems of production. Yet there were production problems, most of them consequent on Tobias Hoheisel's set (see chapter 1, above), which kept the action distant from the audience. At that distance the events seemed unimportant, disengaging the audience when the playing encouraged engagement.

More than previous productions I have discussed, this *Richard III* was explicit about its interpretation. In an interview,[6] David Troughton, Pimlott's Richard, spoke of the need to construct the character by working backwards from the soliloquy at Bosworth (5.5.131–60), the need to find a reason for that outbreak of conscience. In a director's programme-note, a rare phenomenon in RSC programmes, Pimlott identified the speech as the discovery of despair, placing it in 'the same tradition as the final soliloquy of Faustus':

Conscience has brought Richard to this point of realisation. He looks within himself and finds only emptiness . . . Richard, utterly alone, facing the truth of who and what he is and deciding his course: 'I *shall* despair' – that is the decision he takes, to condemn himself.

It suggests a strongly psychologistic reading of character, not a devil or a vice but a man at the limit of his mental strength.

The cause of Richard's actions was here firmly located in his relationship with his mother (Diana Coupland) and that, in turn, identified as the result of his birth. Troughton had consulted an obstetrician and learned that a breech birth could produce a hip injury so that Richard's spinal deformity could have been the result of compensating for the continual hip pain. Deformed by his birth, his costume suggesting a child in short trousers, Troughton's Richard yearned for his mother's love and found only her hatred. After the exit of the court with the dying King Edward in 2.1, Richard found the crown and tried it on, sitting on the throne until, at his mother's entrance, he became sheepish at her glare of disapproval. Once crowned king, Richard found he was unable to sit comfortably on the throne.

For his meeting with his mother in 4.4 he placed himself, with great awkwardness, on the ground, his head in her lap. Wanting her blessing he received only her curse, following her appalling account of his childhood (4.4.166–75), a speech which came from her loathing of her own son ('Thou cam'st on earth to make the earth my hell', 167). Pimlott identified it as 'a peculiarly terrible scene, a mother cursing her child in a way that is unique in Shakespeare'. Though his mother's hatred does not 'exonerate him . . . [it] presents reasons why he is as he is'. Open-mouthed with horror, Richard hurled himself away from her and towards the crown which he had placed on the ground. The brutality of the scene with Elizabeth which follows came directly from that horror and despair, ending with a 'true love's kiss' (361) planted aggressively on Elizabeth's mouth.

The viciousness of this wooing contrasted all the more sharply with the playing of the wooing of Lady Anne (1.2), where Troughton avoided most of the opportunities for cynicism and wit to create a thoroughly convincing lover, with a long and passionate kiss at 'both of them are thine' (193). Yet here too the relationship harped on Richard as abandoned son, playing the sulky child as he asked her 'Bid me farewell' and she responded as a benignly mocking mother with ''Tis more than you deserve' (210). His reaction to the wooing, 'I'll have her', was a wondering triumph of sexual power ('have' spoken as unequivocally meaning 'have sex

25. *Richard III* 4.4, RSC, 1995: Mother and son, Duchess of York
(Diana Coupland) and Richard III (David Troughton)

with' here), before he broke the mood with the off-hand cynicism
of 'but I will not keep her long' (217).

The coherent detail of this psychological reading of character
was set against the emphasis on Richard as actor. At his first
entrance, he came to the front edge of the stage, waving at his
shadow as he spied it 'in the sun' (1.1.26), raised an expectant
finger, and opened his mouth to begin his speech when, with a
blast of trumpets, the whole court entered on the gallery dressed
for a masquerade. Richard grumpily limped off stage, reappearing
with jester's cap and bauble, to perform the first thirteen lines as
a comic party-piece of welcome for the court, before they froze as
the lighting switched to the inner hatred at 'But I' (14).[7]
Elsewhere Richard controlled the stage with mysterious efficiency,
asking 'who comes here?' (122) with his back to the entrance
through which Hastings came. To meet the citizens in 3.7, Richard
turned his attendants into clerics and the three robed up from costumes in a wicker props-basket in the space under the gallery,

while the citizens gathered above, unable to see the preparations for the performance of piety.

This performative mode defined the play's ending. There was no battle. As the ghosts of his victims entered on the gallery, a pageant to echo the court in the first scene, Richard made his way towards them. His speech drew on Richard's soliloquy in *Henry VI Part 3* (3.2.174–81), an image of Richard's long search through the 'thorny wood'. As he put down the sword and the crown, he offered, as his climactic realisation, a phrase divorced from its context early in *Richard III*, 'all the world to nothing' (1.2.225), the full comprehension that all the world had dwindled to meaninglessness and emptiness. The withered arm shook down to its full length, the actor gave up his part and ambled to the corner of the stage and sat down, gazing up at Richmond in the gallery and, when Richmond had completed his long speech of healing, Richard clapped his performance, slowly and hollowly.

Alongside these two perceptions of Richard – son and actor – Pimlott placed a third structure: the ghosts of the dead. The corner where Richard ended his performance, downstage audience left, had, through the course of the production, become identified as the ghosts' place, a space with its own door through which Richard's victims made their final living exit and in which the ghosts frequently gathered to watch the action unfold. The nightmare of the ghosts' curses (5.5) followed Richard's placing of bread and a goblet of wine beside his dagger planted in the ground so that its hilts became a cross and the scene a diabolic parody of communion while Richmond prayed. Richmond himself became a figure in Richard's dream, the ghosts' blessings on him something which horrified Richard even more than their curses. Margaret (Cherry Morris, also Margaret in Sam Mendes's 1992 RSC production) was from the start associated with the ghosts' corner, a living link with all the dead of the tetralogy, the play's memory of the longer sweep of history.

But the production gave most of the cast little opportunity to develop interesting characters; too often they were subordinated to the director's will. What was consistently missing in the production's strong reading was an edge of danger. Only when Richard smashed to pulp the Bishop's bag of strawberries as if it contained Hastings' head was there the violent passion so completely missing elsewhere. Though less dictatorial than Purcarete's *Tempest*, the very strength of the director's interpretation had partly buried the actors.

Watching Terry Hands' production of *The Merry Wives of Windsor* on the Olivier stage at the Royal National Theatre was like meeting up with an old friend whom you never expected to see again: the reunion is full of nostalgia but you cannot help thinking that the world has moved on since you last met. Hands directed the play for the RSC in 1968 and the production was a revelation; it was his first Shakespeare production for the company and stamped him as a brilliantly talented young director. It was revived in 1975 alongside his explorations of both parts of *Henry IV* and *Henry V*, creating a cycle of Falstaff plays. In 1995 Hands chose the same play to mark his debut at the National, working again with the same designer, Timothy O'Brien. Even the casting had its own echo of his earlier thoughts: Brenda Bruce, Mistress Page in 1968, reappeared transformed into Mistress Quickly; Tim Wylton, Bardolph in 1975, was now Doctor Caius. In many ways it was as if the National had simply borrowed the RSC for the event: by Michael Billington's count, seventeen of the twenty main parts were played by ex-RSC performers.

It was certainly worth telling the new generations of theatre-goers what Hands had uncovered in 1968, the richness of his depiction of the life of a small Elizabethan town. Throughout the production, Hands covered scene changes with the town band processing across the stage, while troops of Sir Hugh's school-children played leapfrog or catch, chanting playground rhymes. Mistress Page and Mistress Ford compared Falstaff's letters at the market, while other townsfolk were buying cauliflowers or turning over the clothes on the Renaissance equivalent of an Oxfam stall. Bardolph was no sooner turned tapster than he could be seen at the back of the stage, serving beer to a table of workmen.

All of this detailing, finely in place, suggested the bustling density of town life against which the action was played. Yet, where O'Brien's sets in 1968 had put a town street on stage, Windsor had now become much more rural. Backed with a field of ripe corn and with a Thames ketch moored upstage, the play's houses were vestigial frames in a pastoral landscape. The play's contrast of town and surrounding fields had collapsed into a vision of Merrie England closely modelled on Hofnagel's painting of *A Fête at Bermondsey*, used for the production's publicity. All the characters apart from Falstaff and Fenton now spoke in a rustic accent, setting off the Received Pronunciation of the newcomers all the more sharply but also prone to sound too like stage Mummerset, voices for the audience to mock affectionately for their strange sounds.

O'Brien and Hands were of course right to remind audiences that an Elizabethan town like Windsor was little larger than a modern village but their choice of autumnal colourings, however much justified by the play, took on its own overtones of nostalgia. The Windsor of Hands' *Merry Wives* now looked disconcertingly like a living museum, part of a Shakespeare theme-park, a stop-off on the 1990s Heritage Trail. In the warm glow of the production's benign enjoyment of others' folly, the audience could relish the comedy but lost sight of that firm and validated sense of community without which the play's strata have little meaning.

Yet the production was richly enjoyable in its exploration of what Hands sees as 'Shakespeare's warmest and richest comedy'. Hands tried scrupulously to avoid cheap gags: the audience laughed at lines and situations, not at extraneous pratfalls. When, for instance, Alan David's Sir Hugh, a gentle Welsh parson, sang to himself to keep up his spirits while nervously waiting for his duel with Doctor Caius, it was gloriously right that he should end up conducting an enormous imaginary Welsh male-voice choir. Denis Quilley's Falstaff, huge of girth and orotund of voice, would naturally attempt press-ups (his arms on a stool, not of course on the ground) as he anticipated his strenuous encounters with the two wives. Quilley's preening vanity was one of the production's pleasures, a man so sure of himself that it took little for Mistress Quickly to massage his ego until he agreed to visit Mistress Page again, even after his watery experiences in Datchet Mead.

But beside the gallery of expectedly comic characters both play and production set the far more troubling figure of Ford. Richard McCabe started as a melancholic man, dressed in a tightly buttoned-up customary suit of solemn black like some Puritan Hamlet. The jealousy churning within him always risked exploding as words were spat out with venom and the grimace became increasingly like a manic rictus. Shedding both clothes and dignity, Ford in his obsessions twisted his body into the representation of what he feared, wrenching his hair into two huge cuckold's horns, his tongue also taken over by his imaginings. His search of the buck-basket – a word that he could barely manage to get past his lips – produced the usual flurry of dirty linen but McCabe catapulted himself into it so that it ended upside down on top of him as he crawled around the stage like some bizarre tortoise. His matter-of-fact statement, 'Well, he's not here I seek for' (4.2.145), both superbly counterpointed the preceding freneticism and served to underline the mad rationality of his search. It also predicted the moving calm with which he would finally balance love and jealousy. Once he had heeded Page's warning, 'Be not as extreme in submission / As in offence' (4.4.10–11), McCabe's Ford could settle into a trusting and loving embrace of Geraldine Fitzgerald's bright-eyed Mistress Ford, at last calm of mind, all passion spent.

Hands' *Merry Wives* was a comforting return to the old; Deborah Warner's *Richard II* had the brilliant shock of the new. This, her first Shakespeare production in England for five years, was a startling demonstration of her talented work in an alternative mode of Shakespeare, far away from the comfortable effects of Terry Hands' work. As the audience entered the Cottesloe Theatre for *Richard II*, they found the action already under way: down the length of the playing-area stood a series of pedestals, each surmounted by a small and enigmatic object, guarded by a figure in black who, as the moment of performance approached, collected the objects, storing them in a reliquary, and carefully took away all the pedestals. It is not common for the set to be dismantled before the play has properly begun and the effect here was bemusing, the only moment in the performance when the director's intentions were unclear.

Meanwhile, behind a light gauze at one end of the theatre, in a space lit by wall-mounted candles, servants were robing Richard in his royal regalia; underneath the robes, Richard's body was wrapped in bandages like some medieval mummy. Somewhere above the audience's heads, a group of female singers began a haunting requiem which would punctuate the performance throughout its four-hour length. Only at the end, as Exton single-handedly dragged on to the stage a rough wooden coffin and tipped off the lid to reveal the corpse of Richard, would the bandages and the music (as the choir sang 'dona nobis pacem') make

26. *Richard II* 3.4, Royal National Theatre, 1995: The playing area during a dress rehearsal

final sense: from first to last Warner's *Richard II* was an elegy for the loss of Richard and with Richard his entire world, a medieval world of ordered ceremony and religious mystery, now irrevocably lost, replaced by the banal *realpolitik* of Henry IV. By the interval, the candles on the wall had all guttered and died and were not replaced in the second half, a simple effect of great power, a symbol suggesting the dying of Richard's rule.

As a view of the play there is nothing radical in this. Indeed, it opens a space for suspicion about its overly benign view of Richard's world. Behind the steel-hard clarity of Deborah Warner's directing, a style which suggested a superficial sympathy with Bolingbroke's cold rational pragmatism, the production revealed an unexpected nostalgia for a different, lost way. While most of the immediate responses to the production inevitably concentrated on the cross-gender casting of Fiona Shaw as Richard II, it was the production's politics that were more remarkable, tinged with a reactionary mood that teetered on the edge of but never crossed over into sentimentalism, overborne by its deeply humane concern for individuals who were all disturbingly lost in the political world that underpinned every moment of the performance.

The theatre itself had been transformed by Hildegard Bechtler's rigorous design into a traverse, a narrow playing area of light wooden floor and low walls that stretched the full depth of the theatre with the audience ranged along the two long sides, facing each other. It encouraged confrontation, characters set oppositionally, unable in its tight width to pass by each other. Most obviously ideal for the lists at Coventry, where, with powerfully detailed ritualistic ceremony, Bolingbroke and Mowbray prepared for their fight, kept apart by Richard and his court who occupied the middle of the theatre, the stage-space proved itself, over and over again, able to offer each scene the energising dynamic it needed. In 1.2, for instance, the entire scene was controlled and shaped by the slow progress of the aged and crippled Duchess of Gloucester down the theatre, leaning heavily on two sticks, while John of Gaunt stood immobile. Indeed the staging of this scene precisely enabled Paola Dionisotti's outstanding performance as the Duchess, brutally hard in her vindictive grief, confronting Graham Crowden's Gaunt, as every step of her progress and every movement of her body underlined the words with the utmost intensity.

The shape of the playing area also encouraged multiple perspectives. In 3.3, for instance, Struan Rodger's Northumberland, a figure dangerously manic in his aggressive pursuit of Richard, stood isolated in the middle of the empty, darkened stage, far in advance of Bolingbroke and the others, while Richard, Aumerle and his attendants clustered at a distance on a small golden balcony. The moment of connection between the two was not Richard's own descent; instead, at 'down I come' (177), he draped a sheet over the edge of the balcony, threaded the crown on to it and let it slide slowly down the sheet which he then let go so that it dropped to the ground to strange music heard in the air as the others stood shocked at the sight and sound – an image, as so many in the production, both simple and powerful.

Every scene contained details of speech or movement, of blocking or effects, that warranted recording, moments that marked the language, emphasised spoken thought, in a fashion that is necessarily rare, for staging of this quality cannot but be unusual. The style may have been simple but it was based on a full comprehension of the flexibility and rapidity of transitions in Shakespeare's language so that the action coloured but never covered the lines, revealing the meaning of speech, never denying its sinuous effect. Playing a full text (at least I failed to note any significant cuts), Warner demonstrated the coherence and inner necessity of every line, its demandingly intense accumulation of argument across the vast expanse of the play. The rigour of her work, always in service of the play, always demonstrating its profoundly considered respect for the playwright, was an object-lesson.

Warner's scrupulous intelligence was supported by her cast, all playing to their limits. If I single out Michael Bryant's York it is only because his performance showed an actor achieving such comfortable ease with the language that, at moments, it took on edges of a reality that made the others appear to be only acting. Richard Eyre has described Bryant's work in rehearsal:

To hear him talk you would imagine he is a carpenter or a farmer, and is as reluctant to theorise about acting as about a piece of wood or a cow. He has as much interest in 'experiment' and 'research' as a farmer has in veterinary science or a carpenter in tree surgery . . . [He] matter-of-factly builds his character like a detective assembling a case until one day, sometimes alarmingly late in rehearsal, the character is there – complete.[8]

Whatever we may mean by that strange sense of life in Shakespeare's characters was perfectly present in Bryant's York, a complete character. York wandered through the play's political confusions with his values completely integral to his existence so that, after berating Bolingbroke for the rebellion in 2.3, he could not help himself from turning back and becoming host ('So fare you well— / Unless you please to enter in the castle', 158–9), embarrassed by his own hospitality but totally incapable of suppressing his generosity and social obligations. Such consummate playing took the domestic comedy of Aumerle's conspiracy in its stride: the 'boots' scene (5.2) allowed all its farce without for a moment losing sight of the threat to Aumerle's life and to the throne, the clash of family and state fully and appallingly present.

As Richard was carried in for the lists, the production music took on a rare irony as the choir sang 'Rex tremendae maiestatis'. Shaw's Richard was here appealingly boyish, the child-king, desperately unsure what to do. As the preparations for the duel reached fever-pitch and the drums and trumpets thundered, Richard could be seen in complete panic, desperate to find something to save Bolingbroke. He threw his warder down as a last-second reaction, surprising himself as much as anyone else by his action. There was no trace here of a pre-planned strategy, only a terrified bid to protect the object of his desire.

Reviewers were troubled by Shaw's performance but it was a female critic who was most vituperative: Rhoda Koenig complained in the *Independent* that 'Shaw's Richard is a stereotyped girlie', that Richard was 'unlikely to be such a giggling prat' and, as her culminating insult, complained that 'Shaw doesn't have enough maleness to play Peter Pan'. But the absence of 'maleness' in Shaw's performance had nothing to do with her own gender. Instead her Richard was precisely Peter Pan, a child forced unbearably to have to grow up, until, in the scene of the murder, Richard had finally and agonisingly reached the limits of experience. The earlier playfulness had now become a distant memory but from the start it had been accompanied by a febrile gaucheness, trying to make jokes ('Our doctors say this is no time to bleed', 1.1.157) but using the mirror, in which he was forever checking his appearance, to cool his face and neck. The jokes could be light-hearted, as, for instance, the idea of leading the army into Ireland produced a fake 'Oirish' brogue (doubly funny, given that Shaw's natural voice has an Irish accent) and had Richard leading his followers in a mocking Irish jig. But the wit could take on darker hues: Richard arrived too early at Gaunt's deathbed, wearing a black armband and clutching a funeral wreath which he tried to hide behind his back. At the lists, after Mowbray's dignified exit, Richard darted to the door to check Mowbray had gone before he cut the length of Bolingbroke's exile, the cheeky little gesture in itself enough to justify Gaunt's anger. Such joking was still there late in the play, in the cheery little wave to Bolingbroke after Richard had descended from the balcony in 3.3.

In the deposition scene (4.1), Richard entered with the crown in a shopping-basket and placed it on the floor between himself and Bolingbroke, undercutting the solemnity of the ritual by trying to play pat-a-cake with him. But the game was now too painful and he responded to Bolingbroke's question, 'Are you contented to resign the crown?' (190), with an off-hand 'Ay', then turned and buried his head in the lap of the seated York and screamed 'no'. Miming the reverse coronation through tears, Richard prostrated himself full-length before the crowned King Henry, then punched at him until Henry embraced him and calmed him. The childishness was an adult's retreat from the awareness of uncontrollable circumstance and ineradicable pain. From then on, the joking was lost, especially after 5.1, when Richard was dragged in on a blanket, filthy, thirsty and cowering from his tormentors. In his last scene, tied to a rope in the centre of the stage, Richard killed two of his executioners but, with a wry irony, he reached the literal end of his tether and Exton, out of Richard's reach, could stab him.

Richard's desire for Bolingbroke, his mirror-image, was held within this framework. Never explicitly homoerotic (since Richard did not here have the maturity to contain an adult sexuality) the depth of emotion was effectively naturalised by Shaw's gender so that the embraces, stroking, kisses and other gestures of affection were both between two male characters and between a male and female actor, the latter removing the *frisson* that displays of homosexual emotion produce for a mostly heterosexual audience. It gave the scenes with Queen Isabel (Brana Bajic) a certain distance as the two were kept apart by the performers' gender, evading a lesbian embrace of performers but also keeping the married couple strikingly apart. But Shaw's gender was never an intervention: rather, her femaleness and Richard's boyishness combined to create a character who was in so many ways 'not-male', as, Shaw has argued, kings are 'not-male' in Renaissance political thought, their gender invisible behind their regality.

Beside the intensity of Shaw's performance, David Threlfall's Bolingbroke was deliberately underplayed, so that his takeover of power was a shift to an emptier state, ruled by a remarkably benign man who no longer wore the splendid robes of kingship and whose elaborate throne was now covered with a simple green baize cloth. The contrast was acute with Richard, who, when he sat on the throne, found that his legs did not reach the ground and left his feet dangling, again like a child.

Warner's *Richard II* is an apt conclusion of the English productions I have considered in this volume. There is perhaps no need for a retrospective conclusion: Deborah Warner's *Richard II* sums up all the virtues of Shakespeare production that I have tried to value highly throughout. Its consistent intelligence, its refusal to accept tradition for its own sake, its creation of a particular and flexible space for actors and audience to share, and, above all, its unfailing understanding of and respect for the complexity and power of Shakespeare's writing, all these strengths exemplify the very best in English productions of Shakespeare.

CHAPTER 9

Festivals and foreigners

A Midsummer Night's Dream (Georgian Film Actors' Studio, Tbilisi); *The Merchant of Venice* (Goodman Theatre, Chicago); *The Tale of Lear* (Suzuki Company of Toga); *Romeo and Juliet* (Itim Theatre Ensemble, Tel Aviv); *King Lear* (Detsky Theatre, Moscow); *King Lear* (Malaya Bronnaya Theatre, Moscow); *Hamlet* (Comédie-Française, Paris); *La Tempête* (Tramway Theatre, Glasgow); *Romeo and Juliet* (Düsseldorfer Schauspielhaus)

In October 1994, the Barbican Theatre played host to the 'Everybody's Shakespeare' Festival. The Festival seemed to be sprouting tentacles in every corner of the complex: sets and story-boards from the Animated Tales in the Stalls Gallery; glass and silver goblets with Elizabethan overtones in the Craftspace; 'How to be Bottom, or The Interactive Shakespeare Show', complete with massed ranks of computers to play with, in the Concourse. As at the Edinburgh fringe, dedicated festival-goers needed to plan carefully with stop-watches, timetables and packed lunches to be sure of catching everything: on one Saturday a platform show of 'Short Shakespeare for Busy People' was followed hard by Peter Weir's company demonstrating 'Improvised Shakespeare'. They in turn were succeeded by the Original Shakespeare Company performing the first 600 lines of *The Two Gentlemen of Verona* under the direction of Patrick Tucker who believes that Shakespeare's company never rehearsed, and who proved conclusively that good actors pumped up with adrenalin can think fast and excitingly when, having learned their roles only from cue-scripts, they have no idea what the other actors in the scene may be about to say. The frenetic pace of the 'Everybody's Shakespeare' Festival went with a peculiarly British attitude to culture: a certain degree of chaos; good humour and bonhomie amongst actors and audience alike;

a winning amateurism from some and a Messianic zeal from others, especially from Tucker, whose enthusiasm and energy produced exhilarating work from his terrified company.

Shakespeare was neatly turned into consumable chunks of popular culture. It matched many of BBC Television's accompanying offerings (called 'Bard on the Box'): a wry documentary on the claims of Baconians, Oxfordians and an American woman who used computer images to prove that Shakespeare was really Queen Elizabeth; and 'Bardbrain', a Shakespeare quiz-show won by a bank manager whose impressive knowledge was offset by the manic gleam in the eye of a competitor for whom winning was the only thing that mattered.

'Everybody's Shakespeare' seemed expressly designed as the answer to every cultural materialist's prayers, not least in its dominant publicity image of faces appearing from behind half-masks from the Droeshout engraving, chosen with impressive statistical care to represent old and young, gender balance and a politically correct range of ethnicities. If the 'Everybody' of the title was supposed to connote the full range of British society, then the most eloquent symbol of the endeavour was unquestionably Michael Bogdanov's extraordinary documentary for television, recording his intrepid voyage to inner-city Birmingham. Initially greeted with deep suspicion by local residents, Bogdanov found his language of the academy, full of abstract exposition of the imperialist aims of establishment Shakespeare, met by mocking incomprehension. Yet his perseverance resulted in enthusiasm and, more significantly, recognition. There were, in the filmed fragments of plays that resulted, not only talented performers but also a connection between speeches and actors' circumstances that was genuinely troubling and hard-won. It is hardly surprising that some young men could be persuaded to play out the Romeo–Tybalt fight, nor that Juliet's Nurse's speech can translate superbly into black patois; but the emptiness of a man quietly speaking Caliban's 'This island's mine' with eloquent understanding, against a background of a building-site, was a powerful affirmation of the subversive potential of *The Tempest*, denying the government's belief in the divine right of Toryism to appropriate Shakespeare for its version of English culture. If, at the end, one was left worrying what the consequences of Bogdanov's cultural foray were for those he encountered, encouraged and then abandoned, the worry was far

more about the waste of imagination among people that the politics of establishment culture ignores than about the remaining
shreds of condescension hanging on the project. Set alongside a
programme as thoughtful and provocative as this, the BBC's one
new production of a complete play, David Thacker's *Measure for
Measure*, was bound to look signally uninteresting.

Somewhere in the hubbub at the Barbican, though, the osten-
sible heart of the Festival was a series of productions brought over
from Germany, Israel, Japan, the United States and Georgia. To
end my survey of English Shakespeare productions, I want to see
what other Shakespeares have looked like from an English perspective. If the surrounding events of the Festival were defiantly
British, in the community of that sort of 'Everybody' who might be
expected to turn up at the Barbican, the productions themselves
suggested a fundamental tension in the idea, making plain a
curious mixture of both xenophobic suspicion at the sheer
unEnglishness of the work and a vein of cultural elitism that means
Shakespeare in Japanese is somehow bound, by its sheer otherness, to be more impressive and significant than anything the
conventions of English Shakespeare production might be
expected to generate. The xenophobia was most marked in the
theatre reviewers' reactions to the productions, represented, at its
most extreme, by Charles Spencer's comment in the *Daily Telegraph*
(1 November 1994):

Although it is stimulating to be exposed to different views of
Shakespeare, there is something coals-to-Newcastle-ish about importing
foreign-language productions to England: there we sit, following an
edited version of the script in surtitles while listening to the performers
delivering the matchless poetry in an incomprehensible tongue. It's cultural heresy to admit this, but it is a faintly ludicrous situation.

Spencer's parochialism was widely echoed, though rarely in so
extreme a form. Watching Shakespeare, rather than listening to
Shakespeare, offered critics a means to see how a production is culturally located but few took the opportunity. The productions
negotiated their own cultural specificities and the act of inter-
cultural communication in ways as widely varying as the languages
in which the plays were performed.

Mikhail Tumanishvili's *A Midsummer Night's Dream* for the
Georgian Film Actors' Studio in Tbilisi, for instance, marked
its connection with its own culture as a form of deliberately

maintained distance from the experience of the collapse of Sovietism. There was nothing trivial about the conjunctions of statements in Tumanishvili's comment on the development of the production: 'We rehearsed the play while Tbilisi was shattered by shootings in the street. Many people were killed, buildings destroyed. The theatre was freezing cold.'

Alexandru Darie, in his production for the Comedy Theatre of Bucharest, seen in London in 1991, used *Dream* to explore Romanian tyranny as Serban Ionescu's tripling of Theseus, Oberon and Quince showed the dictator's protean power. This Athenian wood was peopled with shadowy secret policemen. At the end, the workers performing 'Pyramus and Thisbe' understood only too well the courtiers' insults and, when Theseus threw them a bag of money at the end of their show, left the money lying there, staring back in a piece of passive resistance that was painfully resonant of the politics of the company's own country. Yet Darie's production had energy, lightness, eroticism and comedy in abundance, counterweighting the savagery of the political system it exposed.

Tumanishvili's response was more straightforwardly celebratory of the pleasures and possibilities of theatre. If the phrase is a cliché of the critic's vocabulary for anything exhilarating, then the work of the Georgian Film Actors' Studio reinvested it with a meaning it has often lost. The company's delight in the play and their excitement at the opportunity to communicate that delight meant that the horrific conditions in which they had worked on it could be overcome. Respect for the play turned actors, designer and director into its servants in a context of performance where a search for dominance would have been seen as a denial of the joys of collaboration in making theatre. Hence there seemed an especial point in the unusually subdued playing of Bottom by George Margvelashvili, intentionally insignificant beside the huge bulk and brilliant comedy of Revaz Imniashvili's Flute.

Tumanishvili's *Dream* revealed a tension in the concept of Shakespeare for the global spectator, the kind of corporate interculturalism that Dennis Kennedy has brilliantly analysed.[1] The production may have seemed generalised, divorced from the specificity of the culture and historical moment which had generated it and hence prey to the accusation of a cheap globalism and commodification, a capitulation to the dominance of Western theatre practice. Yet the generalisation was part of the production's politics; the invisibility of the circumstances of its creation was provoked by the production's exhilaration at the possibilities of social change. That the English theatre critics liked the production may have demonstrated its cross-cultural accessibility but it does not deny the specificity of its cultural production.

Throughout the run of this *Dream*, at exactly the same moment as the audience were excitedly leaving the theatre after a non-stop performance of a little over two hours, the audience in the main theatre were reeling out for the interval in Peter Sellars' four-hour production of *The Merchant of Venice*, and many of the latter joined the others on their journeys home. The sheer arrogance of Sellars' production was shocking when set beside the modesty and humility that underscore Tumanishvili's work. Where the Georgians saw no need to highlight their own society in order to explain why playing *A Midsummer Night's Dream* mattered to them, Sellars' work exemplified in its defiant aggression all that the image of American imperialism embodies, even while he was ostensibly using the play to reveal the ethnic tensions in America's backyard.

Sellars set the play in Los Angeles with jews played by blacks, Venetian Christians by Hispanics, and Belmont peopled by Asians. But the effect was to patronise ethnicity. I was not really troubled by such bizarre intrusions as Jessica pregnant by Lancelot Gobbo or Portia at the end giving Antonio not news of his ships' safe return but a large cheque to buy him off from posing a demand on Bassanio's bisexuality. I was not perturbed by the brashness when Portia's dresses for the casket scenes were colour-coded and when she so subtly suggested which casket Bassanio should choose by standing on it, or when Bassanio and Antonio rolled round the floor of the courtroom in a final defiant embrace. I was not even surprised by the contempt for the audience displayed in the production's frequent *longueurs* and the general ineptness of the over-the-top acting, with Paul Butler's Shylock an honourable exception.

It was the TV screens that I could not get over. Fifteen monitors on stage and suspended over the audience showed either home movies of Los Angeles (basketball at Venice Beach, a tour round the outside of Portia's home in Bel-Air or, during the trial scene, newsreel footage of the riots – in case anyone had managed to miss the point) or close-ups of characters on stage filmed by the video

27. *The Merchant of Venice* 3.2, Goodman Theatre, Chicago, 1994: Nerissa (Lori Tan Chinn), Portia (Elaine Tse), Bassanio (John Ortiz) and a TV monitor

camera of Salerio and Solanio, played as parodies of American TV newscasters. Since the stage was usually lit in sepulchral gloom, at least the close-ups made it possible to see something but it was also an explicit denial of the audience's place in the theatre. Where theatre directors try to encourage the audience to concentrate on one particular part of the action by blocking and acting but also know that they cannot fully control the audience's gaze, film defines what may be seen, selecting and thereby manipulating. Sellars was determined the audience should not look elsewhere but he also made the TV material into the blandest of commentaries: during the trial scene, for instance, when Shylock reminds the Duke 'You have among you many a purchased slave' (4.1.89), the camera focused on one of the black police guards, and when Antonio, staking his own claim to Bassanio, instructs him 'Commend me to your honourable wife' (270), the close-up was of Portia.

Such control is deeply contemptuous of the audience's intelligence, its ability to watch the play, but it is equally deeply distrustful of theatre itself. Since the actors seemed far more comfortable when acting to camera than on the spaces of the Barbican stage, especially when cluttered with camera cable, it was far from clear why Sellars had bothered to direct the play for the stage at all, why he had not simply made a television film in which the specific construction of meaning through television in America could have been much more powerfully explored. Sellars was attempting to use the Shakespeare play as a means of illuminating the conflicts and confusions of Los Angeles. Yet the result offered interesting approaches neither to *The Merchant of Venice* nor to the LA riots. Each seemed trivialised by the analogy posed to the other.

Sellars' domination over the play, the over-determined interpretative authority of the director, was strongly echoed by Tadashi Suzuki's *The Tale of Lear*. The production was first seen in 1988, a collaboration between Suzuki and four American repertory theatres, taking American actors and training them in Toga, the home of Suzuki's company. The Japanese-language version shown at the Barbican used Suzuki's own actors, senior members who have survived Suzuki's punishing and brutal teaching method. The result was a rigorous and ascetic piece of theatre, stripping the play of any trace of reassurance: there was no room here for Kent or for Lear's reconciliation with Cordelia.

Framed as a tale read by a nurse to a dying man in a mental hospital, the narrative existed both in its own right and as a dream projection of the old man. The concept was fierce and powerful but the execution, in its strict method and fragmented scenes, its all-male cast and restricted movement, its monotonous barking voice-work and minimal set, generated a surprisingly dispassionate response. I have never felt so uninvolved in the action of *King Lear*. After all, if the play-text is cut down to a running time of less than two hours (and the length of each production in the Festival was the clearest possible marker of the production style), there are only edited and manipulated highlights left, allusive fragments suggesting the need to recognise the omissions as strongly as the need to engage with what has been left in. In that respect the production marked a cultural connection to the stripped-down version of *King Lear* directed by J. A. Seazer for his Banyu Inryoku Company, shown in London in October 1991 as part of the Japan Festival. Suzuki's *Lear* was crushingly emphatic about its appropriation of the play into the director's vision of a despairingly bleak world where, as he commented, 'all men and women are patients in a hospital'.

Yukio Ninagawa's production of *The Tempest*, brought to London in December 1992, made demands through its use both of Japanese theatrical forms and of the social history of those forms, setting the play into a context of Noh as a rehearsal by the exiled Ze'ami, one of the great creators of Noh traditions, on Sado island.[2] Its problems for the audience were primarily theatrical, not cultural. But Suzuki's theatre foregrounds its cultural difference. Seen at the Barbican it seemed almost aggressively Japanese and its appropriation of *King Lear* significant only for its argument about the forms of Japanese society.

At ninety-five minutes, Rina Yerushalmi's *Romeo and Juliet* with her Itim Theatre Ensemble from Tel Aviv was even shorter than Suzuki's *Lear* and much less than half the length of the *Romeo* from the Düsseldorfer Schauspielhaus. Resisting the obvious option of jewish Montagues and Arab Capulets since 'it did not begin to resemble our situation', Yerushalmi allowed the racial patterns to be echoed in multiplying and mirroring actions, so that, as the action was catapulted towards its end, there were more and more Romeos and Juliets, including Ben-Azar Noam's troubling, white-faced Chorus (an eerie echo of Emcee from *Cabaret*), dying all over the stage, until the entire cast united in an achieved reconciliation, an accomplishment of a social desire for peace that went far beyond the tensions of the play. More dream-like than passionate, this *Romeo* expressed a cultural yearning far more than a narrative, the play a means to plead for the fulfilment of the company's hopes for their country.

These Festival productions made the Shakespeare text a means of defining the company's cultural situation, at least as perceived by the director. There are moments when a particular play seems culturally and theatrically necessary as a response to a social problem or social change. This was particularly visible in two productions of *King Lear* in the repertory of Moscow theatres in 1994. Sometimes the fashion for a play seems little more than theatrical imitation. Rumbles along the theatre networks can also be a fruitful source of suggestion. The sudden rash of new productions of *Troilus and Cressida* in Germany in 1993 – in Bochum, Hamburg and Düsseldorf – seemed to have been provoked in this way, as well as being a response to the time-gap since Dieter Dorn's successful production at the Münchener Kammerspiele in 1986, widely seen when televised.

The two Moscow productions of *King Lear*, though, had precise external resonances, generated by the rapid political transformations of the Russian state. In India *King Lear* has become a crucial play for the exploration of the family as the play that represents 'filial ungratitude' in its most acute form. The assumption that parents must be respected and the failure of children to accept that moral duty is so centrally and, at present, so anxiously enshrined at the centre of the family structures of Indian society that *King Lear* seems a perfect expression of that social malaise. The function of *King Lear* in India is as a text that can witness the consequences of such behaviour, minimising Lear's own responsibility and throwing it unquestionably on the evil of Goneril and Regan. In Russia such concerns do not figure at all. Instead, both productions were centrally concerned with the moral and political consequences of the break-up of the Soviet state. There was a fantastical rumour, widely joked about in Moscow in 1994, of a production which would star Mikhail Gorbachev as Lear. In terms of current Russian views of the play it was an entirely logical proposal.

The ability, highly developed under Soviet totalitarianism, of reading between the lines – so that 'Something is rotten in the state of Denmark' always received a spontaneous outburst of applause in Russian *Hamlet* productions – had changed to the openly political productions in the new world of post-Soviet Russia. What also changed, though, was the audiences' interest. The theatre had stopped being the site of political and social discussion. Audiences sought simpler entertainment and serious plays now often played to half-empty houses.

The two productions of *King Lear* were directed by Sergei Zhenovach at the Malaya Bronnaya Theatre and by Alexei Borodin at the Detsky Theatre. Zhenovach took two years to rehearse his production, the longest continuous rehearsal period I have encountered. Borodin started rehearsal considerably later; one of the members of the permanent company at the Detsky was already involved in Zhenovach's production and performed the remarkable double of playing Fool for Zhenovach and Edmund for Borodin, thereby ensuring the performances could never be played on the same night.

Borodin's production, the weaker of the two, set out to document the chaos resulting from the collapse of arbitrary central power. Eclectic in style, it accumulated materials randomly from a wide variety of theatrical modes, deliberately creating what Borodin calls a 'collision of styles'. Played on a stage filled with costumes and props and a heap of metal containers that could be used to build walls, to hide in or behind and to crash at appropriate moments, the production grabbed whatever it needed whenever it chose, denying any coherence of design in search of the possibilities and resonances that the materials enabled it to generate. Its theatrical method was of a piece with its argument: the theatrical chaos witnessing the need for associative meaning that the politics of Russia searched for. The aftermath of Lear's actions was, for Borodin, an exploration of the carnivalesque, a whirling world of freedom without responsibility that took on its own momentum.

Yet the production argued that responsibility for chaos lay with the past generation. *King Lear*, seen by Borodin as marking a cataclysmic moment in the development of Western society in the early seventeenth century, had its obvious connections with the equally cataclysmic changes in late twentieth-century Russian society. In this period of rapid social change, what Borodin saw as the set of normative values in which children have responsibility towards their parents was now reversed. The allocation of blame was entirely towards Lear and Gloucester with a compensatory exoneration of Regan and Goneril. Sergei Zhenovach's production exactly reversed this process. All he saw Lear wanting from the love-test was a polite 'thank-you' from his children, the courtesy that parents deserve. Cordelia's refusal was not therefore the refusal of an unreasonable request. From this little moment of miscommunication sprang the machine of the play for Zhenovach.

Zhenovach stripped the play down. The Malaya Bronnaya Theatre holds 520 but for *Lear* the auditorium was left empty and seating for an audience of 80 was built on to the stage, a space shared by actors and audience. The audience entered through the yawning blackness of the empty auditorium, a space that already marked the vacuum within which the play takes place. Zhenovach had excluded all sound effects: this was *Lear* without any sound of storm at all. The set of a few carved oak beams, carved by the actors themselves during rehearsals, marked the framework of a house. This *Lear* was not about a king losing his kingdom but about a family losing its home. In this state, as in the Russian state inside and outside the theatre, there was nothing else left to be given away. As Zhenovach's dramaturg Alexander Sverov argued, in the world of this production, there was nothing left but family relationships, the weak and vulnerable links that are the bones that keep the world together. The visual minimalism was not therefore an aesthetic or theatrically stylistic decision but a precise referent for the political meaning of the production.

By the end of the play, it was Edgar's role that had become most remarkably politicised. The experience of being Poor Tom, of living outside the social world of court and town, began to be preferable. Edgar became, for Zhenovach, some form of wholly admirable Timon of Athens, an ecological hero who at the end of the play walked out on the remaining characters, not, like Kent, towards death but towards a retreat from the world and a rapport with nature. In Grigori Kozintsev's film of *King Lear* Edgar spoke the last lines of the play straight to camera as, behind him, the people began the work of reconstruction after the war. Zhenovach, using the Quarto version which gives the final lines to Albany, saw the play as more hopeless for society, more encouraging for the individual.

Zhenovach conceived of the production's engagement with its audience as a form of elevation: not to bring *King Lear* down to the arena of relevance but to raise the discussion of the future of the Russian state to the level of *King Lear*; not, as a theatre critic commented, to make Shakespeare our contemporary but to make us Shakespeare's contemporary. Incisive and profound, Zhenovach's *King Lear* achieved both its functions. It was as subtle an account of the play as any Shakespearean could wish and as thoughtful an exploration of the place of the play in contemporary Russia as the Russian audience could wish.

Zhenovach's production had been proposed for inclusion in the 1994 'Everybody's Shakespeare' Festival but it was feared that its delicacy and precision would not transfer well across cultures. Cultural specificity may be resistant to cultural exchange. The production's purpose and the cultural work that the production seeks to accomplish – in Zhenovach's *King Lear* or in Suzuki's *The Tale of Lear* – may become indecipherable to those outside its culture, especially within the bland circumstances of an international theatre festival.

Dennis Kennedy has suggested that 'Shakespearean performance after the war . . . tended to discover contemporary

28. *King Lear* 3.4, Malaya Bronnaya Theatre, Moscow, 1994: King Lear
meets Poor Tom

themes and to stress the spectator's inclusion in those themes' and summed up the trend as follows:

> In general terms, by the mid-1960s Shakespeare performance, both Anglophone and foreign, sought a message in the play; whatever the message might be, the production almost always achieved its utterance by limiting the manifold possibilities of the raw text.[3]

I appreciate why Kennedy presents this narrowing in productions in such negative terms, setting the 'limiting' of the particular interpretation against the seemingly inexhaustible potential of the Shakespeare play. For Shakespeareans the recognition of 'the manifold possibilities of the raw text' is an article of faith. It is a position close to the ideal outlined by Georges Lavaudant, the French director of *Hamlet* which opened at the Comédie-Française in February 1994. In his programme-note, Lavaudant describes the perfect *Hamlet* production:

> The ideal, impossible to realise, would be to go through *Hamlet* bringing out every interpretation possible – romantic, marxist, psychoanalytic – the maddest, the most improbable, the most absurd, and in the end there would only remain the obstinate and enigmatic brutality of that challenge to all interpretation: *Hamlet*.[4]

But the ideal cannot be realised. Interpretations may co-exist in the language of the play but they often cannot co-exist on stage. Action, the physical event that Shakespeare incompletely prescribes, becomes a necessary choice at each and every moment of performance, one choice inevitably excluding many others.

An example from Lavaudant's *Hamlet* may make the point. In the last scene, after Laertes has identified Claudius as the source of evil, 'Le roi, le roi est coupable' in Yves Bonnefoy's translation used for the production,[5] Hamlet turned to kill the king. Claudius grabbed Gertrude's dead body, holding the corpse from the back in front of himself, Gertrude's face towards Hamlet, using Gertrude as a human shield to protect himself from Hamlet's rapier. It was an effective action but it was not the action that Andrzej Seweryn, who played Claudius, had wanted. He believed that Claudius was deeply in love with Gertrude and he had wanted to seize Gertrude's body because he could not bear to be parted from her as he faced his own imminent death. He wanted to hold Gertrude with her face towards him, embracing her, not using her as a shield. But during rehearsals the corpse was turned round to

be face outwards. It may have been the wish of the director or of
Christine Fersen who played Gertrude – I suspect the latter. As
Seweryn recognised, much to his disappointment, the meaning of
the gesture was reversed as the body was reversed. The result
offered one of the possibilities of the text while closing off another.
Neither Seweryn nor Lavaudant is to blame for this: theatrical
action is limiting.

Lavaudant's production was disappointingly bland, seeking not
so much to present the inclusion of every possible interpretation
as to leave that remaining challenge to interpretation that
Lavaudant described, trying to leave open the possibilities inher-
ently present. This respect for the text's openness monumental-
ised *Hamlet* into an uninteresting object. The production did more
than translate the play; it treated it to the full Comédie-Française
style of slow, ponderous declamation so that a heavily cut text still
took nearly four hours to perform. By comparison, Terry Hands'
production of *Hamlet* with Francis Huster (which opened at the
Marigny theatre in Paris in March 1994) used far more of the text
in a performance of little over three hours, the actors speaking at
a most un-Racinian speed. Shakespeare did not write *tirades* like
Racine and only rarely did the declamatory style of Lavaudant's
production respond to the play, in for example Fersen's narrative
of Ophelia's death when the control of the *tirade* was entirely
appropriate. *Hamlet* had become a mountain which must be
climbed simply because it is there and it had been fifty years since
the Comédie-Française last made the expedition. Yet the clash of
play and the specificities of French theatre culture seemed irre-
solvable: Terry Hands' production only succeeded by making
French actors uncharacteristically English.

In 1990 French-language Shakespeare, however, exemplified
the possibilities of globalised Shakespeare in Peter Brook's *La
Tempête.*[6] Working against the traditional Eurocentricity of productions of the play, Brook cast an African Prospero (Sotigui Kouyaté)
opposite a white German Caliban (David Bennent). The deliberate inversion of colonialist readings underlined Brook's aim of a
non-political production in which the ethnicity of the performers
would resist politicisation in favour of theatricality. Brook's astonishing theatrical invention, his use of music and props, his exploration of conflicting forms of movement and gesture and the
physical presence of his performers, was thrilling.

But the notion that the production, as a specimen of Shakespeare offered for worldwide consumption, was therefore depoliticised was false. The otherness of Prospero as magus was embodied in the otherness of the physical presence of Kouyaté as performer; the latter's racial alienness to Western culture – exemplified by the rituals he used for performing Prospero's magic – tried to authenticate the magic by offering the actor's culture as one in which magic exists. This is unquestionably orientalising, a Western appropriation of cultural otherness. Brook's production may have sought to remove the play's argument about colonialism but it replaced it by its own colonialism, its own annexation of other cultures for its aesthetic ends. Even in a production like Brook's, which wished to occlude its cultural origins in its celebration of world theatre, the originating impulse of Western cosmopolitanism commodified the other cultural forms it utilised.

The first production of the 'Everybody's Shakespeare' Festival was the one that most sharply divided the critics. Karin Beier's ambitious *Romeo and Juliet* for the Düsseldorfer Schauspielhaus responded with imagination to every shift in the play's tonality, the production's eclecticism and discontinuities reminiscent of the jagged style of Peter Zadek. It should have offered something for everybody, even as it risked fragmenting into a form of consumerism by allowing the audience to deconstruct the production into acceptable chunks. With no attempt at the achievement of unified seamlessness of Brook's *La Tempête*, Beier's eclectic approach was fully aware of the culture it represented, the range of theatre it absorbed and the detail of the Shakespearean play it exposed.

For some, the rough edges of abutting styles (like the singing chorus-line of Paris's servants juxtaposed on stage with the numbed and traumatised figure of Juliet) only dismantled the performance into elements too disconnected from each other and from what is conventionally assumed to be the play's coherent tragedy. But Beier was thrillingly and sensitively responsive to the play and its own myth, particularly at the end: as Juliet was still dying, Friar Laurence began his speech of apology to an onstage audience of the Prince alone but was drowned out by a blaring and banal modern rock song about 'Romeo und Julia' sung by two aging German rock stars, as upstage a statue of the lovers was trundled on. If the effect sounds harsh, it was also overwhelming in its

29. *Romeo and Juliet* 5.3, Düsseldorfer Schauspielhaus, 1994: The death of
Juliet (Caroline Ebner)

emotional force and fully aware both of what the play does and of
what it has come to mean.

At the heart of the production was the outstanding performance
of the whole festival, Caroline Ebner's Juliet, taking terrifying risks
with the character and her own body and miraculously overcoming them. She began as a child playing at an imaginary
conversation between her two shoes while her father negotiated
with Paris. When Juliet was caught between Nurse and mother
when the marriage to Paris was first proposed, Lady Capulet laid
claim to her daughter by giving Juliet her first pair of high-heeled
shoes and teaching her to balance in them, to become, in effect,
an adult like herself. But, at the ball, while everyone else danced
with robotic awkwardness, Juliet and Romeo charged around,
bouncing off the walls, like children larking around under the feet
of the grown-ups. After their one night of love, Ebner's Juliet
became a sulky wife in the dawn: the whole of her married life collapsed into the rows and reconciliations over the lark and the
nightingale. From that point on Juliet was traumatised, locked into
isolation by her secret pain. Ebner charted with precision and

imagination every moment of the transition from child to adult that Juliet has to make with such breathless and unfair speed. Juliet's death could not here be a neat stabbing; instead she slit her arms with the dagger and (with no blood visible) sat and bled to death.

As often, the play became 'Juliet with Romeo' but it was also at times almost 'Juliet and Mercutio'. Bernd Grawert's demonic Mercutio only fought Tybalt as a means of taunting Romeo into becoming involved, demanding, in effect, that Romeo acknowledge his desire for his male friend over any other commitment he might have been negotiating, and Mercutio killed himself deliberately on Tybalt's sword to stake his final claim on Romeo. After death, Mercutio continually reappeared, as the Apothecary for instance, helping Romeo towards death and hence towards himself.[7] This ghostly presence emerged out of a fiery performance of Shakespeare's Mercutio. Grawert made 'Queen Mab' into a tormented self-revelation, a field of imagination unglimpsed by any other character.

Mercutio became a key part of the play's mechanical fatalism. Florian Etti's set, a cold white tunnel with sections of concrete sewer-pipe, allowed for depth[8] and hence for different planes of action: Paris and Lady Capulet embraced lasciviously downstage while upstage, in another world, Romeo and Juliet nakedly but chastely wrapped their arms round each other. But the set also suggested claustrophobia with its heavy panelled roof, a remarkable device which lifted off as the lovers found each other and closed down on the action in its later phases.

The production did not demand assent to glib iconoclasm but it required from the audience a sustained evaluation of the viability of its thoughtful responses. Where *Romeo and Juliet* can too often appear to be a play designed only for an audience of adolescents, Beier used youth culture, its stamping rhythms and its insecurities, to set beside the smug world of the adults and thereby proved conclusively that *Romeo and Juliet* is really a play for adults. In its heterodox but illuminating responses to the play, Beier's *Romeo* stands as the convergence of all that made the five productions of the Festival encouragingly provocative to the safety of English Shakespeares, making the play exhilaratingly unfamiliar, rightly showing us that not everybody's Shakespeare is the one we possessively think we know.

Beier's production was freed from a reverential obeisance to the English text, though she had previously directed the play in English for her semi-professional Cologne company Counter-check Quarrelsome. English Shakespeare productions, at their worst, are inhibited by Shakespearean language but, at their best, are liberated into a space of thought and feeling that matches the language's demands. Deborah Warner's *Richard II*, my final example of English Shakespeare in chapter 8, has much in common with Beier's apparently more radical work than might at first appear: both rigorously mine the text for its possibilities; both place the theatrical at the service of Shakespeare. Service, as Kent well knew, is not a passive acquiescence. The best Shakespeare productions work hard to validate their approaches, work hard to make Shakespeare immediate in the theatre. Directing Shakespeare is never easy.

Notes

PREFACE

1 *Shakespeare Quarterly* 36.v (1985) pp. 531–669.
2 Barbara Hodgdon, 'Looking for Mr. Shakespeare After "The Revolution": Robert Lepage's Intercultural *Dream* Machine' in James C. Bulman, ed., *Shakespeare, Theory, and Performance* (1996) p. 68.

1 MEASURING PERFORMANCE

1 Henry James, *The Tragic Muse*, in Henry James, *Novels 1886–1890* (Library of America, New York, 1989), vol. I ch. 4, pp. 748–9. I owe this reference to my colleague Jean Chothia.
2 Letter to Philip Gaskell, October 1975, quoted in Philip Gaskell, *From Writer to Reader* (Oxford, 1978) p. 260.
3 In a seminar discussion at the Shakespeare Centre, Stratford, in January 1996.
4 Letter of 29 March 1904, quoted in Ronald Hingley, ed., *The Oxford Chekhov* vol. III (1964) p. 330.
5 Brian Cox, *The Lear Diaries* (1992) p. 4. See also Brian Cox's comment 'The Lear I did in London was a very contentious performance, because it wasn't a performance that was based on keeping everybody safe. It was challenging, and the London audiences on the whole don't deal with that particularly well' (Murray Cox, ed., *Shakespeare Comes to Broadmoor* (1992) pp. 52–3).
6 Ralph Berry, *On Directing Shakespeare* (1989) p. 60.
7 *Ibid.*, p. 61.
8 *Ibid.*, pp. 61 and 63.
9 Interview for the BBC World Service, December 1993.
10 Berry, *On Directing Shakespeare* p. 61.
11 Quoted in David Addenbrooke, *The Royal Shakespeare Company: The Peter Hall Years* (1974) p. 182.
12 *Ibid.*, p. 174.
13 Ralph Berry, 'The Reviewer as Historian', *Shakespeare Quarterly* 36 (1985) p. 595.

14 *Ibid.*
15 *Hamlet* (1676) sig. [A]2a.
16 Irene G. Dash, *Wooing, Wedding, and Power: Women in Shakespeare's Plays* (New York, 1981).
17 See, for instance, Bernice Kliman's fine analysis of cutting in the BBC's television *Hamlet* of 1980 in her *Hamlet: Film, Television, and Audio Performance* (1988) pp. 62–86.
18 Grigori Kozintsev, *Shakespeare: Time and Conscience* (New York, 1966) p. 215. The passage is quoted in Jay Halio's provocative piece, 'Finding the Text', *Shakespeare Quarterly* 36 (1985) pp. 662–9.
19 Halio, 'Finding the Text' p. 666.
20 Patrice Pavis, 'Theatre Analysis: Some Questions and a Questionnaire', *New Theatre Quarterly* vol. 1, no. 2 (1985) pp. 209 and 211.

2 1989–1990: THE ROYAL SHAKESPEARE COMPANY AND THE ROYAL NATIONAL THEATRE

1 See Michael Bogdanov and Michael Pennington, *The English Shakespeare Company: The Story of 'The Wars of the Roses' 1986–1989* (1990).
2 Quoted in Sally Beauman, *The Royal Shakespeare Company: A History of Ten Decades* (Oxford, 1982) p. 244.
3 *Ibid.*, p. 245.
4 See Cicely Berry, *Voice and the Actor* (1973) and *The Actor and His Text* (1987). Berry's work receives a hostile analysis in Richard Paul Knowles, 'Shakespeare, Voice, and Ideology' in James C. Bulman, ed., *Shakespeare, Theory, and Performance* (1996) pp. 92–112.
5 Beauman, *A History* p. 354. See also David Addenbrooke, *The Royal Shakespeare Company: The Peter Hall Years* (1974).
6 Ralph Berry, *Changing Styles in Shakespeare* (1981) p. 7. See, for a redefinition of that position, Alan Sinfield, 'Royal Shakespeare: Theatre and the Making of Ideology' in Jonathan Dollimore and Alan Sinfield, eds., *Political Shakespeare* (Manchester, 1985) pp. 158–81.
7 See Robert Smallwood's discussion of 'a phenomenon surely on the increase in recent Shakespeare production – the little directorial dumb-show (and sometimes not altogether dumb) that so often begins the evening' in '"Beginners, Please"; or, First Start Your Play' in *Shakespeare Jahrbuch 1993*, pp. 72–84 (p. 73).
8 See Carol Rutter, *Clamorous Voices,* ed. Faith Evans (1989).
9 Brian Cox, *The Lear Diaries* (1992) p. 7.
10 René Weis, ed., *King Lear: A Parallel Text Edition* (1993) p. 34.
11 On Dexter's performance, see also Carol Rutter, 'Eel Pie and Ugly Sisters in *King Lear* (Part Two)', *Essays in Theatre* 14 (1995) pp. 49–55.
12 See Ian McKellen, *William Shakespeare's 'Richard III': A Screenplay* (1996). My review of the film appeared in *TLS*, 10 May 1996.

13 Richard Eyre, *Utopia and Other Places* (1994) pp. 162–3.
14 McKellen, *A Screenplay*, p. 13. If this suggests the quintessential Englishness of the production, Eyre saw the production's 'spiritual home' as Bucharest, where, McKellen noted, 'when Richard was slain, the Romanians stopped the show with heartfelt cheers, in memory of their recent freedom from Ceaucescu's regime' (See Eyre, *Utopia*, p. 162, and McKellen, *A Screenplay*, p. 13).

3 1989–1990: POPULAR SHAKESPEARE AND THE SWAN THEATRE

1 Rupert Christiansen, 'Good Times, Bard Times', *Harpers & Queen* August 1994, p. 154.
2 Stanley Wells, 'Shakespeare Productions in England in 1989', *Shakespeare Survey* 43 (1991) p. 201.
3 Ben Jonson, *Works*, eds. C. Herford and P. and E. Simpson (Oxford, 1925–52) vol. I, p. 144, lines 420–3.
4 On the Swan, see Ronnie Mulryne and Margaret Shewring, *This Golden Round: the Royal Shakespeare Company at the Swan* (Stratford-upon-Avon, 1989) and my article, 'Style at the Swan', *Essays in Criticism* 36 (1986) pp. 193–209.
5 Quoted in Sally Beauman, *The Royal Shakespeare Company: A History of Ten Decades* (Oxford, 1982), p. 113.
6 See Dennis Kennedy, 'Shakespeare Played Small: Three Speculations about the Body', *Shakespeare Survey* 47 (1994) pp. 1–13.
7 Quoted in Alan Sinfield, 'Royal Shakespeare: Theatre and the Making of Ideology' in Jonathan Dollimore and Alan Sinfield, eds., *Political Shakespeare* (Manchester, 1985) p. 169.
8 *Ibid.*, p. 170.
9 The description is conveniently reprinted in the Wells–Taylor *Complete Works* (p. 1168); see also their reproduction of the woodcut of Gower on the title-page of George Wilkins, *The Painful Adventures of Pericles Prince of Tyre* (1608).
10 Simon Russell Beale has described the role in 'Thersites in *Troilus and Cressida*' in Russell Jackson and Robert Smallwood, eds., *Players of Shakespeare 3* (Cambridge, 1993) pp. 160–73.
11 See my article, '*Troilus and Cressida* and the Rate of Exchange' in Yasunari Takada, ed., *Surprised by Scenes: Essays in Honour of Professor Yasunari Takahashi* (Tokyo, 1994) pp. 86–104.

4 1991: A NEW TAXONOMY

1 S. T. Coleridge, *Table Talk*, ed. H. N. Coleridge (1835), 27 April 1823.
2 Robert Smallwood, 'Shakespeare at Stratford-upon-Avon, 1991', *Shakespeare Quarterly* 43 (1991) pp. 349–50.

3 Philip Brockbank, ed., *Players of Shakespeare* (Cambridge, 1985); Russell Jackson and Robert Smallwood, eds., *Players of Shakespeare 2* (Cambridge, 1989); Russell Jackson and Robert Smallwood, eds., *Players of Shakespeare 3* (Cambridge, 1993).

4 Michael Billington, *RSC Directors' Shakespeare: Approaches to 'Twelfth Night'* (1990) p. xvii; compare Stanley Wells' praise of it as 'a classic' (in *Royal Shakespeare* (Manchester, 1977) p. 44).

5 Smallwood, 'Shakespeare at Stratford-upon-Avon, 1991', p. 346.

6 But see also my analysis of the 1995 revival of that production in chapter 8, below.

7 Anne Barton, Introduction to the play in *The Riverside Shakespeare*, ed. G. B. Evans (1974) p. 145.

8 Smallwood, 'Shakespeare at Stratford-upon-Avon, 1991', p. 353.

9 Michael Bogdanov and Michael Pennington, *The English Shakespeare Company: The Story of 'The Wars of the Roses' 1986–1989* (1990) p. 241.

10 Shakespeareans might wish to know that Tubal and Old Gobbo were doubled by an actor named Gary Taylor who was also to be seen as Sir Politic Would-be in *Volpone*.

11 Quoted in John Willett, ed., *Brecht on Theatre: The Development of an Aesthetic* (1964) p. 265.

12 Stanley Wells, 'Shakespeare Productions in England in 1989', *Shakespeare Survey* 43 (1991) pp. 195–6.

13 My first responses to this production appeared in *TLS*, 15 March 1991.

14 Quoted in Walter Benjamin, *Illuminations*, ed. Hannah Arendt (1970) p. 249.

15 *Ibid.*

16 *Ibid.*

17 On the balance between Angelo and the Duke in productions, see Ralph Berry, '*Measure for Measure*: Casting the Star' in his *Shakespeare in Performance* (1993) pp. 119–25.

18 Ralph Berry, *On Directing Shakespeare* (1989) p. 164.

19 *Ibid.*, p. 165.

20 For a view of Stephens' Falstaff as more straightforwardly sentimentalised, see Alan Dessen, 'Resisting the Script: Shakespeare Onstage in 1991', *Shakespeare Quarterly* 43 (1992) pp. 477–8.

5 1992: PRODUCTIONS AND SPACES, LARGE AND SMALL

1 The best account is still Colin Chambers, *Other Spaces: New Theatre and the RSC* (1980).

2 This and subsequent quotations are taken from the anonymous programme-note.

3 All quotations are from a facsimile of Q1 (here sig. B3b) but see also the aggressively packaged version edited by Graham Holderness and

Bryan Loughrey in their series *Shakespearean Originals* (Brighton, 1992).

4 I. Wardle, *Theatre Criticism* (1992) p. 41.

5 'If a classic could be defined once and for all it would immediately cease to be a classic: impaled on a definitive production like a moth in a display cabinet' (*ibid.*).

6 *Ibid.*, p. 43.

7 'Stylized: The reviewer cannot name the style and probably does not understand what is going on' (*ibid., p. 42*).

8 'Complaints about "unfulfilled expectations" come from people who want always to be told the same old story' (*ibid., p. 43*).

9 'What a cry came with, "O, she's warm!" It is impossible to describe Mr Macready here. He was Leontes' very self! His passionate joy at finding Hermione really alive seemed beyond control' (Helena Faucit, in *On Some of Shakespeare's Female Characters* (1893), quoted in Leigh Woods, *On Playing Shakespeare* (Westport, 1991) p. 157). Helena Faucit played Hermione opposite Macready.

10 The Petruccio-actor's response, 'It's all right; it's only a play', was at the same dismal level of linguistic invention as the Induction. The equivalent passage in *The Taming of a Shrew*, 'My lord, this is but the play. They're but in jest' (Additional Passage C, l.6), had to be rewritten to fit the defiantly twentieth-century mode of the frame materials.

11 Robert Smallwood, 'Shakespeare at Stratford-upon-Avon, 1992', *Shakespeare Quarterly* 44 (1993) pp. 348–9.

12 This is a good example of the common problem of a director reading the play back to front. Audiences were likely to be bemused by the basket in 1.2, having no reason to know that the Soothsayer would be the Clown and hence that, in effect, Cleopatra had the asps ready from the beginning of the play. Viewed from the perspective of the end of the play, the basket in 1.2 made perfect sense, provided one remembered it by that late stage.

13 Hesketh Pearson, quoted in Ralph Berry, *The Methuen Book of Shakespeare Anecdotes* (1992) p. 123.

14 Since my intense dislike of this production aligns me with the broad mass of English theatre reviewers whose vituperation knew few bounds, see Barbara Hodgdon's vigorous analysis of their – and my – xenophobia in 'Looking for Mr. Shakespeare After "The Revolution": Robert Lepage's Intercultural *Dream* Machine' in James C. Bulman, ed., *Shakespeare, Theory, and Performance* (1996) pp. 68–91.

15 Wardle, *Theatre Criticism* p. 53.

6 1992–1993: LONDON AND STRATFORD

1 Niky Rathbone, 'Professional Shakespeare Productions in the British Isles, January–December 1991', *Shakespeare Survey* 46 (1994) pp.

191–203. My count is based on excluding all adaptations and all visits by foreign companies. The RSC figures include transfers to London of the previous year's Stratford productions as well as continuing tours.

2 Niky Rathbone, 'Professional Shakespeare Productions in the British Isles, January-December 1992', *Shakespeare Survey* 47 (1995) pp. 209–19.

3 Shrapnel's Claudius had cautiously eyed Hamlet earlier, leaving a pause after 'And now' before taking the easier option and turning to Laertes (1.2.42).

4 See the fascinating comparison of reviewers' comments of Branagh 1988 and 1992 in the *Independent*, 23 December 1992, p. 15.

5 *Sunday Times*, 13 December 1992, 8/20.

6 Some props seem peculiarly 'in' some years: a supermarket trolley could also be seen in Rutter's *Richard III* as the source of the 'rotten armour', mostly plastic, in 3.5.

7 This included outstanding productions, in the Swan, of Eliot's *Murder in the Cathedral*, Wycherley's *The Country Wife*, Goldoni's *The Venetian Twins* and, at The Other Place, of Ibsen's *Ghosts*.

8 Compare John Barton's comment on a workshop exploration of 3.1: 'It's what [Tubal] thinks of Shylock that perhaps tells an audience how the Jewish community look at Shylock. It seems to me that this scene often goes wrong because Tubal is played as a snivelling, sympathetic side-kick to Shylock. What both of you did as Tubal was to be dispassionate, detached and in the end disapproving. And that's terribly important to maintain the right balance of sympathy in the play' (*Playing Shakespeare* (1984) pp. 178–9).

9 See also Carol Rutter, 'Eel Pie and Ugly Sisters in *King Lear* (Part Two)', *Essays in Theatre* 14 (1995) pp. 60–1.

7 1993–1994: THE PROBLEMS OF HISTORY

1 Thomas Postlewait, 'Historiography and the Theatrical Event: A Primer with Twelve Cruxes', *Theatre Journal* 43 (1991) pp. 157–78.

2 George Bernard Shaw, *Our Theatre in the Nineties*, 3 vols. (1932) vol. III, p. 200.

3 The financial burden of running a building proved too much for Talawa's fragile funding and they left the Cochrane Theatre soon after *King Lear*.

4 On the history of black actors playing Shakespeare, see Errol Hill, *Shakespeare in Sable* (Amherst, 1994).

5 In *The Merry Conceited Humours of Bottom the Weaver* (1661) the cast-list recommends that Snout, Snug and Starveling 'likewise may present three Fairies' (sig. [A]2b).

6 Angela Carter, 'Overture and Incidental Music for *A Midsummer Night's Dream*' in *Black Venus* (1985) pp. 63–76

7 *Henry V*, ed. Gary Taylor (Oxford, 1984) pp. 32–4 and 4.6.37.1.

8 Oscar Wilde, *The Importance of Being Earnest*, ed. Russell Jackson (1980) 3.178–80.

9 Peter Reynolds, *Pericles: Text into Performance* (National Theatre Education, 1994), p. 11.

8   1994–1995: TWO BY TWO

1 Hall had used the same double in his production at the National Theatre in 1975, with Denis Quilley as the brothers.

2 A similar use of a ghostly Mercutio was made in Karin Beier's production for the Düsseldorfer Schauspielhaus seen in London in 1994, a possible source for the idea here. See chapter 9, below.

3 The production was reviewed alongside Gregory Doran's production of *Titus* for the Market Theatre of Johannesburg by Jonathan Bate, *TLS*, 28 July 1995, pp. 18–19.

4 See Dennis Kennedy, 'Shakespeare and the Global Spectator', *Shakespeare Jahrbuch* vol. 131 (1995) pp. 50–64.

5 For an attack on the production, see John Peter's fulminating review in the *Sunday Times*: 'how many liberties can you take with a play in order to interpret it? What is the difference between interpreting a play and making it say what *you* want it to say? Do dead playwrights have rights?'

6 *Kaleidoscope*, BBC Radio 4, 7 September 1995.

7 Ian McKellen, in his film performance, similarly made the first part of the speech public and the rest private. The film had not been released when Pimlott's production opened but rumour might, I suppose, have travelled from film to rehearsal room.

8 Richard Eyre, *Utopia and Other Places* (1994) p. 103.

9   FESTIVALS AND FOREIGNERS

1 See Dennis Kennedy, 'Shakespeare and the Global Spectator', *Shakespeare Jahrbuch* vol. 131 (1995) pp. 50–64.

2 *Ibid.*, pp. 59–63.

3 Dennis Kennedy, ed., *Foreign Shakespeare* (Cambridge, 1993) p. 13.

4 Georges Lavaudant, 'Un défi à toutes les interprétations', in the programme for *Hamlet*, Comédie-Française (1994), p. 17 (my translation).

5 W. Shakespeare, *Hamlet; Le Roi Lear*, trans. Yves Bonnefoy (Paris, 1978), p. 209.

6 On this production, see also Kennedy, 'Shakespeare and the Global

Spectator', pp. 56–8. I saw it on its visit to the Tramway in Glasgow in 1991.
7 For the reappearance of this device in an English production, see chapter 8, above.
8 The stage of the Düsseldorfer Schauspielhaus is strikingly deep. For performances of the production that I saw at the Barbican and at Bochum, the set had to be severely truncated.

Index

Plays are listed alphabetically by title. A number in italics indicates that a photograph shows the actor in this role. All productions are indexed by director, play and theatre company.